This IS Your Life

Achieving Success
in the Wake of Tragedy

Sylvia Booma Carroll

DEDICATION

I dedicate this book to my beloved and now departed husband. We had an incredible life together, in spite of all he suffered and all we had to overcome. He is still the light of my life.

PREFACE

There was a post on Facebook a while back. It said something like, "If the person you love became disabled, would you stay with them?"

Many people may have considered this scenario, but I never did. Then, when it actually happened to me, I didn't have time to think. I just had to go into action.

My husband was a world-famous scientist, at the peak of his career when he had an accident that instantly left him a paraplegic, paralyzed from the chest down.

After Doug's accident, there was a drastic change in our lives and a permanent one. I never expected anything like this to happen to us. Who does?

It was such a shock, that I lost 25 pounds in just three weeks.

When we married, my husband was 18 days older than me. I knew women usually live longer than men do, so I thought by not marrying someone older than me, I'd have my husband around longer. I never considered him becoming disabled.

At first, there were many times I found myself wishing that, instead of being paralyzed, either he had died or I had. Then, at least, the other person would have been able to just get on with their lives and raise our two boys.

Fortunately, however, we found ways to adjust, survive, and even thrive. My husband went on to greater accomplishments in his career and I created a loving, happy home for our family. This book is the story of how we did that and all we had to learn in the process.

Once when I was feeling particularly beat down and defeated, I said something like, "I can't believe this is my life!"

My younger son, Steve, answered me, "Mom, this IS your life. What you're doing right now. This is it."

Steve knew I didn't particularly like my life at the time, especially when I was having a bad day, but somehow I kept living it, one day after another. Eventually I learned to enjoy my life. I realized this wasn't a dress rehearsal. This was the real thing and I had to make the best of it, because I would never get that time back.

I've met a lot of young people who hear my story and they're amazed. They ask, "How could you stay married so long and do all that?" That's what I want to share with you.

I want to help other people learn from the experiences I've gone through. I've also met other people who would say, "Oh, so and so had a spinal cord injury accident. Would you be willing to talk to them and their family?" I'm always glad to.

I'm writing this book for everyone who has had tragedy in their lives. After my husband died, the only books I kept were the ones he had written and a few by other people who were in our situation. One very touching one was by Christopher Reeve, *Still Me*.

In it he says that, when he became a quadriplegic, he wanted to die. It was his wife who talked him into living. I happened to meet Christopher and his wife Dana at a restaurant in Williamstown, Massachusetts. They were beautiful people and very inspiring.

I also kept another book by John Hockenberry, *Moving Violations*. He's a writer with the *New York Times*. My son Steve and I also met him at a restaurant in New York City. It helps to know these people are real and they're living what they've written about.

There's one more quadriplegic radio personality in Philadelphia, Daniel Gottlieb, whom I have to remember. He wrote a book called *Letters To Sam,* for his autistic grandson. It's short stories containing his philosophy of life, "a grandfather's lessons on love, loss and the gifts of life." I heard him speak in person and was deeply touched by his wisdom.

I kept these books because they were relevant to me. They were all by people who had suffered great tragedy. I've been moved by their stories and I hope I can do the same for my readers. You never know what you might accomplish by sharing your story and your view of life.

Other people's experiences have helped me, as I went through the hard times in my life. It would be great if my book could do the same.

When I told my sons I had decided to do this, their reactions, like their personalities, were very different. My older son, Greg, was amazed. He said, "You are gonna write a book?" He couldn't imagine it.

You see, his father wrote many textbooks and articles all his life, while I never wrote anything more than my diary. Greg wasn't objecting, he was just surprised.

My son Steve, on the other hand, said, "Well, I don't know why you need to write a book." He's a very private person.

So I just said, "Because I want to." I guess that's a good enough reason, right? Evidently it was, because he didn't object.

I realize a lot of the things I have to say may be unpleasant for some.

But it's my story. Of course, there are many private things I don't want everyone to know about but I'm opening up my whole self to the world.

I'm not a writer. I do keep a diary, however. It's been very handy to keep track of events and details. My idea is that when I get real old and have nothing to do, I'll read my diaries and remember all I did.

I also have a whole suitcase of letters, including the Christmas letters our family sent out every year. My husband wrote those in his inimitable style. He was very long-winded, as many scientists are. One year he did 25 pages, handwritten and double-spaced on lined paper, which we had to edit down to two pages.

So I've drawn on all these resources to reinforce and refresh my memories. The interesting thing is, if you had just read our annual Christmas letters, you'd think we were a very normal family. We cheerily reported how all year long we had engaged in all kinds of normal activities. But when I think about the reality of our lives, I remember it was very different and much more difficult.

An old college friend, Sid Mittra, also wrote his life story, *Yes, the Bee Can Fly,* an incredible book. When I asked him how long it would take me to write my book, he said, "Oh, that's the first wrong question to ask. If you're going to write your life story, you have to put everything in it. It doesn't matter how long it takes."

He honestly didn't think I could do it, because my life had been so full and unusual, it would be impossible to put everything in.

I told another couple of old friends, Tapas Sen and his wife Sondra, that I was writing a book and Sondra said, "Oh, you will definitely learn something about yourself." I hope we all learn something here.

When I talk to people about my life, they always say, "Oh, you should write a book!"

So, here we go.

Chapter 1

In your life on this crazy planet, there may be one day, or perhaps one moment...in which everything changes. All your priorities, plans and dreams are suddenly obliterated – replaced by – you don't know what.

Now you have to live your life to find out who you will be.

That moment came for me on February 18, 1979. This is what I wrote in my diary that day:

"The worst day of my life. About 2:10 this afternoon, Doug went out of control skiing in icy conditions down the Flying Mile. He hit a tree and broke his back and neck. It paralyzed him from T-4 down. I started freaking out, when I saw him lying there in the snow, in front of a tree. He immediately said to me, 'Sylvia, it feels like my back is broken.' I immediately thought, *Oh, my God, will he ever walk again?"*

The answer was no. He never walked again.

Looking back on it now, I see my whole life up to that point had prepared me to deal with this tragedy...but I didn't know it at the time. Only going through the actual experience led me to a greater understanding of how strong I could be.

I was born in Waterbury, Connecticut on January 21, 1939.

The card game, bridge, was always a big thing in my family. In fact, my parents were playing bridge while they waited for my mother to go into full labor and give birth to me. Appropriately, they were playing with the doctor who was to deliver me, along with his wife, at their home, which was something of a mansion.

When my mother's contractions got serious enough, they all took her to Waterbury General Hospital. I was the happy result. You could say I was learning how to play bridge while still in the womb.

My earliest memory though is lying in my crib when I was a baby, probably less than a year old, in our home in East Hartford. I remember the room I was in. I could hear airplanes flying over the house. I guess I knew what airplanes were, even though they weren't that common then. I wasn't scared. I just remember hearing the noise.

I was an only child. My parents had dated for nine years before they finally married in 1929. My father was a well-to-do stockbroker before they married. I've seen beautiful photos of fancy cars, clothes, and more. They were quite a dapper couple at the time, but unfortunately, my father lost a lot of money in the Crash of '29, just about all of it. After that he held various jobs to survive the Depression.

It was another nine years before they got around to having me. My mother was about 36 by then and my father about 40. I always knew my parents were older than most of my friends' parents. They had a lot more going on in their lives than just me, so I grew up very independent.

My father was a Shriner. For their honeymoon, my parents had gone on a six-week Shriners' excursion to California. There they happened to meet a doctor and his wife who were celebrating their fifth wedding anniversary. This doctor worked at Waterbury General Hospital in Connecticut.

The two couples remained friends, so, nine years later, he was the doctor they chose to deliver me. That's how they all ended up playing bridge until my mother went into labor. And that's why I was born in Waterbury, even though my parents lived in East Hartford, about 35 miles away.

We lived in a two-story house on Chapel Street, near my grandparents' home, until I was almost six years old. I remember running joyfully down the sidewalk to meet my father, as he was returning from work at Pratt & Whitney.

My parents were very loving parents. They were both business people and had lots of friends. My father was outgoing and gregarious, while my mother was somewhat conservative, but pretty.

The strongest image I have of my father is that he was fun, happy-go-lucky, and not terribly responsible. My mother was the responsible one. I remember her as being very loving and concerned about me. She always wanted me to have a good life, go to college, be successful, get married...all the things I eventually did. She was sweet.

My grandparents on my father's side passed away before I was ever born. My middle name was Stevens, which had been my father's mother's maiden name. She died just a month before I was born.

My grandparents on my mother's side, I loved very much. My grandfather worked at Pratt & Whitney in East Hartford. He had a huge garden in his back yard, with all kinds of vegetables and flowers. He taught me how to play cards when I was little. He was very kind.

My grandmother was nurturing to me. After we left Connecticut, she took care of me every summer, when I came back to visit. After my grandfather died, she moved to live near us in Miami. Once I got my driver's license, I took her grocery shopping, running errands, and so on until she died. She left me some money in her will, so I could fulfill a life-long dream of going to Europe.

I loved both of my maternal grandparents as much as I did my parents. These were the four people I truly cared for as a child and I loved them all equally.

In fact, when I was about 12 years old, I thought, *If I die, I want whatever money I have to be divided equally among all of them.* That would be my will. I only had a couple of hundred dollars in the bank, but I was already thinking about what to do with it.

Chapter 2

In January of 1945, my parents decided we should take a vacation to Miami. They'd never been down there before. We were driving, so it was going to be a long trip. There were no Interstates then.

At the time, I had a pet cat, which I dearly loved. As we were leaving, I was sitting in the front seat of the car when, all of a sudden, I heard my cat meow. There was a duffel bag on the floor in front of me. My cat was in there!

I asked my father why he was in the bag and he said, "Oh, we're going to drop it off, so it can find a new home."

Then he just drove to a neighborhood near our house and let my cat out of the car. I was very upset. That was my cat and I had lost him forever. A few years later, something similar would happen with a pet dog I had. People back then didn't have the same compassion for animals they do now.

I got over my heartbreak and we made it down to Miami. For my father, it was love at first sight with that city. Everything was very different then than it is today. It was booming after the war.

They were building roads and putting in the causeways to connect Miami Beach with the mainland. I think my father saw it as a land of opportunity. So just like that, my parents decided to up and move down there. We arrived just before I turned six, on January 21, that same year, 1945.

When we moved to Miami, I did get a new kitten named Boots, which I was happy about. She survived and thrived till I went off to college, over 12 years later. My parents took care of her while I was at college. After my mother died, my father even continued taking care of her until Boots eventually passed away too.

We started out living in an apartment in the Shenandoah neighborhood of what was then southwest Miami. I went to Shenandoah kindergarten. That first summer, my mother and I went up to East Hartford to finish moving everything permanently to Miami. We had had beautiful, heavy, velvet furniture, which we got rid of, along with a lot of other household items.

After we settled in Miami, my father worked at a florist shop for a while and did some other things to keep food on the table. Eventually, my parents began a children's furniture business. My mother had worked in a bank in Hartford, so she worked right along-side my father in their new business. She kept things organized and on track. She was the financial person in the business.

Their store was on NE 40th street. It was called Babyland Juvenile Furniture. Later, we moved to an apartment on NE 54th street to be closer to the business.

One strange thing happened when we were living on 54th Street. When I was a child, I was afraid of the dark, but I never had any scary experiences or apparitions. One time, however, I did sleepwalk.

We had an enclosed porch there with wicker furniture. Somehow, I got up in the middle of the night and just started walking, without even being aware of it. I ended up out on the porch, sleeping on the wicker couch.

When my mother went into my bedroom the next morning, she panicked when she saw I wasn't in bed. Of course, she was always very nervous anyway.

One time she dropped a dish in the kitchen and I couldn't believe how upset she got that she had broken that dish. I said to myself, I will never be like that. After all, it was only a dish. I couldn't see any reason to be so upset.

That attitude has helped me all my life. If something is broken, fix it. If you can't fix it, forget it and just get on with things....

So thank God, my mother finally found me out on the porch, before she called the police or woke up the neighborhood or something. Major disaster averted.

Eventually we moved to NE 40th Street, to another apartment just a block from the family business. While we were there, the year I was eight, there was a hurricane, which was pretty scary. A woman who lived in the building where our business was, called my mother during the storm, to tell her the roof had blown off the whole place.

Meanwhile, my father was still over there inside Babyland! All I could think of was that we had lost him. I was sure he had been blown away in the hurricane.

Well, it turned out, my father had been sitting on the toilet in the bathroom out of harm's way, when the roof blew off. He was perfectly safe. He always was a lucky guy.

Around that same time, probably in second grade, my parents gave me my first two-wheel bicycle. They told me this would be the only bike I would ever get from them, so I better take good care of it. You can believe I did. I was really responsible anyway.

For example, when we moved to 40th Street, I had my own garden. That's when I learned how to raise gardenias, which is a pretty difficult thing to do. Gardenias are tricky plants, which are very particular about their growing conditions. They require consistent maintenance to stay happy and beautiful. A lot of people give up on them, because they're so finicky.

So it was the man next door who taught me how to grow them. You were supposed to have peat moss for them. Since I didn't have the money to buy peat moss, he told me I could boil dirt in water, to sterilize it. So one day my mother came home from work to find me boiling dirt on her stove. She wasn't thrilled about that.

I also even started a little business of my own. I gathered coconuts and then opened them by throwing them on concrete. I would crack them and then pull them apart by hand. I could sell them for ten cents apiece, which was a pretty penny – or dime – in those days.

My favorite card game was gin rummy, which my grandfather taught me to play, when I was about seven years old. He and I had many great games together over the years. I also really enjoyed checkers and Monopoly.

When my parents went over to their friends' house to play bridge, they would take me with them. I'd go into the bedroom and listen to *The Lone Ranger* on the radio, while the adults played in the other room. I never caused a problem.

I was a latchkey kid, so I learned how to take care of myself and of my responsibilities. When I got home from school, I would practice the piano for an hour, then go outside to work on my garden. Besides the gardenias, I had other flowers and vegetables, like zinnias and nasturtiums, tomatoes, and so on. I would water and weed them. Then I'd come inside and do my homework. I'd usually still be doing that when my parents got home from work.

I had a lot of homework. Some nights I would be out on the breezeway, still working away at 12:30 at night. My mother would come out and say, "Sylvia, when are you ever going to finish up? It's late. Do you have any idea what time it is?"

Besides piano, garden, and school, I also did Brownies for a while, then Girl Scouts. I also went to church and Sunday school every week. I was a good girl.

In fact, my father thought I was such a special child that he was always getting items published in the newspaper about me. He didn't work for the paper, but he was a natural PR man, who was always promoting himself, his business, and his family. He loved publicity. He was proud of us and he had no problem letting everyone know about it.

My father was a real socialite, actually in the Social Register. He felt that everything he did was newsworthy. He was always the life of the party and was good at networking. He eventually became president of the Florida Furniture Dealers Association.

It was amazing how he could get so many little things into the Miami Herald. For example, when I was in grammar school, I wrote a little story about my dog. My father saw it and got it published in the local newspaper. I think they had a section where they did little items from the local schools, kids' birthdays, and so on.

Another time, when I was eleven years old, I had to fly alone up to Connecticut for the summer and he wrote a feature about that as well, which appeared in the Miami Herald: "Eleven Year Old Girl Flies to New York Solo." Later on when I was an adult, he would even get mentions in the paper whenever my husband and I came to visit him. That was just his thing.

I even found one of the items he got published, still living on the Internet after all these years. This was that story I wrote about my dog.

It said, "One day I was down stairs and in my yard I saw a dog sleeping. He was gray and white. I named him Skippy. When I went away in the summer, Skippy was taken away. He had puppies but I couldn't get one and I am broken hearted."

So, in retrospect, I realize now "he" must have been a "she."

Poor Skippy was the only dog I ever had. When we went up north on vacation the summer after she showed up, we left her behind. Someone called the Humane Society and they came and took her. I guess I was too young to realize something like that would happen if you just went off and left your dog alone for a long time.

Chapter 3

Around the time I was in fourth grade, we moved to Miami Shores, which is an older suburb of Miami. It had and still does have a nice feel to it, with wide, tree-lined streets and a calm, quiet atmosphere.

It was a pleasant, upper middle class community, a good place to grow up. My parents rented our first house there at 55 NW 107th Street. I was glad to be in a house again, and not in an apartment. I went to school at Miami Shores Elementary.

During this time, around third, fourth or fifth grade, I also started taking piano lessons, which I continued for quite a while. I did very well. My piano teacher, Mrs. Brown, who had gone to the Boston Conservatory, wanted me to become a teacher too. But I thought piano teachers always ended up as old maids and I sure didn't want that, so I didn't pursue her dream.

I did, however, play pretty well. Mrs. Brown actually put me on the radio one time, which was quite an honor. This was before TV got to be popular, so the radio was pretty close to the height of fame then. I played an excerpt from the ballet, "Raymonda," and another piece from an operetta. That was the peak of my piano career.

This period, however, also marked a true low point in my young life, perhaps my most embarrassing moment ever. It was the only time I ever got in trouble at school. My sixth grade teacher was Mrs. Gahn. She was very skinny, rigid and strict. I have never liked that kind of person. Maybe because of her!

Anyway, after lunch every day, we would come back to the classroom, where we were supposed to have quiet time for thirty to forty-five minutes. Mrs. Gahn wouldn't be there then, but she would usually appoint someone to be a monitor. If anyone spoke during quiet time, the monitor was supposed to report the person to her.

One day, when we came back, nobody knew who the monitor was supposed to be. Somebody said to me, "Sylvia, why don't you be monitor today?" So I said okay.

When Mrs. Gainer came back into the class, someone – probably trying to get me in trouble – asked her, "Was Sylvia Booma supposed to be the monitor today? Because she was."

Mrs. Gahn looked around, startled, wondering what was going on. Had she lost control of her class? Slowly she said, "Noooo...Sylvia was not supposed to be the monitor."

Then her eyes landed on me and she barked, "Sylvia, stand up. I want everyone to hear this."

Sheepishly I rose to me feet beside my desk, as everyone stared at me. I stood there cowering before her. *I was only trying to help out*, I thought to myself. Then Mrs. Gahn began her interrogation.

"Sylvia, I didn't appoint you to be the monitor, did I?"

"No, Mrs. Gahn."

"Well, then why did you do it?"

"Um, because someone asked me to."

"Mmmm hmmm, and what if someone asked you to jump out the window into a burning fire? Would you do that too?"

"No...."

"So why did you just do what somebody asked you to today?"

I couldn't answer. Case closed. She really showed that little sixth grade girl who was boss.

She was a tyrant and she really embarrassed me, the one girl who was always trying to be good and do the right thing. It was terrible for me. Today it seems like a trivial matter, but back then, it was traumatic.

Fortunately, life goes on. I had lots of friends when I was young and my parents liked them all. My best friends were Elaine, Janet, Priscilla, and Leighton. They never got me in trouble. We were good kids. Oh, yes, except for that one terrible time when Elaine and I made coffee....

I wasn't supposed to drink coffee. My father was dead-set against it. He didn't think anyone should drink coffee, because it made people nervous. He never drank a drop till he was 40 years old, but my mother did like it.

Sometimes when it was cold in January, my mother would heat up milk for me to warm me up. I didn't care for milk that much, so mother would put a little coffee in it, because she knew I liked that flavor. Then I would drink the milk. So I was sneaking coffee from an early age.

My friend Elaine liked coffee too. So one cold winter's day, we decided to make a pot of coffee in my mother's percolator...on the living room carpet. Thank God, we got away with it. I never did it again. That would have been a catastrophe if the pot had spilled on the living room carpet.

One other very interesting thing happened when I was in the sixth grade. And I must confess, I did do something a little naughty on that occasion as well.

Our class was taking a trip to Cuba over Easter weekend. This was before the revolution of course, when Cuba was still a popular tourist destination. My father didn't want me to go, but since I was now twelve and did want to, I was learning to get my way.

My mother was excited to go. Plus my father's sister and her husband were visiting from Hartford and they were enthusiastic about the idea. So all four of us took off for Havana. We stayed in the center of the city in a nice hotel.

One night the adults went to the Tropicana nightclub. My classmates and I had to stay in the hotel. I was with some girls in our hotel room, where we were all reading comic books. There were some boys in the room next door.

We weren't supposed to unlock our door, but we wanted to trade comics with them, so we did open the door. We didn't do anything more than that, but we got some new comic books out of the night.

So, okay, that was kind of naughty too. I never said I was perfect!

Chapter 4

I went to Horace Mann for junior high. It was on NW 2nd Avenue, about 20 blocks from our home. It's still there, although now they call it "middle school."

Around this time my parents bought a brand new house at 149 NW 107th Street, just a block from where we had been renting, on the same street. They were putting up a lot of new houses in that neighborhood then and this one had just been built. It was a nice ranch-style house with a breezeway. My parents paid $18,000 for it. The house is still there and looks very nice.

That's the home I remember the most. It was a two bedroom, one bath home to start, but we added another bedroom and bath later, so that my grandmother could come live with us.

I rode my bike to school, hair blowing in the wind. I always had very fine hair, medium length. Before I left home, I would fix it just right, but by the time I got to school, it was all blown to bits. The only time my mother gave me a ride to school was when it was raining.

When it was cold outside in winter, we suffered, because that house had no heat, except for a little gas burner in the breezeway. My father liked to brag to his friends up north, "Oh, we live in Miami, so we don't need any heat." Maybe he didn't, but my mother and I were freezing.

It wasn't like we couldn't afford it. My parents' financial status was basically upper middle class. Both my parents worked. Anything I wanted, I got. Miami Shores, where we lived, was nice then and it still is now.

I was raised as part of a very conventional family. Both my parents loved me dearly and I was able to do all kinds of things and participate in all kinds of activities. Still, I spent a lot of time by myself, so I grew up independent. It was in my blood.

We attended church. As a baby, I was originally baptized in a Congregationalist church in East Hartford. When we moved to Florida, we went to a Methodist church for a time. Then, when we moved to Miami Shores, we switched to a Baptist church. That's what I grew up in.

It was a somewhat strict Baptist church. You weren't supposed to drink alcohol, even though some people did. When I asked my minister if it was okay to dance, he said, "Well, that is a personal choice."

So I chose to dance. Some people might have thought I was dancing with the devil, but I loved it. Of course, premarital sex was not a personal choice. It was a big no-no.

My parents, for the most part, only drank alcohol when their friends from Hartford came down to visit. They'd make highballs like Canadian Club and ginger ale, pretty traditional stuff. When they went out, my mother liked to order something called a Ward 8. It was a drink that had supposedly been invented in Boston after a city election in 1898. It was whisky, grenadine syrup, rock candy syrup, and lime juice, all blended, shaken and strained. Pretty tame.

My parents never smoked, of course, even though back then, most everyone else did. Everyone had ash trays in their homes. People smoked at the dinner table, in the bedroom, in the kitchen, you name it.

That is one other naughty thing I have to add to my list of misdeeds, now that I think of it. Being as independent as I was, I had to try everything for myself, so I did try smoking. I did it with Elaine, my usual partner in crime. Somehow we got our hands on a cigarette and decided to try it out. Fittingly enough, we held our grand experiment in the dingy ladies room of a local gas station. How seedy!

My parents didn't smoke and there were no drugs in those days, so I certainly didn't do that. It turned out smoking didn't do a thing for me and I didn't get addicted. Fortunately, my parents never found out about my brashness either. Yeah, I grew up pretty clean and straight.

I also helped around the house, doing chores, like mowing the grass. My father would pay me $1.50 for that. He depended on me for it. One time he went to do it himself and he couldn't even figure out how to start the lawnmower!

With those old power mowers, you had to wind a rope around this circular metal piece and then pull it hard and fast, so the engine would turn over. I showed him how. I don't remember who taught me, but I taught him.

Keeping my room clean was my other big responsibility. If my mother needed help, I would chip in, like for Thanksgiving dinner, I'd set the table, that kind of thing.

My first allowance was 25 cents, then 50 cents, then up to $1.50. I never got much, so I would supplement my income with little side jobs.

My first job was babysitting, mainly for the people who lived behind us, Bob Loft and his family. I probably made about 50 cents an hour for that. Years later, Bob became famous in a tragic kind of way.

He was a pilot for Eastern Air Lines, when a plane he was flying crashed in the Everglades on December 29, 1972. They made a movie out of it.

Evidently, one of the wheels on the plane wasn't coming all the way down, as they were preparing to land in Miami. The crew was focused on figuring out the problem. Meanwhile, unbeknownst to them, the autopilot was slowly taking the plane down and down, until they crashed in the Everglades. Most of the passengers survived, but poor Bob died, along with several of his crewmembers.

It's a well-known story. There were even tales about ghosts being sighted afterwards. These stories got turned into a book and another movie. The crash happened long after I had left Miami, but when I heard about it, I realized it was the Bob Loft I knew.

Turning to happier thoughts, summers were always a treat for me. My parents had their business to run and couldn't leave it. My mother could leave for a while, but my father had to be there year-round.

Since they were busy and I wasn't in school, my parents didn't want me staying alone all day for the entire summer, so they would send me off to my grandparents in Connecticut.

I usually went up north by car. Once, at the tender age of eleven, I actually flew up there by myself. Of course, this occasioned the Miami Herald article from my father, which I mentioned in Chapter 2.

When we drove, my mother usually went with me, but she wouldn't stay the whole summer. She had to get back to help my father with the business.

My grandmother and grandfather took really good care of me. When I was about nine and ten, my parents arranged for me to go to camp up there for a couple of weeks. Then I would come back to my grandparents' house and enjoy being with them. At the end of the summer, my mother came up to drive me back home again.

One summer, my English teacher, Miss Colin, drove me up. She was going up to Massachusetts for the summer, so I hitched a ride with her. I had a pet canary named Putney that I took with me. I had taught him tricks. He was very smart and I really liked him.

As we were going through Richmond, Virginia, it was really hot. This was before cars had air conditioning, so we decided to stop and see a movie, in order to cool off in the movie theatre's air conditioning.

When we got back to the car, poor Putney was dead from the heat. I hadn't realized that might happen. I had bad luck with pets as a child. Eventually I got another bird, Putney 2, but he was never as smart as the original.

It was around this time, when I was in the sixth grade, that I first began to realize I was near-sighted. I was sitting towards the back of the room and realized I couldn't see the blackboard very well. My girlfriend, Elaine, who was my oldest friend from fourth grade, had just gotten glasses. So when I told my mother I was having trouble seeing the blackboard, she didn't believe me. She thought I just wanted to be like Elaine.

Then, a little later, my mother was letting me drive the car coming home from somewhere. My parents weren't irresponsible for doing this. A lot of kids started driving before the legal age back then. It was how you learned. In fact, when we drove north in the summer, from an early age, my mother would often let me steer the car. She'd be at the steering wheel, but I was controlling it. It was fun.

Anyway, this time I ran a stop sign. It was on NW 2nd Avenue and 103rd Street. I still remember to this day. Then she finally realized I was definitely near-sighted.

So I finally ended up getting glasses, but I hated wearing them. I didn't like the way they looked. If I went to a dance, I definitely wouldn't wear them while I was dancing. I wouldn't wear them at school either, even though that's what I first got them for.

My vision was like 20/450, which is very near-sighted. I had to wear glasses to see anything at a distance. I suppose some people must have thought I was a little conceited when I didn't acknowledge them right away, but the truth was, I couldn't see anyone until they got right up in front of me.

One thing I saw the next year, which I never wanted to, was my grandfather's death. When I was thirteen, my grandfather was dying from colon cancer. So my mother and I went up north early in May, to be with my grandparents. I actually went to school up there for the last six weeks to finish out the school year. My mother and I were there for the end. Then my father came up for the funeral. It was really hard to see my grandfather go like that.

The next summer, when I was 14, I went to Connecticut again, since my grandmother was still living there. Now that she was alone, she was getting ready to move to Miami. My mother was an only child and we all wanted her closer to us.

She and grandfather had owned their house, a three-story home. They lived on the third floor and rented out the first two. So she sold that house and paid cash for another little house near us in Miami.

My last summer up there, I went to a parade in Hartford. There were some sailors in the crowd and I met one of them, Dwaine Leroy Sutton. He asked me to go to a movie with him that night. I told him I had to get my grandmother's permission, so he took the bus with me back to her house. There, he asked her if he could take me to the movies.

Of course, she was very nervous about it. If anything happened to me, her daughter would kill her. I was her only child, not like my grandmother, who was the oldest of 11 children. She finally did let me go, as long as I came right back afterwards. She was very protective of me. Fortunately, Dwaine was a gentleman. I arrived home safely and my grandmother remained in my mother's good graces, so she could move to Miami the next year, when I was fifteen.

Chapter 5

After junior high, I had two choices for high school: Miami Edison, which was top-notch back then, or North Miami High, which had just opened and was brand new. I chose Miami Edison. I did well there, becoming a member of the National Honors Society, debating in the National Forensic League, taking a lot of Spanish, and continuing to play the piano.

The National Forensic League met on Saturdays. We went to other high schools and debated them. I remember, one of the topics we had was whether Hawaii and Alaska should be admitted into the U.S. as states. That was a big question at one time.

One Saturday when I was probably about 15, my mother was up north and my father couldn't drive me to the debate, so he let me drive our car to the high school where our debate was. I didn't even have a license at the time, but that was the only way I could get there. It wasn't legal, of course, but my father could be a little loose sometimes. Plus, people were a lot more lax about teen-agers driving back then. It was kind of accepted.

In high school, I always liked the academic side of things, but what I really liked most was socializing. So I was very concerned with my appearance. Besides thinking glasses would ruin my looks, I was very picky about clothes.

I even took tennis in high school, instead of phys-ed, just because I didn't want to wear the phys-ed gym suits they had. These monstrosities were one-piece, white, with bloomers for legs, and snaps all the way up the front to close them. Horrible.

I already fancied myself something of a glamour girl. I had started out by just talking to a couple of boys on the phone every now and then in junior high. My first real date was when I was 15. Then I dated all through high school.

In junior high, my friend Elaine and I had already started going out on Saturday nights to El Portal, a little village south of Miami Shores, for their dances. These were record hops, where a DJ played records and the kids danced. It was only 10 cents to get in. My girlfriend and I were both pretty precocious and met a lot of boys. We especially liked guys from high school.

One of the boys I met and dated was a high school football player.

Because I belonged to the Spanish Honors Society, I got to go on a several-hour cruise on a boat. Our Spanish teacher was giving us this trip as a reward. I invited him to go with me.

The first and second decks of the boat were enclosed, but the third deck was open to the air and the sky. Towards the end of the cruise, my football player friend talked me into going up to that third deck to "look at the stars." Once we got there, he started kissing me. Then my Spanish teacher came by and caught us.

She said, "Sylvia, would you like to come up for air now?" I was so embarrassed.

Another guy I dated was Cuban. His name was Rolando Jimenez. In fact, when I moved back down to Miami, I actually tried to get in touch with him after all those years. I found out he had been the postmaster of Miami. I called his phone number and had a nice conversation with his wife. Unfortunately, he had died about three or four years earlier, so there was no rehashing of memories with him.

I also liked another guy named Jim Hill. He actually asked me to go steady, but I wasn't really the steady girlfriend type. I told him I wouldn't be able to go steady for at least two weeks, because I had a date with another guy that weekend.

Well, Jim understood, so we waited and started going steady after my other date. He was actually the only guy I ever went steady with. He was a year older than me and invited me to his senior prom at Miami Edison High. I was a junior, but I got permission from my parents to stay out all night, because there was going to be a beach party after the prom.

It was supposedly going to be well supervised. We were just going to have hamburgers and such on the beach, no drinking. Still though, I would be on Miami Beach all night with my boyfriend. My parents actually agreed to it. They must have really trusted me.

After the dance, we were at someone's house, changing out of our prom outfits into regular clothes. Jim was messing around, pretending to be playing football with another guy. Somehow, the other guy accidentally hit him in the nose and broke it. Jim was in real pain and had to go to the hospital.

So instead of carousing on the beach, I spent prom night sitting in a hospital. We got back to his parents' house about 7:30 in the morning. Then I went home and told my parents we never made it to the beach party. They were probably relieved.

20

Eventually Jim and I broke up in August of that year. It was a nice relationship, but I really wasn't good at being with one guy. I liked to date different guys. A few years ago, when I was cleaning out my house to move down to Miami, I found a beautiful, old love letter from Jim. I read it again and was touched, but I didn't keep it. I've had a lot of love in my life.

I was never infatuated with a teen idol either. I wasn't the type to idolize anyone. I prefer reality. In fact, when I was a little girl and had a couple of dolls, I didn't even like them. I wasn't crazy about dolls the way some girls were. They made me feel too girlish and maternal, not like me, free and independent.

Besides dating, my other big passion in high school was Rainbow Girls. I had been in the Brownies and the Girl Scouts, but Rainbow Girls was something else. The organization is a branch of the Masonic Order, under the Shriners, for teen-age girls.

My father was a Mason and a Shriner. He received the 33rd degree in Masons and another degree, which was supposedly the highest you could go. He even had a sterling silver Masonic sword that was about two and a half feet long.

In those days, the Shriners included most of the prominent citizens in a community. It was mostly a social, fun group that also did charitable work. My mother was in the Eastern Star, which was the women's branch of the Masonic Order.

Rainbow Girls was very influential in my upbringing, probably the most significant influence outside of my parents and grandparents. A girl can hold different offices or "chairs" in her local group. Each one requires some memory work and a show of character. They represent a level of maturity. These chairs include Faith, Hope, Charity, and Worthy Advisor.

I went through all of the chairs, to eventually become the Worthy Advisor of the Miami Shores Rainbow Girls. That was being president of our local chapter. Becoming Worthy Advisor was one of the most memorable achievements of my teen-age years.

When I became the Worthy Advisor, I had an installation ceremony in a big hall. I was probably only about 15 years old, and I had to wear a formal gown, so it was a big deal to me. My gown was long and white with a pink sash.

During the ceremony, I especially honored my parents for all they had done to bring me to that point in life. There was a song, "I'll Be Loving You Always," which was very popular at the time. I adapted the lyrics of the song, to make them refer to my parents, instead of a romantic lover.

Then I had a vocalist sing the song to my parents. A girlfriend of mine was the pianist. It was really beautiful. When my mother died, about five years later, I felt it was very significant that I had honored them like that.

Come senior year, our prom was at the wonderful, luxurious Fontainebleau Hotel on Miami Beach. My mother said to me, "What are you going to do when you grow up? You're having all these wonderful experiences already!" Well, of course, I went on to do a lot more, but she never got to see most of it.

I invited Charles Leighton Reynolds as my date. He was in Demolay, which was the young men's counterpart to Rainbow Girls in the Masonic Order. We had met at joint events when the two groups socialized together and we had dated a little.

After the prom we went to a party on the beach. That night I wrote in my diary, "Leighton kissed me tonight. Wow!" We continued to date and hang out together for a while, but nothing much came of it.

Later on, Leighton became the chief of police in Port Saint Lucie, Florida. He was also very helpful to me later in life, when my father's time was coming to an end. But I'll save that story for later.

I liked popular music but didn't have any special favorites. I liked a lot of Harry Belafonte's tune and I had some favorite songs, like: "The Great Pretender," "Love Letters in the Sand," "Memories Are Made of This," "Secret Love," "The Twelfth of Never," and so on.

I loved dancing to those songs. When I was 16, I used to hang out with a fellow, Sid, whose mother was the housekeeper for the man next door. I was friendly with my next-door neighbor, so he introduced me to Sid, who had just come back from the service. He was 23.

I would invite Sid over to my house and we would play these 45s on my record player. We'd dance to them in the dining room. We got pretty close. He actually thought I was 18, though I'm sure I have no idea where he got that notion. He actually wanted to marry me. He was ready to get married, but, of course, I wasn't, so I told him I had to go to college.

One time, he took me to the 79th Street Causeway, which overlooks Biscayne Bay, to watch the "submarine races," as he said. That was a joke we had back then…an excuse for making out. We didn't do much more than make out. As far as I was concerned, we were mostly just friends who danced together.

My parents would both be at work while we were dancing. Looking back, they probably knew about it. If they had asked, I wouldn't have lied, but I didn't offer it.

My parents always trusted me. Still, if I went out on a date, they were always there when I came home. They made sure I didn't stay out later than I was supposed to. They had nothing to worry about. I never really misbehaved. I was basically a good and honest daughter.

Chapter 6

Most of my childhood, I was a Baptist and I took it seriously. I went to Sunday school and church service every Sunday morning. There I was taught to never indulge in alcohol or premarital sex. Those were the two big no-nos. Dancing, well, that was a personal choice.

So I was always a little scandalized when I saw my parents drinking. If they had company visiting from up north, they would serve and drink cocktails. That confused my young mind.

My parents never drank when it was just the three of us at home, except for maybe a little at Thanksgiving or Christmas. Then my father would pour some Manischewitz wine. That was a terrible tasting, sweet stuff and evidently had some kind of religious significance.

But to just drink cocktails and socialize? That seemed all wrong. I was shocked and a little upset seeing it. In my mind, because of my religious upbringing, it seemed to me they must be sinning. Still I didn't say anything.

Then, in 1957, during my senior year of high school, with college approaching, I began thinking about what it would be like to be out on my own. I knew a lot of kids did start to drink in college, so, as I was having dinner with my parents one night, I asked them if they thought it would be okay for me to drink in college as well.

My parents were pretty understanding. Without much thought, they said, "Yes, Sylvia, it would be fine for you to drink at college." Well, that sounded good.

Then, as fate would have it, that very same night, I was over at the home of our neighbor, Bob Loft, for a baby-sitting job. He was the pilot who later got killed in the crash in the Everglades. This night, however, the Lofts were celebrating before they went out.

They had just gotten their car painted and, because it was the paint company's 40th anniversary, the Lofts received a free bottle of champagne. They were opening it up when I arrived, and they asked if I would like a sip.

Because my parents had just that night told me it would be okay to eventually start drinking, I decided to say yes. It seemed like too much of a coincidence!

I had never had a drink before, so I took just a little bit. It tasted good and felt good. I didn't feel tipsy or anything, but I did like it.

24

Unbeknownst to me, this would be the first of many drinks I would enjoy in my lifetime.

Then, just to show you how weird life is, the very next night, as I was having dinner with my parents again, my father said, "Well, your mother and I discussed a little more what you asked us last night, and we changed our minds. We decided it would probably be better if you didn't have any alcohol in college."

Oh, Lord, I had already done it!

I felt guilty. In my mind, it was like virginity. Once you do the thing, it's over. Your innocence is gone. I had betrayed my Baptist upbringing. I felt like, once you have a drink, that was it. You could never go back and say, "Oh, I've never had a drink in my life," like a blushing bride could say, "Oh, I've never had sex with a man."

Maybe it was because my church's teaching always linked alcohol and sex together. Both were forbidden. Now I was no longer a virgin with alcohol...why shouldn't I just go ahead and have more? I had lost my alcohol virginity...just like that.

Well, I didn't tell my parents I had already had my first sinful drink of champagne the night before. It had been like I couldn't wait to get that alcohol in me! I felt guilty and confused, so I just kept my mouth shut. I figured, the less I said, the better.

Of course, these panicked thoughts were just the foolish innocence of a young girl starting to make her own way in the world. Fortunately the guilt didn't last long.

Once I got to college, I did enjoy drinking. Alachua County, where the University of Florida was located, was a totally dry county. Everyone had to drive about 30 miles south to Ocala, to get liquor. A favorite place was a store named Ruby's. That's where most people went. There was also a pizza place that served 3.2% beer. That was popular too, even though it wasn't much alcohol.

Drinking was a big social thing at colleges everywhere in the late '50s, just as it is now. I drank at football games and fraternity parties, and so on. I usually only drank when I was socializing. I didn't keep alcohol in my room or anything like that.

When I did drink, it was usually just vodka with grape juice or something similar. Some people actually drank bourbon, but I always hated it. That's where I drew the line.

One of the busboys in my sorority house – who may have been

Mexican or Latin – gave me some tequila once to try. I did the whole ritual, with licking the salt off my hand, taking a shot of tequila, and then sucking on a lemon wedge. That was different, but a lot of work.

Meanwhile, I hadn't completely abandoned my Baptist beliefs. I was still at least a Sunday Baptist! It was really hard for me to understand how the girls in my dorm could so free and easily not even think about going to church on Sunday morning.

I'd walk down the dorm hall, getting ready to go, dressing up in my Sunday best, and these other girls would be just lying there, hanging out doing nothing...or maybe recovering from drinking the night before.

I was brought up going to church every Sunday morning. Sometimes my parents and I would go out for dinner or lunch afterwards, so Sundays were a real family occasion. The whole religious disconnect at college really bothered me at first.

Still, this experience helped me realize other people grew up differently and thought differently. The world wasn't all like my family and my childhood.

College definitely changes people. It's a real eye-opener. You see there's a whole new world out there you know nothing about. If someone had told me then all the things I would do in my later life, I would have sworn they were talking about someone else!

I went to the University of Florida. All my friends were going there. It was a great deal, because as a state school, it was tuition-free back then. There was a $75 activity fee my parents had to pay, plus books, dorm, food and so on, but that was nothing compared to what college costs today.

At one point, my father had wanted me to go to Baylor because it was a Baptist school. Imagine, if I had gone there, my life would have been totally different!

There was also another Baptist school my father kept talking about, Stetson, in Deland, Florida. Maybe I had already subconsciously checked out of the Baptist thing, but I had no desire to go to either of those schools.

My parents would have had to pay tuition there, since they were private schools, so that helped sway them in the direction I wanted. My social life was important to me and all my friends were going to UF, so that was the only place I applied.

I originally wanted to become a medical technologist, but UF didn't have that program then. They had just opened their medical school. They had an MD program and a nursing program, and that was it.

I went to see my guidance counselor and he said medical technology wouldn't start till the following year. He suggested transferring to a technical school, if I really wanted to pursue medical technology.

That wouldn't work for me. All my life my parents had instilled in me that I was going to go to college...not technical school! I wanted a college degree and my parents wanted me to have one even more – so I could have the good life, which would come with that degree. Plus I did like learning. So I stayed at UF.

I eventually decided to go into nursing, even though I didn't want to ever work in a hospital. For one thing, I hated uniforms. In the College of Nursing, for clinical duties we had to wear the full nurse's uniform, even the cap. Terrible. They don't require that any more, not even white uniforms. It's all just colored scrubs now, which are much more comfortable and practical.

Another reason I decided to go into nursing was because I always liked to travel and I wanted to be able to live and work anywhere in the world. I later did that, thanks to my nursing degree. I didn't really want to be a nurse, but I did want to learn about life and about the body. My mother thought it would be a good career for me, so it seemed like the right choice for the time.

If I had it to do it all over again, I'd probably still go the same way. I ended up working in medical research, which is what I really wanted to do. The only other path I ever considered was becoming a clinical psychologist, but that would have taken a PhD, which would have meant another four years of school. If I had gone that route, I never would have married Doug, so I'm happy I did what I did.

Chapter 7

I was very popular in college. I had lots of guys to date, too many, in fact. My dorm room was at one end of the hall and the only phone was at the other end. I got more calls on that phone than any other girl in there.

Every time I got one, somebody would yell out my name and I would have to walk all the way down the hall, as everybody looked on. I didn't know whether to be embarrassed or proud. I was sure all the other girls were wondering who all these guys were that I was dating?

Well, it was a funny story. When I first got to school, I had just met three different boys that summer at a Baptist retreat in Asheville, North Carolina. Believe it or not, all three of them were related to each other, two brothers and a cousin.

They knew that I was going to the University of Florida, which they liked, because that was where they were all going as well. Somehow they each found me and asked me out, one after the other.

Being a good Baptist girl, these were the first guys I went out with. Of course, to start with, they were the only ones I knew, but that didn't last long. And neither did they.

I dated the first one and eliminated him. Then I tried another one, who also didn't work out. Finally, number three quickly helped me realize why I had put him off till last.

I didn't like any of them because they didn't hold my interest. I guess I was ready to expand my horizons. They were all very religious and I still was too, but I soon discovered I preferred dating guys who were going on to graduate school, more intellectual guys. That was my type.

Brains really appealed to me, even at a young age. I was in the National Honor Society and I especially liked men who were very intelligent and going somewhere.

I dated guys who were studying medicine, dentistry, law, engineering, and so on, men who were headed for advanced degrees. The guys I went out with were all really smart. The one I married was the smartest one of all.

When I married my husband, Doug, he had his PhD and worked with famous PhDs from all over the world. In my life, I too have worked in medical research with PhDs and MDs at the top of their professions.

Yet in spite of all that intelligence around me, not too long after I started college, I pledged a sorority, Alpha Omega Pi. I joined as a freshman and moved into the sorority house my sophomore year. The sorority sisters were fine. One of the girls, Jenny, is still my best friend here in Miami, but I soon realized I didn't like living in a sorority.

My father was paying all this extra money for me to live in that house. I think a lot of the money went to all the food they prepared for us. There were three big meals a day, juicy pies, delicious snacks and more. You could gain a lot of weight if you ate everything they put in front of you.

It was too much temptation for me. Just the crust of a slice pie, I heard, had 300 calories by itself. People who like to eat a lot might like that, but not me. I never ate much anyway, because I don't have a high metabolism and I had always watched my weight. To have to sit and eat with these girls, looking at so much food, when all I wanted was a little bit…well, that wasn't much fun.

Plus, they were always having meetings, which we were required to attend. Sitting in all these meetings really interfered with my social life. I got fed up and actually moved out of the house back into the dorm for a semester. Then I figured, *Oh, well, I might as well be a sorority girl* and moved back into the house for my junior year.

Then came the final straw.

My boyfriend at the time, Charlie Horn, had come over to an open house at my invitation. He brought a joke book with him, so we were upstairs in my room innocently reading this book and laughing together. Meanwhile, all these people were walking past my open door, making noise. and disturbing us. So I closed the door.

I didn't know I could get in trouble for that. It was forbidden to shut your door if there was a man in your room. So I was brought up before the sorority standards committee.

I guess I didn't meet their standards and I felt they didn't meet mine. I knew what I had to do. I resigned from the sorority. They gracefully released me and let me keep my pin.

I was much happier out of there. I was too independent for a sorority. I had a girlfriend, Lois Tourtelot, who was studying nursing with me and had an apartment by herself off-campus. She wanted a roommate, so she invited me to come live with her. I loved it.

I had no curfew. I could stay up till 2:00 or 3:00 am, if I wanted to. I could invite guys over, whatever. Don't get the wrong idea. Despite the fun and freedom, I still wasn't having sex with these guys. I didn't believe in that at the time.

In fact, that's why Charlie Horn and I broke up. I had started dating Charlie in my junior year. He was actually the third guy I met and fell in love with during college. Doug, my future husband, was the second, but that's another story. The first guy later became a dentist, but we didn't really go very far together in college.

I really liked Charlie. I was actually thinking I would marry him when we graduated, if he asked me to. Then, one night soon after our joke book escapade, while I was still living at the sorority house, he was bringing me back from a date.

It was late, after my curfew. I would get in trouble if I came in then, so I decided to just stay out all night with him. I figured my roommate, Jenny, wouldn't turn me in, and she didn't.

Charlie and I went back his apartment. For some reason, me being out all night with him at his place was just too much for him. He wanted to have sex and he wanted it bad. I wouldn't do it…because I loved him. I thought if I gave in, he would never see me as wife material.

My strategy backfired. Charlie got mad at me when I wouldn't surrender my virginity and, because of that, we broke up. I loved Charlie, but felt he just wouldn't respect me enough to marry me if we had sex together. That's the way people thought in those days.

I don't know if I was right or not in my assessment. Maybe we really just weren't right for each other. Many years later, when I was in my 50s, I called Charlie, but it was a big let-down.

He was still living near Gainesville and I was in the area. We talked on the phone for almost an hour, but he said he didn't want to see me again in person. He said he just wanted to remember me as I was. I thought that was awful.

One more life-changing thing that happened at college was that, during my freshman year, I met a girl who wore contact lenses. They were still pretty new then. They had only been introduced in 1948. At first, they were hard, plastic lenses that just covered the corneas. She told me, "Oh, gee, yes, they're great. You ought to get them."

I suddenly saw how I could be freed from wearing glasses. That summer I decided I wanted to buy contact lenses. I had some money saved up from my summer job at a bank and that's what I wanted. My mother said it was fine, but my father was always suspicious of certain things.

He was usually a lot of fun, but he had a few prejudices, like not wanting me to drink coffee. Contact lenses were another bugaboo for him. He just couldn't accept how you could put something like that in your eyes.

Well, since it was my money, I just went ahead and got them anyway. And I loved them. I wore contacts all my life, till I got Lasik surgery about fourteen years ago. Eventually contacts became gas permeable, which made them more comfortable.

As I got older, my optometrist adjusted my prescription, so I had monovision. I could see distant things with my right eye and close things with my left eye. When I got the Lasik surgery, the ophthalmologist did the same thing, so I wouldn't have to use reading glasses after the surgery.

The extracurricular activities I enjoyed most in college were the Foreign Student Club, cultural events, tennis and, of course, dating. Sometimes I combined them, by going on tennis dates.

One good friend I met at the Foreign Student Club, as a freshman, was Sid Mittra. He was from India and was working on his doctorate in Finance. He would send me articles he had written and ask me to review them, to see if they were good enough for *The Gator*, our college newspaper.

I couldn't understand why he asked me, because I was a Nursing major, not an English major. Still, we became good friends and continue to be after all these years. Knowing him made me want to go to India, to see where he grew up, which eventually turned into a trip around the whole world years later.

Sid wrote three pages about me in his autobiography, *Yes, the Bee Can Fly*. It's a very interesting book. My picture, which I had autographed for him when I was a freshman, is featured in there. He was even nice enough to say I was the most popular girl at the University of Florida at the time, although that may be a stretch.

Once he and I were working on a project together, when he told me he needed a date for a fraternity party he had been invited to. Being a nice person, I offered to accompany him.

In his book, he said that, at first he declined my offer because, "Sylvia was extremely popular and boys were always chasing after her." I guess he was a little intimidated, but finally he accepted.

His description of the party we went to and how he reacted to it is hilarious. A conservative upbringing in India had not prepared him for the wild goings-on at a college fraternity in America.

After college, I didn't hear from Sid for 50 years. Then, after I moved to Miami, he called the University of Florida, got my email address and sent me an email.

I happened to have a date the night his email arrived, but I checked my computer when I came home and there he was...after 50 years! I was astonished. I couldn't believe it. I was ecstatic. I didn't know what had happened to him.

So I asked him for his cell number and called him. That's when he told me he had written his autobiography and he wanted to send me a copy of it, because I was in it.

When I opened it up, I saw he had autographed my copy of his book, with the following dedication: "To Sylvia Booma Carroll, for a friendship lasting half a century. Best, Sid Mittra."

I'll have to send him an autographed copy of this one.

Chapter 8

It's a really interesting story how I met my husband during my freshman year at college. It was all because my father was going to be installed as president of the Florida Furniture Dealers Association.

My parents had had a lot of success with their furniture business. They had moved from their original location on 40th street to Biscayne Boulevard near 79th street. Then they moved again to a bigger location a few blocks west, near 79th street and 2nd Avenue. That area is not very nice now, but it was in those days.

They had also changed the name of the business to Babyland Booma, to feature my father's last name, another stroke of marketing genius. With all his success, my father had worked his way up the ladder of furniture dealers in Florida and had been elected president of their association.

The meeting where he was to be inaugurated was to be in Jacksonville, Florida on the weekend of May 2, 1958. My parents invited me to come, since UF was only 75 miles away from Jacksonville. Since I was still in the sorority at the time and dated a lot of fraternity guys, I knew one fellow whose father was also in furniture sales. I invited him to go as my date, thinking it would be a natural fit.

Well, this guy couldn't go and another fraternity guy couldn't either, so I didn't know what to do. I happened to drop into the Baptist Student Center. There I ran into a casual acquaintance, Reese Waters, whom I knew was from Jacksonville. I didn't particularly like him as someone to date, but I was running out of options.

So I asked Reese, "Would you give me a ride to Jacksonville this Friday? My parents are going to this big function there and I want to join them."

He said he could, so then I said, "I have a dinner to go to Saturday night with my parents. Would you like to go with me?"

He said, "Well, I don't know if I can do that. I may not be in town Saturday night, but don't worry, Sylvia, I know a lot of guys from Jacksonville and I can fix you up with someone."

Well, that sounded pretty good to me. Problem solved.

Sure enough, Reese managed to arrange everything. That Friday afternoon at 4:00, four guys came by my dorm to pick me up for our grand adventure.

Now, picture this. Back in the late 50s, cars still had bench seats in the front, just like they still do today in the back. It was all one seat, like a sofa, so there was room for someone to sit in the middle. That's where I was stationed.

The driver, on my left, was Ronnie Braswell, who later became a professor at Florida State. In the back was Reese. Another guy, Hank Gran, was back there with him. To my right, was Doug Carroll. He was 6'4." I had always liked tall guys. I liked Doug. Plus, the fact that he had very twinkly, blue eyes made him interesting and intriguing to me. There was a glimmer in his eyes I didn't see in most people's.

I still had no idea who the lucky guy was, who was going to be my date, but all the way to Jacksonville, Doug was talking to me non-stop. I found out that even though he was just 19 (18 days older than me), he would be graduating college Phi Beta Kappa in just three more months. He was completing school in two and a half years, after entering early, and had a fellowship to get his PhD at Princeton.

Doug had been valedictorian of his high school class, even though he was only 16 when he graduated. His fellowship at Princeton had to do with Educational Testing Service (ETS), the organization that developed the SATs and many other exams. They were headquartered at Princeton.

Doug had to take a very competitive exam to win this fellowship, which was only awarded to two students each year. Al Kurtz, Doug's faculty advisor, had told him to apply, which he did. And Doug got one. He was obviously a genius.

So I was thinking to myself, *This guy is really ambitious. He's going somewhere in life. I'd like to date him!*

With all this going through my head, just as we got close to Jacksonville, Reese in the back piped up and said, "Oh, Sylvia, by the way, I definitely can't go to that dinner tomorrow night, so Doug's gonna take you."

Bells started going off in my head. I was ecstatic, but, of course, I didn't show it. I just very nonchalantly turned around and said, "Oh, really?" and let it go at that.

When we got to the Washington Hotel, where my parents were staying, Doug said to me, as I got out of the car, "Sylvia, what are you doing tonight?"

I said, "Well, I don't know, let me check with my parents."

When I found my parents, they said, "Oh, there's a cocktail party and

34

dinner tonight. Why don't you invite your friend?"

So that's how it happened that the first time I ever drank alcohol in front of my parents was also the same day I met my future husband. Go figure.

As we all stood there at the party, the waiters were bringing around big trays of drinks. I picked out a whiskey sour and prepared to show off my newfound prowess at drinking.

It felt really weird to drink in front of my parents, but we were at a cocktail party which they had invited me to, so why not? We were all adults, right? As I sipped that sweet and sour libation, I felt like I was really taking a big step in my life. I had no idea just how life-changing that night would truly be.

My parents pretended not to notice me drinking, so everything went well. Later, I even indulged in a Canadian Club cocktail as well.

When the dinner was over, Doug and I left about 10:00 and went to see a movie together, *Teacher's Pet*, starring Clark Gable and Doris Day. It was cute.

Then we went for a ride down to Jacksonville Beach. Doug was really nice. He parked right on the beach and kissed me a couple of times. Later, he took me back to my door at the hotel, where he kissed me again. I didn't get in until 2:30 in the morning.

I wrote in my diary that night, "Doug was the perfect date." Nobody else ever had been.

Saturday evening, Doug came over for the inauguration banquet. My parents, of course, were seated up at the head table, while Doug and I were at another table. After dinner and a floor show, there was dance music. Doug and I danced and talked a lot. I even had a martini. Very sophisticated!

As we were socializing, a woman who was chatting with me said in the course of our conversation, "And so, what does your husband do?"

I was aghast. I thought, *Egads, I only met this guy yesterday and already people think we're married?*

"Oh," I blushed, "we're both just students at U of F. We're just 19 years old." Still, a girl can dream, can't she?

At midnight, the party was over, so Doug and I drove over to the St. John's River, where we took a romantic, moonlit walk along the water. It was so pretty and cool. Doug kissed me some more and then took me back to the hotel at 1:30, where he kissed me good night again. It felt like something was really happening here. I was truly starry-eyed.

The whole weekend Doug and I hit it off really well. The next day, Sunday, he invited me to come over to his home. He would pick me up, so Ronnie, who was driving us back to UF, wouldn't have to make an extra stop at my hotel.

That meant: Not only did my future husband and I meet each other that amazing weekend...we both also met each other's families.

Yes, I believe in destiny or whatever you want to call it. Something definitely seemed to be greasing the rails.

We actually had milk and cookies that afternoon at Doug's parents' house. Doug's father was about six feet tall and very slender. He talked to me a lot, asking things like, what was my major, what were my plans for the future, and so on.

Doug's father was very rigid and set in his ways, stand-offish, and introverted. He wouldn't even let Doug come in the living room when he was playing his records, because he couldn't be disturbed or distracted. Everything had to be just so. He never went to college, but he was self-educated and knew a lot about many different things, because he read all the time.

He wasn't religious. If he ever went to a church, it was Unitarian, but he didn't go often. He was brought up a Catholic and when he married my mother-in-law, his father actually disowned him for marrying a Baptist girl.

Doug was closer to his mother than to his father. His mother was the social one. She was very sweet, but a strict Southern Baptist. She would take Doug to her church, where he was constantly told that if you don't do the right thing, you'll go to hell. Doug only went with her because he loved her.

Still, he must have believed it all to some degree, because one summer he actually ministered as the youth pastor at their church. When he went to college though, he suddenly lost his religion in his freshman year. He said he was just sitting on a toilet when it happened. He had some kind of sudden realization or something, and that was it.

When we first started dating, I got Doug to go to the Baptist church with me in Gainesville a couple of times, but he never liked it. He was done with religion by then. Okay, I'm getting ahead of my story.

When we arrived back at school that Sunday night, Doug very courteously brought my bag into my dorm for me and said we should go out the following weekend. He kissed me again in the dorm lobby and vanished into the mist. What a marvelous weekend it was.

Sure enough, Doug called and asked me out for a date the following Saturday. He also asked me to bring another girl for his friend Dave. He wanted to do a double date. I was fine with that and said I would line someone up

During the week, we got together again and went to the library, where we talked a lot and studied together. My diary said, "He's so interesting to talk to."

Afterwards, he walked me to my dorm and kissed me goodnight. Again, I wrote, "It was so wonderful. It felt like I was floating on a cloud. I like him so much!"

Then another night that same week he called and asked if I wanted to go to a play that same night. I was so mad, because I had a date with somebody else and couldn't go with Doug. He said it was all right, because he should just study anyway. I felt bad. I really wanted to be with him.

Our big double date started out with Doug and Dave Shoen picking me up in the afternoon and driving out to a nearby lake. We went swimming, rowing, taking pictures, and so on. Dave was studying photography and he took many pictures of me.

That evening I showed Doug my sorority house. We sat out on the patio and kissed some more. My diary said, "He is so kissable."

Doug took me back to the dorm at 1:15 am, where there was a lot more kissing in the lobby. Doug didn't seem to want to leave. He said, "You're sweet." That surprised me. I didn't think of myself as sweet.

The next night I ran into Doug by accident, as I was leaving the library and he was entering. I decided to go back in the library with him and "study" some more. Afterwards, he walked me to my dorm and kissed me lightly on the lips to say goodnight.

So by the end of that school year, we were seeing each other all the time. Doug was calling me, we were meeting in the library, or going out on a date. He was definitely chasing me. There was no question about that.

Then school was over and I went home for the summer. I was living with my parents that summer, so I got a job in a bank around the corner from their business in Little River. Then one day in July, just a couple of months after I had met Doug, my mother called me at work and said,

"Sylvia, you'll never guess who's in town…"

"Who?" I asked, mystified.

"Doug Carroll and his parents! They're here on vacation, over in a motel on Sunny Isles Beach." Sunny Isles is actually where I live now, the north end of Miami Beach. I was shocked. I had no idea they were coming.

Evidently, they had been driving to New Orleans for a little vacation with Doug, before he left for Princeton. They had gotten almost all the way there, when Doug's father suddenly said, "You know, I don't really want to go to New Orleans."

And Doug chimed in, "I don't want to go to New Orleans either. I want to go to Miami Beach." So they turned the car around and drove back to Miami instead.

Now maybe that was because I was in Miami, I don't know, but I like to think so. They stayed for three days. While they were here, Doug borrowed the car, to take me out on a date. I don't think I saw his parents.

While Doug and I were out together, he invited me to come up to UF for the Summer Frolics. He was finishing his courses there and planned to graduate in August.

So I went and we had a good time. Then Doug invited me to come back up again for his graduation. That August, I flew from Miami up to Jacksonville and then drove with him and his parents to Gainesville for his graduation.

Afterwards, we drove back to his home with his parents. The next day, we saw him off on the train to Princeton. At Christmastime that year, his family invited me up again for a week and I flew up.

It certainly seemed like this was turning into something serious.

Chapter 9

I had more than my share of tragedy at a young age. My grandfather died when I was 13. My grandmother died in 1958, when I was 19. And eleven months later, when I was 20, my mother died.

After my grandfather passed away, my grandmother moved down to Miami, where she lived in her own house, not far from ours, for about four years. While I was in my freshman year of college, she went into the hospital to get surgery for some kind of cancer. She got through the surgery okay, but in the course of her stay in the hospital, she got a blood clot and died.

We were all heart-broken. She was such a sweet lady. I always called her "Honey." I found out after her death that she had left me $2,000. I decided I would use that money to take a trip to Europe. It was a life-long dream of mine and now, thanks to my beloved grandmother, I had the means to make it happen.

Meanwhile, my mother hadn't been feeling well for a long time herself. She kept plugging away as if nothing was wrong, but she knew it was. She would even go to her doctors in Miami and say, "I think I have cancer," and they would say, "Oh no, you don't have cancer. Don't worry about it."

Finally, towards the end of my sophomore year, out of desperation, she flew up to Connecticut to see our old friend, Dr. Wight, who had delivered me. That same weekend my father, as president of the Florida Furniture Dealers Association, had to be at their annual convention at the Dupont Hotel in downtown Miami.

My mother was originally supposed to be with my father as his first lady, but she was feeling too ill to go with him. She felt she had to get to the bottom of what was wrong and that Dr. Wight was her last hope to do so.

My father called me up in Gainesville and asked me to, please, come home for the weekend and take her place. Of course, like a good daughter, I did.

It was a lovely meeting. People really missed my mother and everyone was asking for her. I wrote her a letter about it later. Then, that Sunday night, after the meeting was over, we called Dr. Wight up in Connecticut.

He said my mother was already jaundiced and it didn't look good to him. He was going to do an exploratory surgery on her the next morning. He also told my father that he should get up there right away. That sounded even worse.

I had to go back to Gainesville, because I was preparing to take my final exams, so I told my father to, please, let me know what happened. We were hoping for the best.

Several days later, my father sent me a postcard. He always used postcards instead of letters. These weren't the tourist postcards with a picture. They were the old fashioned, U.S. Mail postcards, which you could send for a few cents. They had the whole backside blank to write on, so he could get quite a bit on there.

Anyway, he had written my mother's diagnosis on this postcard. It didn't sound so bad. It said my mother had "an over-active enzyme system." Supposedly, that was what was wrong with her.

My father didn't tell me she was actually dying and had just a short time left. The doctor and his wife had counseled him that, if he told me my mother was dying, I probably wouldn't be able to get through my finals. Which was true. I wouldn't have been able to study or concentrate. I probably would have just come straight home to be with her.

Puzzled by that postcard, I wanted to get to the bottom of what was going on, so I asked one of my nursing instructors, "What is an over-active enzyme system?"

She looked at me quizzically and said, "I don't know. I never heard of such a thing." Looking back, I know now, it probably doesn't even exist. I think it was just something the doctor made up for my father to tell me.

Well, not knowing any better, I decided to just stay optimistic. I took my finals, got a ride back to Miami on May 30th, and walked up the sidewalk to our front door. When I opened the door and saw my father, I almost went into shock. In the three weeks since I had last seen him, he had lost 25 pounds. He looked awful.

Then I noticed there was a couple there, who were friends of my parents from New Jersey. They had been matron of honor and best man at my parents' wedding. Normally, they would visit Miami in January or February, never in the heat of June. Obviously something was up.

I stepped slowly inside and down one step into the breezeway. Then my father told me the truth. My mother was dying. She had cancer of the pancreas and only three months to live at the most. It's a deadly disease.

There's still no cure for it today. I started shaking uncontrollably. I just couldn't stop.

Then I heard my mother calling me. Her voice came from my bedroom. When she had returned from Connecticut, she had moved out of her bedroom into mine. There were two twin beds in my room. I guess she wanted my father to be able to sleep comfortably in their room.

I went to her bedside. I could see she was in bad shape. They had her on pain medication, so she was fighting off grogginess to speak to me. The first thing she said was, "How did your finals go?"

I said, "They were fine, mother." It felt ridiculous to even talk about that. The second thing she said was, "I still want you to go to Europe this summer." I couldn't believe she would even say such a thing, but she didn't know she was dying.

She did know that I had been planning a two-month, 14-country tour with the $2,000, which her mother had left me. She was fine with the idea, because she liked it better than my alternate plan of buying a car. I guess she thought, if I had my own car, I'd have an accident and kill myself.

I said, "Mother, you are going to need me around the house this summer. Don't worry about it. I'll just go to Europe next summer."

It was a good thing I offered to stay and help her, because later, when I spoke privately to my father, he told me, "We don't want to get a nurse. We don't want your mother to know she's dying, so we'll just let you take care of her."

Now, since I was majoring in Nursing, that may have seemed like a good idea, but I wasn't happy about it. I didn't have any hands-on experience nursing and I didn't want any. Taking care of sick people was not what I got into nursing for. This was a doubly difficult situation and it was all just thrust on me.

In the meantime, my father had to keep working every day, running his business. I was on my own, watching my beloved mother die of cancer. There was no other nurse. I gave her injections, bathed her, fed her, slept in the same room with her...I was the full-time caregiver.

My only escape was to occasionally go out for a couple of hours in the evening, when my father was home. The fellow who had given me a ride from college, Henry Lewis, would invite me out and I would go, just to get away from the grief. It seemed this was how I would spend my summer.

41

Then one day, while I was at my mother's side, a very strange thing happened. As she was progressively slipping away, she had started seeing things. So this day I heard her say, "Now, isn't that nice?"

I said, "What's nice, mother?"

She answered, "Your engagement to Doug Carroll is in the Miami Herald. " That gave me chills.

I didn't know and I still don't know if she was seeing the future. She did like Doug a lot and I did too. At the time, I figured this just meant that she wanted me to marry Doug.

Whatever the case, when Doug and I finally did get married, I was happy that she had known who my husband would be.

Then, a few days later, on June 7, just eight days after I had arrived home from school, came the next tragedy in my life. That night, I wrote in my dairy:

"Dear sweet mother died this afternoon at 1:50. It was really a blessing that she didn't have to suffer any more, since she couldn't get any better. I had given her a bath in the morning at 11:00, a little Jell-O, and some codeine.

"About five minutes later, she said she had a terrible pain, the worst ever. I called Mrs. Thompson and gave her some hot tea."

Now Mrs. Thompson was a woman living across the street, who was a nurse. She had told me after I got home, "If I can help you at all, any time, Sylvia, please, let me know."

Well, if I ever needed help, it was then. Thank God, she was there.

My diary continues:

"When I couldn't get a pulse on her, I called Mrs. Thompson again and she came over. She said, 'I hope the Lord makes me a liar, but she won't see tomorrow.'

"I counted her respirations at 40, 36, 18, 16. She didn't respond to me. I kept checking on her every five minutes, taking a quick two-minute shower at one point. Then I looked in the room and couldn't see any respiration. I called Mrs. Thompson, who checked her and said, 'She's gone.'

"I cried but felt relieved that my mother was out of her misery."

I'm amazed I was able to write all that. We called the doctor and that was that.

My mother was gone. I was in shock.

Chapter 10

I had nightmares for seven years after my mother died. I don't recall them exactly, but they were tortured memories of reliving my mother's death, over and over again. This kept repeating for seven years.

Mother had been the strong person in the family. She kept it all together. She had a sense of responsibility that my father didn't seem to have. She was more quiet and reserved. She was the main person in my life to give me direction. She had always steered me to do the right thing.

I realized now, with a sinking feeling, that I would be more on my own than ever. My father wasn't even there when she died. He was out making deliveries for the furniture business.

Another strange thing. That terrible day my mother died, June 7, was also the exact same date my husband Doug died, many years later. June 7 is not a happy day for me.

The next day, June 8, was my father's birthday, a big one. He was turning 60, but there wasn't much celebrating. I gave him a set of studs and cufflinks as his birthday present. Then we went over to Philbrick's funeral home and picked out mother's casket.

People came by the house all day. Some brought food. Then we were at the funeral home from 7:00 to 10:00, receiving people for the viewing. Many came and brought beautiful flowers.

The next day, just two days after Mother died, my father held her funeral at the Miami Shores Baptist church. About 150 people attended. It was a beautiful service. Everyone was telling me how sweet and kind Mother was, a true Christian.

Then my father and I flew to New York on June 10, just three days after Mother died. He had everything planned. Daddy wanted to hold a second funeral and bury her up north, so all of her friends and family could say good-bye.

We had Mother's body sent by train up to Massachusetts, where she would rest next to her parents in Charlemont, at the foot of the Mohawk Trail. That's where she and her father had been born and where her family was buried.

The train was how most people transported bodies at that time. When my grandmother had died, my mother personally went with her casket up to Massachusetts, but my father sent Mother's body by itself, since he had to stay with me.

Meanwhile, my father and I flew up north to New York for a few days on the way. Trying to cheer me up, I guess, my father said, "Now we're going to relax and have a good time."

We stayed in a nice suite at the Empire Hotel in the City for three days. While we were there, we saw the Rockettes at Radio City Music Hall and ate at Mama Leone's Restaurant, a famous place in the theater district.

We also saw *My Fair Lady*. The show was sold out, but my father gave someone a tip and got them to set up extra seats in the aisle for us. We also went shopping on Fifth Avenue, getting gifts for our friends from New Jersey, who had helped at the end, and for Mrs. Thompson, the nurse across the street.

From there, we took the train for Hartford, where we stayed with friends. We had the second funeral June 13 in Shelburne Falls, Massachusetts. Many of Mother's close friends and relatives were there.

We buried her at Levitt Cemetery in Charlemont. We drove there in a procession. It was a beautiful, peaceful spot, right next to a river. When my father died years later and I had to have him cremated, I sent his ashes up there also, to be buried near Mother.

It didn't seem possible she was really gone. I said in my diary, "It's like a terrible dream and Mother is still home."

After the funeral, I heard my father talking to a married couple, who were friends of my parents. We were staying overnight with them. I remember him saying, "Well, I will never get over this, but Sylvia will."

He didn't know I overheard him, but I felt that was an awful thing to say. The fact is, it took me many years to get over my mother's death.

Her passing really devastated me. It was such a shock. It had all happened so fast. I was only 20, and yet it seemed ridiculous for me to be alive. The future looked bleak. I was sure I was going to end up like my mother, getting cancer and dying at 56 years old. What was the point? Life didn't make sense any more.

We flew back to Miami, my father went back to work, and I just took care of him and the house the rest of that summer. I was very, very depressed. I kept thinking, *The same thing is going to happen to me one day. Why even bother?*

Meanwhile, Doug had written to say he was very sorry to hear about my mother's death. He had just met her the year before, the same weekend he met me. He actually flew down to visit me in Miami, I guess to help me feel better.

He stayed with us from June 23rd to the 29th. We had a nice time, going to the beach, the Fontainebleau Hotel, and so on. It did help some, but then Doug went back to Jacksonville, and off for another year at Princeton.

On July 6, Doug wrote a very gracious thank-you letter to my father and me for our hospitality. Then I didn't hear from him again till August 1. When I did, I noted in my diary, "Boy, was I happy to hear from him!"

It's hard to understand in these days of total, 24-hour connection, but back then, if you were in a long distance relationship, it was hard to stay in touch. There was no email, no chat, no texting, no Skype, nothing. Long distance phone calls were very expensive. Letters were pretty much all we had and they weren't much.

Doug was at Princeton and I was at UF. We were both dating other people. Doug and I weren't going steady and I always dated a lot of guys anyway, so I was just having fun while we were apart.

There was one guy that summer in Miami, Frank, who wanted me to marry him right away. There was another guy, Walter, who was the son of a dear friend of my father's. He was also very interested in me. I had a lot of suitors at any given time.

In the fall, I went back to college to start my junior year, still in a daze from my mother's death. I was in the sorority and everyone was very nice to me, but I was hurting.

Eventually I found reasons to live. One of them was that, because of my mother's death from pancreatic cancer, I resolved to work in the field of medicine, to help find a way to prevent deaths like that. I planned to work in cancer research or in preventive medicine, which is exactly what I did.

Chapter 11

On October 15, I went to Jacksonville with my nursing class to a home for the aged. While we were there, I called Doug's mother to say hello and we had a nice talk.

She said she regularly heard from Doug once a month, but he never said anything about his personal life, so there was no indication of how he was feeling about me. Then she said one thing I was very happy with, "You know how much we think of you, Sylvia."

On November 6, I went to Hank Gran's wedding. He was Doug's best friend and had been in the back seat of the car when Doug and I met. His wedding was held in Jacksonville, with the reception at his parents' house.

It seems weird to me now that Hank got married. Hank hadn't even graduated from college yet, though he did eventually get a degree in engineering. His bride didn't go to UF.

It seemed strange to me, because Hank and I had had a couple of tennis dates just a month or two before and it seemed that he liked me. I thought they were dates, anyway, even though we didn't do anything romantic. Hank and I had a lot in common, more than Doug and I did. We were both very interested in sports.

Hank certainly never said he was engaged or anything. His wife's name was Mary. I don't know how they met. Maybe she was a secretary at school. Even though she was much older than he was, he didn't find that out until she died, when he saw her birth certificate.

I don't know how you could be married to someone for years and not know how old they are. She also couldn't have children, so they eventually adopted a girl and a boy.

Years later, she was actually jealous of me, when Doug and I would go out with Hank and her. I heard about this from Hank's second wife. It wasn't that Mary was worried about me taking Hank. It was that I was so independent and she wasn't.

So anyway, back to Hank's wedding. Doug's parents were there also. I reconnected with them, which was nice. Doug's mother told me I was just as pretty as ever. Later, as fate would have it, I ended up catching the bridal bouquet. I didn't know if that meant something or not, but I was a little embarrassed, because Doug's parents were there and I had been dating him.

Then, not long after that, I received a very disheartening letter from Doug. Even though everything had seemed fine when we were together in the summer, he wrote me a Dear John letter, or Dear Sylvia, whatever you want to call it. We were over. Just like that.

This came completely out of the blue and really shook me up. From the time we had met, the chemistry had been there immediately. Starting that weekend, with him kissing me, then calling me and running into me at school, visiting my home in the summer, going to Summer Frolics, going to his graduation, spending Christmas week with him and his family, spending a week together after my mother died....

Now all of a sudden, he wrote me this letter. It was very rational and highbrow, saying things like, "There's something missing in our relationship. It seems we are just not meant for each other...." and so on.

I don't remember exactly what he said, but the gist of it was that we didn't need to see each other any more. I was upset, very upset. Yes, I was dating. He was up at Princeton and I assumed he was dating too. I wasn't going to not date and just pine away. I was very popular and always had guys asking me out. Why wouldn't I go? I wasn't going to stay home and be a hermit.

But Doug was the one I was waiting for.

Just a couple of months earlier, I had seen a photo of Doug and Walter, the guy I had also been dating that summer. When I saw that picture, with the two of them side by side, I realized how l much I loved Doug. I was even knitting him a sweater with the Princeton name and colors on it when I got the letter.

He was the only guy I had an 8x10 photograph of in my room. I don't remember if I cried or got angry, but I was very emotional about this breakup. I told my friends it was finished with Doug, but I was still in love with him.

So, after losing my mother, now I had lost Doug as well. Still, a part of me remembered my mother's dying words, that she saw our engagement announced in the Miami Herald.

I may have not written anything in my diary about this breakup, because I can't find any entries about it. Maybe it was too traumatic, but I eventually got over it. I've never totally fallen down in life and not been able to get back up again. I always get up and keep going.

I learned later, that Doug had met a girl, Kathleen, up in New Jersey and had started dating her. I don't know if they were having sex or not. I know Doug and I weren't. I was still a virgin.

Maybe it was just that she was so much closer and more convenient, I don't know. She was certainly around and I wasn't. Doug and I were 800 miles apart. Maybe she told him that if he wanted to be with her, he would have to end it with me.

Doug later told me that he eventually broke up with Kathleen because she was Catholic. She didn't believe in birth control and wanted to have a lot of kids. He definitely didn't want that.

Well, life went on. Then, the next February, my first cousin, Ruth, who lived in Hartford, invited me to go skiing at Mount Snow, Vermont. I jumped at the offer. Strangely enough, the best ride I could find up there was to Princeton, so I wrote Doug to let him know I would be in town.

I felt we were still friends and could socialize together at least. I didn't know if our spark would be rekindled or what might happen if we saw each other again, but what did happen was not romantic.

Doug was very friendly on the phone and actually offered to put me up in a hotel. He even fixed me up on a date with one of his roommates. Doug and I weren't dating any more, after all, so there was no reason to be unpleasant.

It actually worked out great. I liked the guy Doug fixed me up with, a chemistry major. Plus, I loved Princeton, which I had never seen before. I thought it was just beautiful. It's still my favorite university.

In fact, I had so much fun, I decided to stay another night. Doug didn't want to pay for the hotel again, so he let me stay in his apartment in the graduate dorm. This was highly illegal and he could have gotten in a lot of trouble, but nothing happened.

His place had two bedrooms for four guys, with a living room in the middle. I slept peacefully on the couch in the living room. The next day I took the train up to Hartford to meet Ruth. It appeared that Doug and I were now truly "just friends."

48

Chapter 12

By the summer of 1960, a year after my mother's death, I was definitely ready for my long-awaited adventure to Europe. I had just finished my junior year, during which Doug broke up with me, I moved out of the sorority, and then Charlie Horn broke up with me too.

What a year! I was ready for a fresh start and looking forward to getting away from it all. I was originally going to go to Europe by myself as part of a tour, but when my girlfriend Jenny heard about my plans, she insisted on going with me. She and I are still best friends. We had all kinds of stories on that trip.

She was recently cleaning out all her old slides and sent me a bunch from our trip, showing all these strange guys. I didn't know who they were or what we did with them, but she was saying, "Remember this, remember that?"

We had a blast. And that was just the first of many, many trips I've taken all over the world.

Our journey began with my father driving Jenny and me from Miami all the way up to New York. There we boarded a ship to Southampton, England, to start our grand tour of the continent. This was a tour for young people, 18 to 25, I think. I found it someplace. We were planning on spending two months traveling to fourteen different countries...almost two countries every week.

I was just 21, with no ties or responsibilities. I was relishing my freedom and ready for adventure. We had plenty. What was nice about this tour was that they would take us sightseeing during the day and then let us do our own thing at night.

Jenny and I would date the local guys. We'd meet them and they'd take us to a restaurant or a jazz club or whatever. Jenny and I never had sex with any of these guys, but we were both attractive and American, so they'd meet us and ask us out, and we'd see things most tourist don't get to. That's why the trip was so interesting and fun. We learned local stuff, not just the historical stuff.

We both gained weight, about five or ten pounds, which wasn't good. Beer was cheaper there than Coca Cola. Plus, we ate the bread everywhere we went. It was so delicious we couldn't resist.

Once in Norway, the travel agent even asked me out on a date. I told him he had to also get a date for my girlfriend. On our date, we went way up high in the mountains to a restaurant there. He asked if I would like to try something typically Norwegian, so, of course, I said yes.

It was steak tartare. Raw chopped beef., with cut-up onions, capers, peppers, and so on. There was even a raw egg on top. I thought, *Oh, my God, I can't eat a raw egg.* But he put it in the meat, mixed everything up together, and it was absolutely delicious. I loved it.

I thought, *Boy, this is great. When I get married, this is what I'll fix for dinner every night. Then I won't have to cook.* I still eat steak tartare all the time.

After that, we took a boat and they even had little miniature steak tartares as appetizers. I couldn't get enough.

In Brussels another time, I met a fellow who was a musician. He took us to this club, where he was the pianist. He was fantastic. I was so proud, thinking, *Boy, this guy is my date!*

So, even with all this gallivanting around at night, everything went pretty smoothly until Jenny and I were in Italy near the end of our trip. Our next and final stop was to be Paris.

My father was supposed to have sent me some money in Italy, but it never came. So I ended up in Paris penniless, with just one franc to my name. Jenny didn't have much more, maybe $10. And Paris was expensive, compared to other places in Europe.

Still, we weren't going to let a little thing like lack of money stop us from having a good time. It was a Sunday and, at that time, you could get into the Louvre for free on Sundays. So we made our way in and there we met two Persian medical students. Or maybe it would be more accurate to say they met us.

In the course of our conversation, we told them about our sad economic plight. We had some bread and jam in our purses, which we had brought along from the train. We showed it to them as evidence of our poverty.

Then, one of them asked, "Well, do you know how to cook?" We said, "Of course...though it might not be up to Parisian standards." So they invited us to their apartment to cook for them.

There we created a sumptuous feast with whatever food they had on hand. It was mostly scrambled eggs, macaroni, wine, bread, and jam, as I recall.

I'll always remember, they were playing all these Nat King Cole records for us. It was fun. And just the kind of thing I went to Europe to experience.

Later, when my father heard the story, he thought it was so interesting, he had to get it published in the Miami Herald…even though it was his fault we ended up in that situation!

I called my father from Paris. It cost $25 just for the call. He agreed to send money for me to a bank in Paris. In the meantime, we went to the loan department at the American Embassy in Paris and each borrowed $100, to tide us over until the money came from my father.

We needed extra money anyway, because we had been told by our tour guides that there was a U.S. seamen's strike, which would it make it impossible to get a ship back to the U.S. Our scheduled ship was now cancelled. We were told we would have to fly home, which would cost more money than sailing.

We didn't want to fly. Aside from the extra cost, Jenny and I had had so much fun on our cruise over to Europe, we definitely wanted to take a ship back again. So we reserved the last two tickets on a cruise from Le Havre to Montreal. From there, we could get down to Florida.

The ship was sailing later than our original departure date, so we had five extra days left in Europe, thanks to the strike. We didn't have enough money to stay in Paris, so we decided to go to Spain instead until our departure.

We had already made a train reservation for Barcelona, when we found out my father had finally sent us some money, about $300. Unfortunately, it was too late to go to the bank and get it that day.

I was very sick our last day in Paris, before we left for Spain. Jenny and I had lost our room, so I was lying on somebody else's bed, hardly able to move. Jenny had to carry the luggage when we left. She got me a sleeper on the train, since I was so sick. She didn't get one for herself.

I was in the sleeper, when she came in and climbed up into my luggage area and tried to get comfortable there. Evidently, it was better than sleeping in a seat. The conductor came by, checking on everything, but she didn't get caught. Then I threw up in the middle of the night, all over my saddle oxford shoes. Fortunately, Jenny was out of the way. What a night.

In Barcelona, Spain, we stayed in a pension. We had a room plus three meals a day for $1.40 per day, per person. In Paris, that would have cost us $70 a day. We were invited to see a bullfight, but we couldn't go, because we had to leave Spain a day early, in order to pick up my money in Paris.

We had to arrive in Paris during the day, to go to the bank, which we did. Finally we had some financial security. Then we got a hotel room on the Left Bank that night. How romantic.

The next morning, we packed everything up to leave Europe. I sent Jenny down to the street to get a taxi to Le Havre, because she spoke more French than I did.

I was staying with the luggage in our room, but Jenny didn't come back for the longest time. Finally I went out there. Jenny said she couldn't flag down a taxi, because they were all full and no one would stop.

She finally resorted to begging some poor guy in a station wagon for a ride to the train station. Sure enough, it worked. He gave us a ride. That was the only reason we made the train to the port on time.

When the nice man dropped us off at the station, we ran up to the window to get our tickets. By the time we finally reached the train, it was already moving. We both jumped aboard and then poor Jenny just broke down crying. It had been that close and nerve-wracking.

What a relief. We would be able to continue our schooling at the University of Florida, instead of having to apply someplace in France.

When our ship arrived in Montreal, we were glad that we were at least back in North America. Somehow I had let my father know we were now sailing into Montreal, instead of New York. I might have written him a letter while we were in Spain.

My father's best friend had a cousin, who lived in Montreal, so this 45-year-old single man met us at the boat to take care of us. My father and his friend had gone to kindergarten together and known each other their whole lives, so I guess they felt they could trust this guy.

Jenny flew from Montreal down to Florida. Meanwhile, I stayed for two or three days with this man. He was very nice. I had never been to Montreal before, so he showed me around. It was a little weird to be staying with a single man so much older than me, but I always did weird things like that.

I don't think he was gay, but he never made a move on me, even though I was a very attractive 21-year-old girl. It was a little nerve-wracking, of course, but all my life, I've taken chances. I don't gamble for money, but I do gamble with my life.

Maybe this guy was just a real gentleman. When it was time, he got me onto a train to New York City, where I stayed by myself in a hotel in the Village for a couple of days. More adventure! Finally I took another train home to Miami. What a trip.

Chapter 13

When I got back to school and started my junior year, I felt like I didn't really want to be a nurse any more after all. I had seen these bus drivers in Europe who really affected me. It didn't seem like they had much of a job, but they were really happy just being bus drivers. It made me realize you have to love what you're doing.

When I thought about it, I didn't think I would be that happy as a nurse in a hospital with sick people. So I changed my major to psychology. I wanted to be a clinical psychologist.

I also took philosophy and a lot of electives I had never had time for before. I even took statistics and had the same professor Doug had had, Dr. Kurtz, his advisor. I only got a C.

At the end of that first semester though, it hit me. I thought, *This is ridiculous. I only have two semesters left to graduate. If I continue majoring in Psychology, I'll have to go to graduate school to get any kind of good position.* I didn't want to do that and end up in school forever.

So I decided I was better off going back to get my degree in Nursing. I didn't necessarily have to work in a hospital. I could always work in preventive medicine or research or something. So I changed my major again, back to Nursing.

Another big reason I decided on a degree in Nursing was that I wanted a field where I could live anywhere in the world. I didn't know where I wanted to live, but I already knew I loved to travel.

Even though I had only been to Cuba and to Europe, I had the bug. I wanted more. I wanted the whole world to be open to me. Anything would be possible with a nursing degree. I've always been governed by reason, not emotion, and this made sense to me.

Because of going back and forth, it took me an extra semester to graduate. I finally ended up getting my degree in Nursing in February of 1962. Before I left those hallowed halls of UF though, there was one other experience I needed to have in order to be ready for the world at large. Sex.

I finally had sex – just once the whole time I was in college – my senior year, right on my 22nd birthday.

With all my worldly sophistication, I just decided I was tired of being a virgin. I made a conscious, deliberate decision to get it over with. That's the way I am. I make decisions on a rational, logical basis, not an emotional one.

There was a guy I was dating on and off at the time, Jack Whiting. I wasn't in love with him, but that was a good thing. My whole experience with Charlie Horn, whom I had been in love with, had brought me a lot of unforeseen grief. Just because I was in love with him. I decided I needed to separate sex from love and just experience sex for itself. I selected Jack as a likely candidate.

I had never had sex with anyone before. Or even gotten close. And then all the planets aligned. It was my birthday. I was turning 22. I had had three or four final exams in just two days. I was definitely ready to relax from all the stress and have some fun.

I had been invited to a house party. There I ran into this Indian fellow, Rao, whom I knew from the Foreign Students club. If anybody worshipped me, Rao did. He really put me on a pedestal back then.

He had a car, a Mercury Comet, which he would let me drive whenever I wanted. Rao had bought this car, but he didn't have a Florida driver's license. I think he had an international license, but he just didn't use his car very much. So he told me anytime I wanted to use it, I could. It was nice.

Rao was the one who had originally introduced me to Jack Whiting, who also happened to be at this party. He was studying engineering. Jack was 26, and I was 22. When we went out on dates from time to time, we'd often go out in the woods and make out, but I wouldn't have sex with him, even though, like most guys, he always offered the opportunity.

That night I just decided I was tired of being a virgin and I should have sex with Jack after all. I was ready. He was there. So we went into a bedroom, closed the door, and finally, finally, finally, I had sex.

What did I feel? How was it? The main feeling I had…was in my head. Not in my body. Not in my heart. Not in my nether regions. You would think I'd feel something more in my body, but I didn't.

This feeling in my head, I don't know what it was. Maybe it was blood rushing in and sweeping away all my old ideas and fears, I don't know. It was some kind of sensation in my head, that's all I can say for sure. The whole thing was just a new experience.

It was kind of light and happy. It wasn't painful, it wasn't joyful, it wasn't sad, it wasn't even that pleasurable. It was just different. I never had that feeling again in my life.

I don't think Jack knew I was a virgin before we had sex, but I believe I bled a little bit during the process, so he may have figured it out. He didn't say anything if he did. Afterwards we went back out and just continued with the party. Then I went home alone. No big deal.

The next day Rao called me, all in a tizzy. He knew what had happened. He said he was shocked that I would do such a thing. Like it was any of his business. I think he was just sorry it wasn't him.

Still, he managed to get me crying over the whole thing, thinking I had done some terrible crime. But it was all my decision. It was my birthday gift to myself. I was old enough now.

At that time, they didn't have the birth control pill yet. I didn't want to get pregnant, of course, so that created some tension. The other thing was that I had been brought up so strictly in the Baptist religion, it was hard to let go of all that guilt and fear.

A lot of girls who saved themselves for marriage came to college and got married in their freshman year. We used to say they came to UF to get an MRS degree. They didn't have to wait that long for their sex.

It was pretty easy for a girl to find a husband, because there were three-and-a-half guys to every girl at UF. As far as I was concerned though, it was really just one guy to one girl.

I figured one guy out of the three would be married; another one no one would ever want; and…what can you do with half a guy? So that left just one. I wasn't worried about finding mine.

Years later, when I was in my 50s, I caught up with Jack. I had gotten a book from the University with all the alumni information in it. I saw he was living in Orlando, so I called his number.

I spoke to his daughter, who said he was in London. She told me when he would be back, so I called again later, after he returned. I told him who I was and mentioned that I would be coming to Orlando to visit a male friend there soon. I invited him to have lunch together. He said, "I don't do lunch," whatever that meant.

Then, he went on to say he was a born-again Christian now. He had been married, divorced, and was now re-married to another born-again Christian. He suggested the four of us have dinner together, my friend and me, with him and his wife.

I had to laugh. The last thing my date would want to do was meet the first guy I ever had sex with. And I was pretty sure his wife wouldn't want to hear about our history together either. So I never did see Jack again.

But I sure did have a lot more sex. And I found that one guy that was there for me.

Chapter 14

During my senior year, I had to buy my own car. It was required as part of the nursing program, because I had to do public health nursing calls. That meant driving to people's homes to see them. So I ended up buying a red and white, '56 Pontiac convertible. Very snazzy, as we used to say.

I bought that car with my own money. It cost about a thousand dollars and was a good one. I kept it for a couple of years. The summer before I graduated, 1961, my friend Lois and I drove that Pontiac convertible all the way out to Los Angeles and worked there for the summer.

I didn't have any car insurance, so I asked my father beforehand if I would need to get some for the trip. He said, "Oh, no, you don't need that." So I didn't get any. Those were the days.

Amazing, when you think about today's society, how you have to have all kinds of insurance for everything, especially if you live in Miami, New York or New Jersey.

I met Frank Sinatra on that trip, as we were passing through Las Vegas. He was at the Sands Hotel with his entourage, so I went up and got his autograph.

After I graduated February 3, 1962, my father was lobbying for me to come live with him in Miami Shores and get a job in Miami. He was even bribing me with the offer of a membership at La Gorce Country Club, where I suppose he thought I could find a suitable husband.

I didn't want to be in Miami though. My father was living by himself and he never took care of anything. I figured I would just end up an old maid, looking after him and the house, while holding down a job. It didn't seem like much of a life. Plus, when you live with your father, you don't have much freedom. And I craved freedom.

I wanted to live up in Connecticut. I enjoyed the summers I had spent up there and I wanted to see what it would be like year-round. My father was always talking about how different it was living up north. He loved the Florida weather, but I wanted a change.

Wherever I went, I also wanted to be in an academic environment. Yale University was in New Haven, Connecticut, so that seemed like a good place to relocate. I wanted to work in an outpatient clinic doing preventive medicine or something like that. I was even thinking about going back to school and maybe getting a master's, but I wasn't sure what I wanted to focus on.

I had to take my state board exams before I did anything though. They were held in Jacksonville. Since I was going to be there, I contacted Doug's mother. I always liked her. I invited her to meet me for lunch while I was in town. She accepted.

When we got together, we were talking and she asked me, "So what are you going to do now, Sylvia?"

"I'm moving up to New Haven, Connecticut, where Yale is," I said.

That's when she told me, "Oh, what a coincidence. Doug is teaching at Yale. You ought to ask him to help you find a job. He can probably also help you find a place to live."

Doug's mother offered all that. She suggested it. I had no idea. I had already chosen to go there completely on my own. Years later, Doug liked to tell people I followed him up there, and it may have seemed that way to him, but I really didn't. I swear I did not know he was there when I chose New Haven as my destination. It was a total coincidence.

Or...was it destiny? You decide.

With my mind totally made up, I asked my father for $100 to help me get up to New Haven, and he obliged. I took that $100 and never asked my father for any more money again. I saw it as a graduation present. With it, I was able to drive my Pontiac convertible up there and start a new life on my own.

I had a girlfriend, Ruth Hagel, who was living in Jacksonville with her family. She invited me to stop off and spend the night at their place. She had dropped out of college for a semester and nothing was holding her.

So, as we were talking together that night, she suddenly decided she wanted to come with me. She packed up some stuff and we took off early the next morning around 6:00 am. She just left her parents a note saying she was going to Connecticut with Sylvia. They must have been really upset when they read it, but that's what she did.

I had Doug's address, because his mother had told me to write him and let him know I was coming. I had written him, but he hadn't answered, so I didn't know what to expect. I figured I might as well find out as soon as we got there.

When we arrived in New Haven, we drove directly to Doug's place. I marched up to the front door and boldly rang the bell. He came down from his third-floor apartment and didn't seem too surprised to see me. I didn't know what to think.

After some pleasantries, he said, "Hey, I'm just preparing a steak for dinner. Why don't you join me?"

I responded, "Well, my friend Ruth Hagel is with me. Do you know her?"

Even though they were both from Jacksonville, he didn't know Ruth. Still, he invited her up. Then he put a chicken pot pie in the oven, to go with the steak he was fixing, and the three of us feasted on steak and chicken. He offered to let us stay there overnight. So we did.

Overnight turned into three weeks

That's how Doug and I got involved with each other again. It only took a few days before the chemistry kicked in again. We started having sex, which we had never done before, and there was no looking back after that.

At first, Doug had given Ruth and me the double bed in the bedroom. Then, at one point, I remember we had sex in the living room. Maybe that was the first time. Once we got back together again, he and I took over the bedroom, and Ruth was out in the living room on the sofa.

Doug's place was generally a mess. I guess in that respect, he was like my father. One time Doug went off on a business trip and I spent all day cleaning the place. I was so proud of myself.

Meanwhile, I was keeping my eyes open for a job. I couldn't really apply for a nursing position until I got the results of my board exams. That would take eight weeks from the time I had taken the test.

Then one day I was walking on the Yale campus, when I saw an ad for a research assistant to a Dr. Alvan R. Feinstein. There was a phone number listed, so I went home and called him.

He had just arrived from New York University. He was now on the faculty at Yale, but his office was at the VA Hospital, where he was doing research. He'd been interviewing people for two months, trying to find the right assistant.

His interview technique was unusual, to say the least. One of the first questions he asked me was, "What's the latest book you've read?"

I was honest. I said, "Tropic of Cancer," which was written by Henry Miller and had loads of graphic sex in it. It was a very scandalous book at the time. So I thought, *Well, now I'm never going to get this job.*

He was undeterred. His next question was, "Do you play bridge?"

Now I was in familiar territory. I had been raised playing bridge. So I said, "Yes, I play bridge."

I guess he didn't know whether to believe me, so he followed up with,

"Okay, what's the Gerber Convention?" That's a fairly advanced bidding technique, which all good bridge players know about.

So I said, "It's a bid of four clubs, asking how many aces your partner has."

He immediately responded, "Great. Can you come in tomorrow?"

And that's how I got my first job. It paid $85 a week, but that was enough to live on.

Dr. Feinstein turned out to be a real perfectionist. One time he went to New York to some medical meeting. I wasn't even supposed to be a secretary, but he left me with an assignment to type up a manuscript of 25 pages.

I had to use our new electric typewriter, which was just becoming popular then. In the whole 25 pages, I left out one comma. He caught that mistake and boy, did I get in trouble for it. That's the way he was. No wonder it took him so long to find an assistant.

The VA was a government operation, so he was supposed to hire the typical government worker kind of person, but he didn't want that. A lot of government people have a bad attitude. They tend to be very rigid and opinionated, the bureaucratic type. If you go to the post office or DMV, you see what I mean. Their mentality is not real intellectual. Many do just enough to get by.

Dr. Feinstein wanted someone more liberal and open-minded, someone fresh out of college, eager and enthusiastic, whom he could mold to what he wanted. He hired different kinds of people.

I was the first person he hired. The second was a black girl, Joyce, who was a pharmacist. The third was another girl, Terry Hatch, who had a degree in English.

One time the three of us all went out for lunch together and, as we were talking, we realized that he regularly called each of us into his office once a month, just so that he could complain about something. It was usually just one thing for each person. He was picky, but he was fair.

I was originally hired to do two projects. The first was reviewing 500 cases of people who had died from lung cancer. The object was to see whether it was worthwhile operating on them, if they were already coughing up blood. It turned out it wasn't. The other project was an obesity study. I used to have to go to autopsies and get adipose (fat) tissue to do this lab study. I liked that.

Dr. Feinstein was actually a great first boss for me, simply because he was a perfectionist. In my nursing program, I had been schooled in a broad, fluid kind of discipline. Nothing was written in stone.

If I had been in medical technology, everything would have had to be very exact and orderly. In nursing, everything was flexible. You might take a different approach, depending on each patient's psychology. Dr. Feinstein taught me to be more rigorous and specialized, which is what I needed for research.

He was quite a character in his own way. One time, he had car trouble and asked me for a ride to work. He only lived five or six blocks from me. So I asked him, "What time should I pick you up?"

He said, "You tell me. Beggars can't be choosers." I thought that was funny. I picked him up about half an hour before we were supposed to be at work. No problem

Every so often he would send me on an errand over to the Yale co-op, to buy a present for someone he had to give something to. In those cases, I would drive his car, a Triumph Herald. One time I forgot to take the emergency brake off as I was driving. I nearly had a fit when I realized what I had done, but I didn't tell him. He never complained, so I guess it was all right.

Another time, Dr. Feinstein had a party, but he didn't have a record player. Doug and I were invited to the party, so I brought my record player over and lent it to him.

He used to smoke pipes and had several of them in his office. One time I admired one of them and he just gave it to me. He said, "If you like it, it's yours." I still have it in my condo today.

My job with Dr. Feinstein was to be for just one year. The next year, he wanted to re-hire me, so he just wrote up the job description to include all my unique qualifications as essential needs. That way no one else could fill the job. He got me back for a second year, but I resigned half way through it, to take off on my next adventure.

My career path had totally changed, thanks to my time with Dr. Feinstein. I never did practice as a registered nurse.

Chapter 15

After three weeks of staying with Doug, Ruth and I found a beautiful apartment, much nicer than his, just two or three miles away. It was only $1100 a year, so we rented it.

That place reminded me of a Florida apartment. It was on the ground floor, attached behind a house, modern, with picture windows all along one side of a sunken living room.

Still, I ended up spending most of my time at Doug's place, so Ruth pretty much lived there by herself. She didn't like that. Even though she dated, she didn't get to know many people in New Haven.

It took Ruth a while to find a job. She had a strong Southern accent. When she called for job possibilities, people often asked if she was black, which was totally wrong, of course. This was in 1962, before the whole civil rights movement, so racism was still rampant.

Eventually Ruth did get a great position, as secretary to the chancellor at Yale, but she didn't like it much. After about six months, she moved back to Florida. So Doug and I moved into that place.

We were definitely in love with each other. In fact, I had fallen in love with him the first day we met and had never really fallen out. At first, he was really chasing me more than vice versa, but I reciprocated, because I liked him a lot. He was a very interesting person. Anyone who ever met Doug would tell you that. He was special.

In his Princeton days, Doug kind of went back and forth about our relationship. Then he wrote that letter and broke it off for a two a half years. After that, I figured I was finished with Doug. Who knows? If I hadn't moved to New Haven, we might have never even seen each other again, much less re-ignited the spark.

Before I got to Yale, the kind of guys I liked and dated were the professional types, doctors and lawyers. Doug was the academic type, a professor Those two categories have totally different kinds of personalities and ways of looking at life. The professionals are more practical and engaged with the world. The academics are more theoretical and stuck in their heads.

Doug was definitely the typical absent-minded professor. In spite of all that though, I did love him. Our relationship was definitely romantic. It was even more so because of the fact that we were living together in secret. We both worked at Yale. If they had found out we were living together without being married, we could have lost our jobs.

Yes, you ran the risk of getting fired from your job if you lived "in sin" with someone back then. We had to be very discreet. We never told Doug's parents we were living together. I don't think they knew, but my father might have figured it out later on.

Today, you can live with anyone legally. Nobody cares. In 1962, it was a very big deal...but racism was okay. Go figure.

I've always been ahead of the curve. Even in college I was told that. I had done some pretty crazy things already. It kept things interesting.

Still, even with my adventurous nature, it had taken me a good long while to get around to having sex. Once Doug and I got started on that, it was on a regular basis, with no regrets.

I wasn't worried about marrying Doug. I was in love with him, but I wasn't planning on marrying him any time soon. At that point, I wasn't really ready for marriage and neither was he.

I wanted him to finish his doctorate before we slipped into wedded bliss. I had heard of too many couples where the wife put the husband through grad school and then, once he was done, he divorced her. He got too good for her.

I heard about that a lot and saw it as a lesson. It was one thing a smart girl didn't do. The other reason I didn't want to get married yet was that I wanted to wait until I spent a year on my own working in Europe. I needed that experience before I settled down.

Even though Doug and I were living together, I still had lots of guys chasing me all the time...as usual. One guy, John Lindbergh, lived on the first floor of the apartment building in New Haven, where Doug and I were living on the third floor. He was a mathematician. I didn't like him romantically, but one day as I was coming down the stairs of the building, he struck up a conversation with me.

Finally he got around to saying, "If you ever give up on Doug, I'm interested in you." What a guy!

Most people, though, didn't even know Doug and I were living together, because we were keeping it secret, so guys would ask me out. I went because it was just something to do. Doug was so busy working on his dissertation almost every night. Sometimes I went with him to type or whatever, but not all the time.

If someone asked me out and I was free, I'd go. I had finished my schooling, so I had lots of free time. I was also considered very good-looking. I wore my hair up in a French twist, which was fashionable at the time. Plus, I was slender and fun. I was a good date.

I never told Doug I was going out with other guys. After all, it was nothing serious to me, just socializing. Of course, I'm sure the guys were hoping for more, but it never happened.

There were a few guys. For example, there was a physicist at the VA Hospital, where I was working. He asked me out on a date one time and we went out to dinner. Another time, I went to dinner with an MD, who was married. Scandalous.

So you see, I'm not an angel. I was kind of naughty. But I was faithful to Doug. He was actually just the second guy I ever had sex with. I never repeated my escapade with Jack Whiting after my first time.

When Doug and I were dating back in Florida, he had tried to seduce me, of course, but I never gave in then. When I stayed at his parents' house, he'd want me to come into his bedroom. I'd go in, but I just wouldn't do anything.

I had all these moralistic ideas from the way I had been brought up as a Baptist. You wait until you're married, young lady! Looking back on it, it's funny–I did marry the second guy I ever had sex with.

I never asked Doug what his sexual history was when we got back together again, but I imagine he probably had some experience, at least with Kathleen.

My whole perspective on many things changed as a result of moving up north. I became much more liberal and open-minded. One big change happened one time when I went to Brooklyn with Ruth. She had a couple of male cousins there she wanted to see, so we drove down for a weekend.

There was a woman living on the same floor where these two guys were, who was a nurse. She was going to Europe and had a bon voyage party, which she invited us to. At this party, there was a black guy.

Now you have to remember, when I was growing up in Florida, segregation was the law of the land. There were separate water fountains, bathrooms, restaurants, hotels, everything. I had never socialized with a black person in my entire life. In fact, the only one I had ever even seen was a maid who came to our house one time to clean.

Anyway, this black guy at the party came up to me asked me to dance. He was very nice and all, but I turned him down, because that's the way I was brought up. Then…I saw him dancing with other girls and realized he was a really good dancer!

64

I have always loved to dance. So the next time he was free, I marched right up to him and asked him to dance. He accepted and, lo and behold, he and I ended up dancing together till 2:00 am.

That was a real breakthrough for me. Then, when my boss hired Joyce, the pharmacist, who was also black, we always got along great and had a good time together. I even went to her wedding and caught the bridal bouquet. My racism didn't last long when confronted with reality.

After graduation, I didn't see much of my college friends. To tell the truth, I wasn't that interested in keeping things going anyway. I was on to a new chapter of my life up north.

I did see Rao, however, one time. He came all the way up to New Haven looking for me. That's how fanatical he was about me. I told him I was living with someone, but he was undeterred. I would run into him again, years later.

During that first year, I also had to get used to being up north in the wintertime. I still had my Pontiac convertible, so when it snowed, that's what I drove to work. Everyone asked how I did, but it wasn't too bad. I didn't know how treacherous driving in the snow could be.

Whenever we had a serious snowfall, people would say, "Don't go out driving in the snow, unless it's an absolute emergency." I was bored silly staying at home though, so my feeling was, *I've got to get out of here, that's my emergency!*

Doug and I often went skiing in Vermont for the weekend. I liked going places and skiing was fun. One time, we took Doug's car to go skiing and left mine in the driveway where we lived.

When we got back on Sunday evening, my car was covered with snow. I asked Doug to, please, go out and get the snow off my front and back windows, so they would be clear for the morning. Since I had a convertible, the back window was plastic.

Doug went out with a broom to sweep the snow off. As I said, he was never really handy or practical as a man. He was good with his head, not his hands. When he came back in, he told me he had knocked a hole in the rear window of my car. Ouch!

I had asked him to go out there and it was just an accident, so I didn't get upset, but I was the one who had to drive that car to work. It was freezing. Driving in the Connecticut winter with a hole in your car window was not pleasant. We tried taping it up, but that didn't work very well.

Then John Lindbergh, the guy who hit on me at Doug's apartment building, invited us to a party he was throwing at his new place down in New York. He had gotten his PhD and was living in Brooklyn. Doug's car wasn't working very well, so we had to take my car, even though it had the hole in the window.

By the time we got there, we were like popsicles, but we had fun while we were there. John was living with his girlfriend, whom he eventually married. There were three couples total there that weekend.

We all went out together on Saturday night. Each couple got to propose something we were going to do. I wanted to go to the Playboy Club, so first we went there. Another couple wanted to go to a Turkish belly-dancing club. And the last couple wanted to go to Harlem. It was three very different activities in one night.

When Doug and I were getting ready to drive back home, it was so cold, that we knew we had to do something about the window. A convertible is not warm to begin with. So we got all this cardboard and tried to patch it up. No luck. It was still freezing all the way back to New Haven.

Eventually I had to but a whole new convertible top. It cost me $75, which at that time seemed like a lot. I was only making $85 a week.

This whole time, Doug was focusing on finishing his dissertation on learning theory. He was going over to his office at Yale almost every night. Sometimes I would go with him.

Since my boss was an MD, he would get all these free samples of Dexedrine and different prescription drugs. Sometimes he would give some to me. I guess he figured, since I had a degree in nursing, I wouldn't do anything too weird with them. Also, people didn't really think of prescription drugs as being that dangerous back then.

One time I gave Doug some uppers when he wanted them. I don't know how many he took, but he went over to the Yale library and checked out about 20 books. He was so high, he thought he could just whiz right through them, I guess. The next day, when he came back down again, he took them all back.

A lot of times, I really had to crack the whip to make him work on his dissertation every night. I even ended up typing his first draft for him. Believe it or not, that was huge.

He had gotten stuck and was having trouble finishing. People do get stuck. Much later, when we had kids, Doug told our two sons that, without me, he probably never would have even gotten his doctorate. Considering all he contributed to his field, that would have been a tragedy.

Here's what he wrote in his dissertation to acknowledge the help and encouragement I gave him:

"Special thanks are due to Sylvia Booma, who devoted countless hours to the unenviable task of translating my most illegible script to typewritten form, and whose constant encouragement provided the impetus without which this paper would most likely be as yet unfinished."

I was glad to be a part of his work.

Chapter 16

I spent a year and a half with Doug in New Haven. Were we in love? Yes, we were in a romantic kind of love. Still, I'm not sure I really understood then what love was or how deep our love would go before it was all over. I sure found out later.

The everyday things that make a man and a woman compatible are probably even more important than sexual chemistry. You can have great sex with someone, but you spend most of your time just living together and doing things together. You definitely have to share a lot of other stuff.

Doug and I had basically the same background. That helped us a lot. We were both brought up as Baptists. We were both only children. We were both encouraged to do well in school. We both liked to go to plays and get out of the house to do things. All this is extremely important.

We had some huge fights at times, but we still enjoyed living together and wanted to stay together. We were already like a married couple and we planned to eventually make it official.

I just wasn't ready to do it yet.

It wasn't only my fear about how so many men would take advantage of a woman's help while they were in school and then divorce her after they got their doctorate. I also wanted to live and work in Europe on my own for a year first.

I figured if I married Doug, but then we had a major fight and broke up, I would say, "You know, I really should have taken that year in Europe." I didn't want any regrets.

While Doug was working on his dissertation at Yale, he was also teaching a course in Psychology there. Even though Yale was a great school, it wasn't a great situation for him. When he first arrived, somehow they thought he had already finished his dissertation, but he hadn't. So he was on the faculty, but he wasn't getting paid a lot.

We weren't married, but we were still living like a married couple. We socialized a lot with other couples. One in particular was the secretary of the Psychology department and her husband, who was working on his doctorate in chemistry.

We played bridge with them a lot. Sometimes we'd have dinner at our apartment and then play cards, or other times we might go over to their place and do the same. It was a lot of fun. I enjoyed our get-togethers.

But I was starting to get restless.

Finally, after a year, I put my foot down. It was time to plan my trip to Europe. I had gone to Europe for two months when I was 21 and I wanted to go again, before I was too bogged down in a routine with Doug. We decided to put any marriage plans on hold for a year, so he could get his career started and I could get the wanderlust out of my system.

I knew I wanted to live in Germany or Switzerland, because the people there work hard and play hard too. I saw it when I was there and I liked it. That was my philosophy as well. That was the way I wanted to live.

This was long before computers made everything so easy, of course, so I went to the library at the VA hospital and researched 15 different top universities and research facilities in those two countries. Then I wrote 15 letters, 11 to Germany and 4 to Switzerland, applying for a position as an assistant in medical research.

I finally got one response from a man named Don Marvin, a molecular biologist with a PhD in physics. He wrote to say that he was coming to New Haven and wanted to interview me. I was ecstatic. My plan was working, even better than expected.

He was coming to Yale to check out the molecular biology department, because he was probably going to be working there in another year. He had received my letter just before his trip, so he could interview me while he was there.

The day he set for the interview was a Sunday. Typically, I had been to a party the night before. I was a little tired, but I met him and did my best to look fresh and enthusiastic. It's a good thing I did. Our interview lasted eight hours. It was like he had nothing better to do that day than hang out with me.

We talked a lot about his work at the Max Planck Institute in Germany. In case you don't know, this place is generally considered the foremost research organization in Europe and the world. Its scientists have earned 33 Nobel Prizes over the years.

Don took me to lunch at the Old Heidelberg Restaurant in downtown New Haven. We just couldn't get enough of that German culture. Later he took me to dinner somewhere else.

By the end of the day, he assured me it was 99% certain he would offer me the position, but he had to go back to Germany to discuss it with his department head before he could.

I won't keep you in suspense. I got the job.

Meanwhile, Doug was finally finishing his dissertation. Once he did, he got an offer from Bell Labs. Again, in case you don't already know, that's a top research facility in New Jersey, considered the best in the U.S. and the world.

It was originally founded by Alexander Graham Bell, the inventor of the telephone. Over the years, Bell Labs has received eight Nobel Prizes for work completed there. This was great for him.

So Doug and I both had really good career opportunities to explore in our separate lives over the next year. We made a solemn agreement that, at the end of that year, we would get married...if we both still wanted to.

I told Doug I wasn't going to have sex with anyone else and he told me the same. Of course, neither of us could keep that lovely promise – which was pretty unrealistic – but it did sound good when we made it.

Doug was nice enough to see me off in New York on the *Bremen*, my ship to Germany. It was a 10-day crossing. I didn't know any German yet, so I started learning it on the ship as fast as I could.

I met a fellow on-board, who was from Munich. He invited me to come visit him for Oktoberfest and stay in his parents' home. I did. It was really nice and turned out to be the only time I ever went to Oktoberfest.

I was excited about what I was getting into. I was off on a new adventure.

Chapter 17

The Max Planck Institute, where I worked in Germany, was in a town called Tubingen, about one hour south of Stuttgart. It's a university town, very rustic and beautiful. The Institute was up on a steep hill. At first I lived up there, near work, in a small room.

My place was right across the street from the Institute, which was convenient, but it was almost like a dorm. I didn't even have a refrigerator. We'd keep things cold by putting them outdoors on the windowsill. It was nice enough, but my landlord was terrible. More about that later.

I was doing virus research at work. My very first day there was the hardest day of the entire year, but it had nothing to do with viruses. It was all about hiking.

It turns out hiking is Germany's favorite outdoor activity. I did not know that. They love it so much that every September they celebrate National Hiking Day. It just so happened that year the holiday coincided with my first day of work.

So, when I arrived ready for research, they told me to go straight home and put on my hiking shoes. The whole lab was going hiking together. I panicked.

I didn't have any hiking shoes. I never have and I never will. Hiking is not my thing. So I went home and put on a pair of flats, determined to do my best to keep up.

It was a real hike. We ended up covering 17 kilometers, which is about 10½ miles. Germany is a mountainous country, so we were going through the countryside, up and down hills, all day and into the night. Thank God, at least we stopped to eat. I didn't get home till about 9:00 pm.

I could barely walk into my room and collapse. I'm not used to that kind of thing. I'm active. I ski, dance, play tennis, do sports, all kinds of things, but I don't do long distance walking up and down hills. Thank God, we never had to do it again.

I didn't speak German when I got there, so I went to the Berlitz School to learn it. Fortunately, most everybody at the Institute spoke English. Still, the little German I learned was helpful, when I had to teach some procedures to people there who weren't professors. They didn't speak English, so I taught in my limited German.

I was only making about $35 a week. This was in 1963, way before inflation got bad, but I still could barely live on what I made. I had brought some extra money with me, about $500, so I could have some fun. My boss let me take both the Catholic and the Protestant holidays, so I had lots of vacation time, and I took lots of short, local trips.

One day I was going to this cafeteria, which was near my apartment. You could get a whole lunch there for just 35 cents, and lunch is the main meal of the day for most Germans. At night they generally just had wurst and cheese and stuff like that.

Anyway, this particular day, on my way to lunch, I met a very nice German guy, Hans Stein. He was working on both his PhD and MD at the Institute. Doug was pretty much in the background at this point. We were each doing our own thing. So I got involved with Hans.

Meanwhile, Hans also had a girlfriend of his own. She was studying to be an MD in Frankfurt, which was about 150 miles away. Hans and I dated in Tubingen during the week, but he could never tell his parents, who lived in the Black Forest, about us...and not just because he had a girlfriend.

The biggest barrier with his parents was that I was an American. His parents were Nazis! I don't know how he avoided being influenced by them, because every weekend he went back home to visit them, but he did. He was poor and an only child, so he needed to maintain that family connection.

Meeting Hans was nice. When I got over to Germany, I was already very used to living with someone and having sex on a regular basis. Now, all of a sudden, I was over there all by myself in a little one-room place. It was tough and lonely at first.

My landlord was so strict that I couldn't have anyone visit me after 10 pm. There was a girl who lived next to me in the same house, Bridget, who was studying to be a dental hygienist and we had become friends. We met these two French officers who seemed nice.

One evening she invited them and me over to her room for wurst and bread and cheese and wine. Nothing rowdy, no hanky-panky. The rule was that no visitors could be in our rooms after 10 pm. So at 10 she told them they had to go, but they didn't actually leave for about fifteen more minutes, at about 10:15. That was our undoing.

Our little soiree took place just before Christmas. Over the Christmas holidays, I went skiing in Switzerland and Bridget went home to Baden-Baden. When we came back, we discovered we had both been evicted...without any warning.

Our landlord just threw us out over those guys staying 15 minutes past curfew. It was like my old sorority again, but worse. What made it worse was that he had taken all my possessions out of my room and was holding them ransom. He claimed I had damaged this little wooden table or nightstand, which was next to the bed.

He said there was a burn in it from a candle and that I owed him 40 marks for the damage. Needless to say, I didn't do it. I never even had a candle. Plus, 40 marks was a lot of money to me. So I got Hans to talk to him.

Hans tried, but he couldn't get anywhere with the guy. This was in the Schwabisch area of Germany, where the people are very rigid and stubborn. Not like Munich, where they are much more friendly. So I ended up having to pay 40 marks, just to get my belongings back.

Then I had to go into town and find another place to live. I actually did get a much nicer place, owned by a woman doctor. It was a studio with a Murphy bed that came down from the wall. It was a lot bigger than what I had had and it even had a piano. I also now had access to a washing machine, which was much more convenient for doing laundry.

The new place was great, but now I had to find a way to get to work every day. It was about a mile up that very steep hill. I would usually take the bus up and back. Sometimes I would even hitchhike, which was still okay to do that back then.

On weekends I often went up to Heidelberg, just to get away. A lot of times, I didn't even know where I was going to stay. Somehow, I would always find people who would put me up. I was very adventurous. Fortunately, nothing really bad ever happened to me. I did have some close calls with sex, but I would just let the guy know I wasn't interested and that was it.

Chapter 18

During the time I worked in Germany, I took some longer trips too. Over the Christmas holidays, while my landlord was looting my place, I went down to Schuls, Switzerland on a 10-day ski trip with a group of people on a bus.

I had previously met an American guy, George, on the ship going over to Europe. He was working at a different Max Planck Institute in Germany. So we decided that maybe it would be fun to get together over Christmas vacation. He was going to St. Moritz, also in Switzerland. He suggested I could meet him down there on New Year's Eve day.

That sounded like fun, so that morning, I took the train from Schuls to St. Moritz. I was dressed in a ski outfit, just in case we wanted to go skiing. George was waiting at the station. He had another American girl with him, who was working in Paris. The three of us hung out together all day, but we never did go skiing.

Like a gentleman, George took me back to the train station when it was time to go back to Schuls. I had taken a direct train that morning, but I took a local this time. I bought a Herald Tribune to read on the way. Ten minutes later, the train stopped. A bunch of people got off and I thought nothing of it.

I continued on for another hour and then I thought, *Well, since it's New Year's Eve, there's going to be a lot of drinking tonight. Maybe I should get something to eat.* I went into the dining car and had some oxtail soup and bread.

There was a man sitting across from me, so I asked him, "What time do we get into Schuls?"

He said, "Excuse me?" I repeated myself. He just shook his head sorrowfully. "Oh, my dear young lady, this train doesn't go to Schuls. It goes to Chur, Switzerland."

I blurted out, "Oh, my God, what do you do there?" I was panicked, wondering how I might spend my New Year's Eve. I was used to a lot of partying and dancing to ring in the New Year.

My worst fears were confirmed when he said, "There's nothing to do there. You just check into a hotel and that's it."

That was all I needed to hear. I wasn't going to celebrate New Year's Eve like that. Then I had a brainstorm and asked, "How do I get to Davos?"

George, whom I had just left in St. Moritz had invited me to come with them to a party in Davos that night, but I had declined, saying, "Oh, no, I'm going back to Schuls for a wine and cheese party there."

So now I ended up taking three more trains to get to Davos. While I was waiting for the second train, I met a man from Lucerne, Switzerland. He was married, but was going home alone to visit his parents, who happened to also live in Davos.

After he heard my story, he took pity on me and said, "If you're willing to go to my parents' home with me, so I can eat dinner, I'll take you out afterwards to find your friends. There can only be three places in Davos where they might be partying."

I still had my ski clothes on. I was dying to change, but I had no other clothes with me, so I decided I'd just go to the party in what I had on. After dinner, my new friend took me out as he'd promised and, lo and behold, around midnight we found George celebrating in some restaurant.

Six hours after he had put me on the train to Schuls, I showed up in Davos. I said, "George, you wouldn't believe the day I've had. Do you have a place you can put me up?"

He said, no. Well, the guy visiting his parents had told me, if I needed a place to stay, I could stay at their place. So he and I hung out and celebrated New Year's together at the local spots. He took me back home about 3 am to his parents' apartment.

Before I turned in, he asked what time I would like to have breakfast. I said 10 am. The next morning, at 10 am, he actually delivered my breakfast—coffee and muffins. Then he took me to the train station at noon to go back to Schuls.

As I stood there waiting for the train, suddenly the world just seemed so beautiful. I was overwhelmed that there could be such kindness and love in Europe. Tears came running down my face. That guy certainly helped me out of a tough spot.

When I got back to Schuls, no one had been concerned about me. I couldn't believe it. I had figured they'd be sending out police or something, but they said, "Oh, no, we thought you were probably just having a good time and stayed in St. Moritz."

So nobody worried about me. Actually, I didn't even worry about myself, now that I think of it. And everything worked out.

Another time, which wasn't so pleasant, I went to Greece on a bus

75

tour. That trip must have been cursed. Every night the bus would arrive at our destination a little later. While we were in Yugoslavia, we hit a horse-driven wagon. The police came and it was a big mess.

Another night we didn't get into Bulgaria until 1 am. The next day we headed off to Greece and the bus broke down at midnight on the Greek border. We were told we would have to sleep on the bus.

Can you imagine? There were 40 Germans, all eating their wurst and cheese and other stuff that stunk to high heaven. There were 10 Americans on the bus and we felt like prisoners in some surreal movie.

Finally, at 3 am two buses came from Salonika, Greece. We ended up getting something to eat at 6 am. I was so exhausted, I swore I would never get on that bus again. Unfortunately, I didn't have the time or energy to get a train ticket back, but, thank God, there were no problems on the return.

Another time, I took a trip because I wanted to see Geneva, Switzerland. As I was coming back on the train, I met a man who lived in Switzerland. He didn't speak any English, so I had to use my limited German for us to communicate.

Still, he understood me and we had a nice conversation. I was planning on spending the night in the Lake Constance resort area, which is in Germany on the southern border, just across from Switzerland. But this nice man invited me to stop where he lived in Kreuzlingen, come home to meet his mother, and have dinner with them.

Of course, always up for a new adventure, I said yes. Sure, he could have knocked me over the head or done anything he wanted, I guess, but back then in 1964, people weren't like that as much as they are now. Or maybe it just wasn't as well-known.

Anyway, I had a nice dinner with them. His mother invited me to sleep over for the night. That felt like it would be imposing, so I said no, I was going to stay in the Constance area. He helped me get back to the train station.

Once I got to Lake Constance, I started looking for a room. I didn't have a reservation, so I just went around, asking in my basic German, "Do you have a room?" I couldn't find one. Everything was booked.

I only had one suitcase, which I was carrying with me. Suitcases back then didn't have wheels like they do today. My suitcase wasn't that big, but as the night wore on, it got heavier and heavier.

Finally, I went to a place that was a bar/restaurant, where they also had rooms to rent. Again, I said, "Haben zie ein zimmer?"

"Nein." So I just threw my suitcase down in frustration. It was midnight and I was exhausted. I didn't know what else to do.

There were a bunch of guys playing cards there. One of them came over to me and said, "You know I have an extra bed at my house. If you'd like, you can come over there and sleep."

I was too tired to worry about my virtue or my safety, so I accepted his offer. He left the card game and walked me over to his place, which wasn't far away. I slept there overnight.

The next morning, he came in and, guess what? He wanted to have sex. I wouldn't, however, so then he just took me to a pub for lunch. Afterwards, he invited me back for another weekend! You've got to admire that kind of persistence.

I never went back to see him again, of course, but the first guy and his mother had also invited me back before I left their place. Even though they didn't understand one word of English and we could only speak German, I did go back and spend a weekend with them later. It was nice. My German wasn't perfect but I got by. I like to do crazy things like that.

One other thing I have to mention is the time I went to a Fasching party. That's another German national custom. It's kind of like the German Carnival or Mardi Gras. They hold it in February and it goes on for six weeks. During this time, people are totally uninhibited and anything goes. It's a fact that there are a lot more babies than normal born nine months later.

It's a really big thing with the Germans, so Hans took me to a Fasching party at the Institute. There was a chemist there, who was married and whom I had worked with one day. He asked me to dance. His wife was close by, but, as we were dancing, all of a sudden he started kissing me!

Don't forget, this is where we worked. I was really embarrassed, but nobody cared. It was all good, because it was Fasching.

Hans was the first guy I got involved with over there and the main one. There were some others, but they weren't long term. I usually just partied with guys, without getting involved.

Chapter 19

If I had wanted to, I could have married Doug before I went to work in Germany. We were really in love, but being married would be defeating my whole purpose in going there. I wanted to experience life on my own.

Of course, Doug and I had promised that we would be faithful to each other, but that wasn't very realistic. At some point while I was over there, Doug asked me in a letter if I had had sex with anyone. So I told him the truth.

He was pretty upset about it, even though he had not really been faithful either. It all worked out for the best though. He wrote me a 38-page letter, in which he revealed a lot of things to me I had never known about him. It was very open and honest. Our letters established a new understanding and acceptance in our relationship, which would carry us through the years ahead.

As he said, "You used to complain about not knowing what sorts of things were going on in my mind. Ironically it seems to require separation and communication across an ocean to enable you to get a clearer, or murkier, conception of this." Strange, but true.

In the end, we both knew we belonged together and loved each other no matter what we had done. This exchange of letters also led Doug to decide he would come over to Germany on a three-week vacation, so we could tour Europe together.

The plan was that I would resign in June, when my contract was up with the Institute. Then we would travel together for three weeks, go home separately, and get married in Miami in September of 1964.

When I went to hand in my resignation, my boss asked if I could stay another six months. I said no, I was going home to get married. He said, "Oh, congratulations!" He was surprised, but he understood.

So Doug flew into Amsterdam and I met him there. We traveled all over Europe, had a great time, and then he flew back. I stayed a little longer, till August.

While I was there, I went down to the French Riviera to see Nice, Cannes and that area. They were having a big parade, Nuit Blanche, which they do every year. I rented a room in some woman's home for a couple of nights. It was a great way to close out my adventures in Europe.

When it was time to go home, I went back by ship on the *Rotterdam* to New York in August of 1964. Doug picked me up at the pier. He was working at Bell Labs, so he had an apartment in New Jersey, close to work. That's where we lived.

It was a two-bedroom, one-bath apartment. Doug had a roommate there, an Israeli guy who also worked at Bell Labs. Doug told him he would have to move when I came. He moved out and I moved in. I even wrote my father and told him he could write me there.

I thought we were going to get married the next month, in September, so I told my father I just wanted to have a small chapel wedding. Then Doug started procrastinating.

Everybody knew Doug was a big procrastinator. This was going to be maybe the biggest decision of his life. So he kept pushing back the wedding date.

At first, he said we couldn't do it in September, because he didn't have any more vacation time to go on a honeymoon. I said, "We don't need to go on a honeymoon. We just spent three weeks traveling all over Europe!"

To tell you the truth, I think he was still upset over the fact that I had had sex with someone else. I'm glad I was honest though. I could have lied, but I didn't want to.

I am sure he had sex with a couple of girls while I was over there, but maybe it was only once or twice. Or maybe he just set a different standard for me than for himself. I don't know why, but he was more upset about my infidelity than I was about his.

Maybe my having sex made him doubt whether I really loved him. But his having sex didn't make him doubt he loved me. That's life.

Meanwhile, Doug's position at Bell Labs was ending. He took a teaching job at NYU in the city. I wasn't sure if we would move into the city or what, so I took a position in the Department of Microbiology at Seton Hall College of Medicine in Jersey City. That was in the middle, between New York City and where we were living, in Summit, New Jersey.

My job at the Max Planck Institute had really opened a lot of doors for me. It was a famous place and I had been there for a year. People really respected that.

Meanwhile, around this time, Doug's parents announced they were coming to visit from Florida. They didn't know we were living together in what his mother considered "sin." So Doug asked me to leave and move in with my girlfriend in New York while they were in town.

I said to him, "Doug, listen, I came all the way back from Germany. I could have stayed there another six months in a great job, but I came back to get married to you. It's your fault we're not already married, so I'm not leaving." And I didn't.

His parents arrived and he tried to tell them that I lived in one bedroom, while he lived in the other. His mother, the Southern Baptist, didn't think that was appropriate and let him know about it.

While they were there, they slept in Doug's bedroom and he slept on the sofa in the living room. I was in the other bedroom, kind of enjoying what Doug had brought on himself. His mother gave him a good lecture about how he better marry me soon. Finally we agreed on a date in January.

I still wanted a small wedding, but I was an only child, so my father decided to go all out. He was a member of La Gorce Country Club on Miami Beach, where he had a lot of women friends. He was very popular there. He was outgoing, good-looking, and a good dancer. Of course, he reserved the club for our wedding reception.

At one point, Doug had wanted us to go to a Justice of the Peace and get married in December, so he could lower his income taxes by filing as a married couple. Someone at Bell Labs had suggested this would be a great idea. Get married a week earlier and claim a whole year's worth of marriage? I wouldn't do it. I'm idealistic.

I said, "That's not fair to my father. He's planning this big wedding and it would be anti-climactic, if we were already married. I won't do it."

I even told him, "Don't worry, if you could have saved a lot of money by marrying me in December, I'll pay the difference." Doug was making a lot more money than I was, but he also spent it. The difference in his taxes only turned out to be a couple of hundred dollars, so it definitely would not have been worth it

Anyway, Doug and I drove down to my Dad's house in Miami Shores from New Jersey on December 30 and 31. We got married on January 2nd.

I rented my wedding gown for $50. It was just exactly what I wanted, really beautiful. I had four bridesmaids and they all rented their dresses too, for $35 apiece.

Doug had wanted his friend, John Lindbergh, to be his best man, but he couldn't make it, so Doug asked his own father to do it. They weren't really that close, but he didn't have anyone else.

At first his father agreed to it, but then he found out the men in the wedding party were going to be in formal tuxes with tails. He decided he didn't want to dress up. Later he finally came around, but he was always a difficult person. He did pay for the rehearsal dinner though.

Doug and I were married in the Miami Shores Baptist Church. My father had beautiful flowers all the way down the aisle, with candles everywhere. It was magnificent.

The minister had been my pastor growing up. Before the wedding, he asked me if I wanted to kneel when we got to the part where they said the Lord's Prayer. I said no, but I soon wished I had said yes.

As I was standing there, feeling all the emotion of getting married, it began to seem like I was giving up my independence once and for all. I was confused. I didn't like that idea, but I wanted to marry Doug. Suddenly tears started coming to my eyes.

I was wearing my contact lenses and, sure enough, the tears caused one of them to fall out and onto the floor. Everybody was looking at me, so I asked my Matron of Honor, Janice, to, please, look for my lens. Thank God, she found it and got it back to me fairly discreetly.

As it turned out, I never really did have to give up my independence, so my tears were all for naught.

We had a small reception at the church right after the ceremony. Baptists don't believe in alcohol, so we just had punch and cake. Later, my father threw his big dinner party at La Gorce Country Club. He went all out. He had hired a band and a photographer. He was a great dancer and put on a real show with me. It was all very elegant, truly unforgettable. In those days, people didn't do that as much as they do now.

My father's friends at the country club were very well off. He wasn't, but he hung out with people, especially women, who were. I often thought he should have married one of them, but he never did. I guess he valued his independence too.

We did go on a honeymoon after all. A woman friend of our family, Irene Redstone, who was a lawyer down on Brickell Avenue in Miami, drove us to the airport. We flew to Nassau, where we spent a glorious week.

While we were there, we bought some Minton Westminster Bone China. We had asked for Lennox in our gift registry, which we got a lot of. We also received a lot of Waterford crystal and other very expensive gifts, because many of our wedding guests were millionaires. I even got a valuable pearl necklace, which one woman gave me.

The Minton china was on sale down in Nassau. It was even nicer and more expensive that the Lennox, so we bought that for about the same price people were paying for the Lennox in Miami. My plan was to have my father return the Lennox and get a cash refund.

So we left the Lennox china in Florida when we went back and took the Minton in the car with us to New Jersey. My father never did get around to returning it, so later I took a vacation for a week, came down, and did it myself.

On that trip, I also bought us some furniture wholesale in Miami, since my father was in the business. I had it shipped to our place. All of Doug's furniture was junk. In fact, one day, his bed just broke under us. Bachelors aren't very particular about their living conditions.

Meanwhile, back in Miami, my father had gotten everything written up in the newspapers, as he always did. It was now official. Doug and I were together for life, for better or for worse.

Chapter 20

In January of 1965, we drove back up to Summit, New Jersey, where we were still living, to start our newly-wed life. I was still working at Seton Hall. Doug was still at Bell Labs.

Like a good young wife in the early 60s, I decided to throw a fancy dinner party, my first. The guests were to be my boss and one of my husband's colleagues, a dear friend, Tapas Sen.

It took me all weekend to put the thing together. I came home from work on Friday and went grocery shopping. Then on Saturday, I cleaned the apartment and prepared the food. I made some Polynesian dish I had never done before. Saturday night, it all came together. Our guests raved over it.

Years later, I was staying with Tapas and his wife and he still remembered that meal. He said it was absolutely delicious...and he is a gourmet cook. I'm not. But I always did enjoy experimenting.

Come Sunday morning, my work still wasn't done. I had to spend the day cleaning up. Monday, I was back to work. The big lesson for me was throwing a dinner party, even for just two guests, was too much work! It killed my whole weekend.

That's why later on, I just threw a party once a year, but it was a big one. I'd invite 100 people, 80 would show up, and in one weekend I would pay everybody back for their invitations over the year. People loved those parties.

In September, about nine months after we got married, Doug took a teaching position at New York University. He had been thinking about continuing to work exclusively for Bell Labs, but they didn't give him a good enough offer, so he started at NYU.

As a result, we moved to a very big, very nice, luxury apartment complex called Washington Square Village, on Bleeker Street. There were four different buildings there, with lots of landscaping between them and underground parking.

Guaranteed parking in Manhattan is like the ultimate perk. This place was owned by NYU and we only got in because Doug was on the faculty. Strictly faculty and administration people could live there, although there were some political people. In fact, some are still living there. They can't be evicted.

So now I was commuting from Manhattan to Jersey City. I took the

Downtown Hudson Tubes, below the Hudson River. Every day I walked through Washington Square Park, which I loved, and across 5th Avenue to catch it.

It was terrible, leaving glamorous Manhattan to go over to Jersey City to work, even though I had a good position there. So I resigned. I didn't have another job lined up, but I figured I could get one in the city. My ex-boss gave me a wonderful reference, as well as the name of someone to connect with at New York Medical Center, but that didn't work out.

I finally landed a position at Beth Israel Medical Center with an MD, who was doing genetics research. I didn't stay there too long though. Believe it or not, he was working on bacterial warfare, and ethically I just couldn't be a part of that.

Next, I got hired at Sloan Kettering, which is the best cancer hospital in the U.S. I was in the Department of Virology there for two and a half years.

We lived in the Village for four years. Doug was teaching at NYU, so it was really convenient to live there. It was great living in the city too, with everything to do there. Meanwhile, Doug was also still consulting at Bell Labs, in New Jersey.

One day, when we were still in the Village, I was crossing 5th Avenue on my way to work and I saw my old friend from college, Rao, crossing the other way. It's weird how you can just run into people in New York like that.

Anyway, Doug and I were having a party later with about 40 people, so I invited Rao. At the time, another friend of mine from college, Tyge, was staying with us. He was from Copenhagen and had a master's in English. He was sleeping on our sofa in the living room of our one bedroom apartment.

The party went well, but at the end of it, Rao had had a little too much to drink and was taking a while to leave. In fact, besides Tyge, he was the last person there. He was getting a little argumentative, so Tyge made a joke. He said, "Come one, there'll be no 'row' tonight."

This was a pun to say no fighting and no Rao. Poor Rao took offense. He was still definitely in love with me. He and Tyge almost did get into a fight out in the hall, but he finally left.

After a year at NYU, Bell Labs finally gave Doug the offer he wanted to go full-time with them. He also had the option to stay on at NYU, so he asked me what I thought he should do.

I said, "You should do whatever is better for your career...but I don't want to move out of the City."

He decided Bell Labs offered the better career path, so he took their offer, but we continued to live there on Bleeker Street for another three years. I was still at Sloan Kettering in Manhattan. Doug was commuting by train to Bell Labs.

When Doug and I got married, I told him that I wanted to go to India within three years. I had two male Indian friends from college, Rao and Sid Mittra, and I wanted to see where they grew up. So we lived on Doug's salary and mine went into the bank. After about two and a half years, I told Doug I was ready to take that trip.

When I started planning for it, I found out the ticket was $1250, which seemed expensive. So I asked how much it would cost to go all the way around the world. They said it would be about the same amount! That's when I decided I was going to go around the world and see India on the way.

At first Doug had no interest in going. I said, "Okay, whatever I spend on this trip, you can spend the same amount of money on something you want."

He said, "Great, I might buy a Lincoln Continental." He was kidding.

But when his colleagues at Bell Labs heard I was going around the world by myself, they said, "Surely you're not going to let her do that...are you crazy?" They thought it was way too dangerous. They didn't know all the adventures I had already had in Europe.

Anyway, Doug finally decided to come along for the ride, but I would have gone by myself. I wanted to do that more than anything else in the world. I was going, one way or another. Even if I didn't live through the experience, it was something I just had to do

I really wanted to see what the other side of the world was like. I had joined Asia Society previously. It was very close to where I worked at Sloan Kettering, so I'd go there after work and attend lectures to satisfy my curiosity.

Doug and I were gone for two months on that trip. We traveled all through Asia and the Middle East. It was fantastic. Doug was normally allotted just two weeks of vacation time, but he had two extra weeks left over from the previous year. Plus, he already had another two weeks, because we had paid our own moving expenses, rather than having Bell Labs do it, and got two weeks in exchange. Then finally, Doug agreed to give lectures overseas, while we were in various countries. That earned him another two weeks travel time.

So that's how Doug, managed to get two months off work, without taking a cut in pay. He did one lecture at the Statistical Institute in Calcutta, where we were guests for two or three nights. He gave another talk in Delhi and another one at Hebrew University in Israel.

We came back alive and well and went back to work. I had had to resign my job to go, but Sloan Kettering rehired me when I returned.

It was about a 23-mile train ride for Doug to commute to work. After three years of that, he was tired of that and wanted to buy a house in New Jersey, closer to his office. Meanwhile, my father had become ill. I thought he might have to come live with us, so a bigger place sounded like a good idea.

Doug started going out on his lunch hour and looking at houses. We ended up buying one on September 17, 1969 with a $15,000 down payment. The money came out of my savings, since we lived on Doug's salary.

My attitude always was, if we had kids one day, I might not be working any more, so we needed to be able to live on Doug's salary. If we couldn't, then we shouldn't be married to each other. Money never really was a problem though.

The house we chose was a five-bedroom, three-bath home on a hill, with an in-ground swimming pool in the back yard.

What are you going to do with all that space?

I got a kitten. I hadn't had a cat since I moved out of Miami and I missed that companionship. Just before Christmas, I said to Doug, "You know what I really want for Christmas? I want a kitten."

He said, okay, even though he didn't really like cats. His one condition was that I had to make sure it was a male, so he wouldn't have to deal with a litter of kittens. Doug lived in fear that his house would end up filled with cats, like the classic cat lady syndrome.

I had seen a phone number on a ShopRite grocery store bulletin board for free kittens and actually memorized it. So I called the number and went to this couple's house to pick out my kitten.

The first one I liked was grey. Remembering Doug's request, I asked, "Is this a male?"

"Oh, no," they said, "that's a female." So I picked up another one I liked and they said, "Now that's a male." I named him Aquarius.

About a month later, I took Aquarius to the vet. He was a very nice man from Estonia, very formal. He always called me Mrs. Carroll. He wanted to be introduced to the kitten, so he asked, "Mrs. Carroll, what is your kitten's name?"

"Oh, his name is Aquarius."

As he was examining the kitten, he said, "Now is this kitten male or female?"

"Well, I believe it's male..."

"Oh, no, this is a female."

"Oh God, my husband's gonna have a fit."

I did my best, but fate intervened. I was afraid Doug might make me give him...or her... up, but he took it pretty well. Sure enough, she got pregnant.

It turned out that she and I were pregnant together, as I was expecting my first child. After we gave away all her kittens, we had her fixed. I didn't get fixed though.

When Doug and I got married, we were both in agreement that we didn't want to have any kids at all. I had a career and he certainly did too. We traveled a lot and we didn't want to be tied down by children.

Then, after we got the house, we decided, okay, we'll have one child. I told Doug I wanted to keep working though. I didn't want to stay home and take care of a baby. He agreed we would get someone to help with that.

Well, we must have really liked that first baby, because a couple of years later, we decided to have another. We had gone to New York one night to see the movie, *Husbands*. It was a cinema-verite film by John Cassavetes about three suburban New York men going through mid-life crises together.

Somehow, that movie got us thinking and talking and prompted us to have another child. We wanted to have the second one within three years of our first and so that's what we did. All because we moved to the suburbs!

Chapter 21

Meanwhile, my father was still living alone in Miami and declining. He never took care of anything around the house. I would visit him, to find the whole place a mess.

For example, there was a spare bedroom we had built for my grandmother to possibly live in way back when. On one visit I looked in there and it had a big hole in the ceiling. I asked, "Daddy, why is that hole there?"

He said, "Oh, well, I haven't had time to get that fixed."

He never had time to get anything fixed. My mother had always done that. Another time, I went down there and the washing machine wasn't working, so I had to get that repaired. He never was very responsible and now he was becoming less so.

At this point, I was responsible for him. There was no one else. I was an only child and all his other relatives were dead. He had been the baby of the family.

Finally in 1968, it got so bad, I had to fly down there. We had been in Warren, New Jersey, staying with a famous researcher from Bell Labs, Béla Julesz, who was studying vision and perception. He and his wife didn't have kids, so they would invite other couples who also didn't have kids to join them for Thanksgiving.

Anyway, when we got home to New York, this woman, who was a girlfriend of my father's, called and told me he had had a heart attack and was in the Miami Heart Institute on Miami Beach.

I took time off from work to go down there. My father still had his business on 79th Street, but there was a man from the Baptist Church who was running it now. He told me he wanted to buy it, if possible. The doctor had said my father really couldn't work anymore, so I had to decide what to do.

My father owed back tax money to the sheriff in Miami. He had to pay those taxes or go out of business. I could choose to either declare bankruptcy or sell the business for what it was still worth, about $900.

Because my father had all these high-class girlfriends at La Gorce, I wanted to spare him the embarrassment of bankruptcy. So I got power of attorney. Irene Redstone, the lawyer who had been at our wedding, had my father sign everything over to me. Now I could handle the business, the house, and all his affairs.

Daddy went through a lot of money towards the end of his life. He lost 30 acres of land he had in Massachusetts. He borrowed money against it and then lost the land, because he couldn't repay the loan. My father didn't know how to handle money and kept borrowing to keep going. He got a mortgage on my grandmother's house, which she had paid for in full with cash.

Meanwhile, the house he was living in, our old home in Miami Shores, was a wreck. It was winter and the house was really cold because there was no heat, except that little gas burner in the breezeway. I was shivering most of the time.

Daddy had even taken out another mortgage on that house as well. After I sold the business, I sold the Miami Shores house and moved him into my grandmother's house, just seven blocks away.

Since Daddy couldn't work any more, there was no reason to stay there, especially since he wasn't taking good care of it. When I did sell the Miami Shores house, I only cleared about $3,000. Everything else went to the mortgage company.

My mother would have turned over in her grave a dozen times if she had seen all the things he did. She was the one who was the financial person in the family, more like me in my family.

When my kids wanted money, they usually came to me, because I was the one who paid all the bills. The first two months we were married, Doug would be writing checks and he'd start groaning. I'd say, "What's wrong, Doug?"

He'd say, "We don't have enough money in the bank to cover all these things."

So I took over, paid all the bills, and kept the budget balanced. If Doug wanted to buy a stock or something, he could make that decision or we might discuss it together, but he had no idea what we paid for most of our regular bills. That was my responsibility.

My responsible mother was coming through me. The fun-loving, party side of me was from my father. I got the good aspects of both my parents and they balanced each other well in my life. Both my parents worked very hard, so I believed in hard work. They were both honest and loving. I grew up in a healthy family.

In certain ways, it might have been nice to be raised differently, of course. I would have enjoyed having my mother around more, but she was a working woman. I really admired the doctor who delivered me, Dr.

Winfield Wight. Sometimes I wished he had been my father. He was well educated, but my father was a lot of fun.

Daddy took me places and helped awaken my love of adventure and new experiences. One time when I was nine, he took me to a little place in downtown Miami, where he ordered a dozen oysters on the half shell for me to try. I ended up eating nine of them. I loved them.

Sunday nights, he and I would eat raw onion sandwiches on white bread, with mayonnaise and a glass of milk. My mother didn't like that kind of food, but we did.

My father was also very generous. If I needed money, he would always give it to me. He kept his money in a clip, not a wallet. When I was older, after my mother had passed away, he would give me money whenever I asked.

I was just 29 when I had to take over for my father. I had already had a lot hit me at a young age. First my mother, then my father.

Next, the attorney discovered my father's Cadillac was not in his name. It was in my name and he didn't nave any insurance on it. All those years I had been married, we could have been ruined if he had had an accident in it and been sued.

Irene told me I had to get that car out of Florida. My father didn't want me to sell it, so after spending two weeks down there, I drove it all the way up to New York by myself. It was an ordeal.

As I was driving from Miami to Jacksonville, the bottom of the car started dragging on the ground. I stopped to spend the night with my in-laws in Jacksonville. The next day my mother-in-law and I went to the Cadillac dealership. I found out this car didn't have springs and coils like most cars. It had air suspension and the air was leaking out.

When my mother-in-law asked if I could drive it back to New York, they told us, "Well, if you stop at a gas station every two hours to fill up the air suspension, you can probably make it."

I had to get back to work, so that's what I did all the way up to New York. I stopped to get air every two hours. Gas stations still had attendants back then, who would help you out. When I told them I needed air, they would ask me which tire and I would say, "It's not a tire, it's the air suspension."

At night, I'd have to stop close to a gas station, so I could fill the air in the morning before I started. I had to get air just to raise the car up off the ground high enough to drive. It was pretty crazy. When I got back to

New York, we had it converted to springs and coils, so we never had that problem again.

Chapter 22

After we bought our house in Bernardsville, New Jersey, in 1969, I resigned from Sloan Kettering. I had really liked working there but it was too much of a commute now.

I got a job at Merck, an American pharmaceutical company, one of the largest in the world. It was in New Jersey, but it was still an hour commute each way, which I drove. My position there was in biochemistry.

Then the next year, in 1970, I got pregnant. My pregnancy, which was planned, coincided with our cat's pregnancy, which was very unplanned.

While Greg was still "in the oven," Aquarius gave birth to a full litter of kittens. We gave away her last kitten just one day before Greg arrived. Doug was ecstatic. Out with the kittens, in with the kid.

We started writing our annual Christmas letters in 1970, now that we had something major to report. We always put pictures of our boys on the Christmas card, from the time they were born. Those letters became a real family tradition.

While I was pregnant, my obstetrician was very strict about weight gain, so I only put on 18 pounds. Nobody knew how pregnant I was. They didn't even know I was pregnant, till I was five months along. During that time, I was down in Miami for two weeks with Doug for meetings and two of his colleagues asked me separately if I was pregnant.

I said, "Oh, no, I just gained some weight from moving to New Jersey." I played it coy at first, but later I realized I had to start telling people.

The night before Greg was born, Doug and I went to the Asia Society for an art opening. There wasn't much food there and I got ravenous on the way home. We stopped at Max's Kansas City restaurant on Park Avenue.

Even though I was scheduled to see my doctor the next day for an examination and weigh-in, I scarfed down a lobster tail, baked potato with sour cream, salad with bleu cheese dressing, and more.

By the time we headed home, it was snowing like crazy. I had driven my car from our house to pick up Doug at Bell Labs, so we could go to the Asia Society together. On our way home in this snowstorm, we had to retrieve his car at Bell Labs and drive home separately.

When we got there, we couldn't get our cars up the driveway. The house we had bought was at the top of a very steep hill. That hill was well-known and feared among our friends, because it was so difficult to drive up and down it, especially in the winter.

When we bought the house, we had been living in New York, so we didn't think about stuff like that. Some people were so afraid of that driveway, that they wouldn't even attempt it.

One time Doug's best friend from Jacksonville came with his wife to visit us. It snowed, while he was parked up by the house. He was afraid to try to drive back down the hill. Doug had to do it for him.

Another time, Doug and I had had a fight one morning. I was upset, when I left for work. The driveway was slick and I was distracted, so I ended up sliding my car all the way down the hill. There was a huge tree right across the street which I almost hit. I turned the wheel and just missed it.

It was a miracle there was no one coming and I got the car turned. As soon as I saw a gas station, I stopped and used the pay phone - this was before cell phones, of course. I had to call Doug and warn him to be careful. Even though we'd had this big fight, I didn't want him to die on that driveway.

This is all just to explain why we had to park our cars at the bottom of the hill the night before Greg's birth and trudge through the snow all the way up to the house.

Then the next morning my water broke. Thank God, Doug was still there, but I thought, *How am I ever going to get to the hospital, walking down this crazy driveway, while I'm in labor?*

As luck would have it, my doctor was off on a vacation in the Caribbean. I got his backup on the phone, who said we should come in at 9:30.

Somehow I managed to walk down that steep driveway to the car without falling or breaking anything. At that time, we had a Volvo and a Cadillac. Doug asked, "Which car do you want to take?"

Of course, I said, "The Cadillac." I wanted to get in the back seat and lie down as best I could.

It would have been about a 10-minute drive to the hospital without snow, but we passed three accidents on the way and it took a lot longer. Once we got to the hospital, the fun really began.

I was in labor for nine hours. I wanted an epidural so bad. I had even told the doctor ahead of time I wanted one, but he said I wasn't dilated enough, so he couldn't give me one when I asked for it.

Meanwhile, Doug was sitting there next to me, reading the New York Times, as calm as could be. He had a whole stack of newspapers to catch up on. I was in so much pain, that I just wanted to die.

I told him, "You're supposed to be helping me. You should be entertaining me and taking my mind off this, not reading the paper."

Doug was just mainly worried about brain damage to the baby from a forceps delivery. When he saw the doctor come in with those, he did come to life.

The doctor finally gave me an epidural. It was the best fix I ever had in my life. I felt nothing after that. We went into the delivery room and Greg was born January 14, 1971, weighing in at seven pounds, four ounces.

I had been planning to leave work at Merck 16 days before Greg was to be born. I went over to personnel and signed up for my maternity leave. When I got back to the lab, my boss, who was a Chinese guy, said, "Oh, could you possibly stay another week?"

So I said, "Well, I'll stay on one condition: that you go and change my maternity leave, because I don't want to go back there and deal with those people again." So he did.

The Merck policy was that you were supposed to be out for four months total: two months before the birth and two months after it. Since I had worked almost right up to the birth, I planned to go back four months afterwards, around June 1.

During my leave, Doug and I went on a two-week vacation to Barbados, Caracas, and the U.S. Virgin Islands. I felt like I never had enough vacation time, because Merck only gave us two weeks a year. Doug had two weeks vacation at Bell Labs at that time, plus he traveled a lot for business. So we enjoyed the time we had.

Then, when June 1 rolled around, Merck wouldn't take me back. I called personnel on a weekly basis, but they kept putting me off. They kept saying, "No, you can't come back right now."

This continued for months. Then someone I knew at Merck told me they had hired a new man in the biochemistry department, where I worked. I smelled a rat...a sexist, male rat.

In the meantime, I was collecting unemployment, but the unemployment people treated me terribly as well. Once they asked me if I was nursing my baby. I said I was and they said, "Oh, well, then you can't work, so you're not eligible for unemployment." They were always looking for an excuse to deny me. They were awful.

At this time, Doug was doing complimentary consulting for an international, non-profit group in New York called Experiments in Arts and Technology (EAT). It had been co-founded by Robert Rauschenberg, the famous artist, along with a fellow who used to work at Bell Labs, Billy Kluver.

Anyway, through this group, I met a woman lawyer who worked with them, Sharon Blasgen. I told her about my situation with Merck. In a nutshell, I had had a baby, I was supposed to go back to work, and instead they hired a man.

She said, "Oh, that's sex discrimination, all right. I'll help you fight it and I won't even charge you." She told me to file a complaint with New Jersey Civil Rights, which I did, and another complaint with the Equal Employment Opportunity Commission (EEOC), the federal agency.

Shortly after I did that, New Jersey Civil Rights found Merck with probable cause. So on May 31, 1972, Merck called me up and asked if I could come back to work the next day.

It felt so good to say, "No, I have a big trip planned within the next few weeks. But I can come back in September." So that's when I went back to work.

You see, while I was out of work, Doug had a meeting scheduled in Tokyo for the International Congress of Psychology. Always looking for a new adventure and with time on my hands, I thought, *You know what, maybe we should go to the South Pacific before that meeting*.

So I scheduled a trip to Tahiti, Bora Bora, Moorea, New Zealand, Australia, New Guinea, Bali, and Japan. We spent three weeks in Japan: one in Tokyo for the meeting, one week in Kushu, and one week in Hokkaido, which was a popular vacation spot for Japanese people.

We had a great trip. We narrowly avoided disaster skiing in New Zealand. We went to the wildest party I've ever seen in Australia. And we saw an amazing mass funeral and cremation in Bali.

The only place we didn't like was Hokkaido. There was nothing to do there. When Americans go on vacation, they usually like to get out and do things. The Japanese, on the other hand, prefer to just relax.

We were in culture shock our whole time in Hokkaido. About all we could do was go for a boat-ride on a lake. We couldn't even watch TV. All they did was keep replaying the events that the Japanese had recently won in the Olympics.

There were baths in the evening, but they were segregated, men on one side, women on the other. They'd bring dinner to our room, which was served Japanese style, sitting on the floor. They'd also serve a little whiskey or sake, but it was just to us in our room. It wasn't social at all. One of Doug's colleagues took us hiking one day, but we didn't care much for that either because we're not really hikers, as I learned in Germany.

From Japan, we went to Honolulu for the American Psychological Association meeting. As soon as we arrived, I heard music coming from a lounge on top of our hotel. I was so happy to be back in Western civilization, with cocktail lounges and music!

When I got home, I became a working woman again. I never sued Merck for money, because I had received unemployment all the time I was out and it was tax-free. I wasn't making that much at Merck anyway. If I got anything from them, I'd have to pay taxes on it, so it all balanced out.

The important thing was I had stood up to them and changed their policy. I felt I was helping fight the battle for women's rights. Everyone knew from then on that a woman could determine her own scheduling of maternity leave at Merck. She could work right up to the day she had the baby, have that baby and then go back to work the next day, if she wanted to. Or she could take off time as she saw fit. It was her choice, not Merck's.

This actually helped my girlfriend who was working there. Her husband was unemployed, so she was the breadwinner. When she had a baby, she couldn't afford to be out of work for four months.

She had been planning to be out for just a week, but she had a Caesarian birth, so her doctor wrote a note that she needed to stay out an extra two weeks to recover. She never did go on maternity leave at all. She got sick leave.

I felt good about what I had done. When I went back to work though, they put me in a different department than I had been in before. It was in the basement and my boss was a real jerk.

He wasn't a PhD and he was always saying all this sexist stuff like, "Oh, you're farming out your child to some daycare center or nanny. You should be home taking care of him." Maybe that was Merck's way of trying to punish me. I probably should have filed another suit against him.

I was still working there when I had my second son, Steve, on February 5, 1974. I took another maternity leave then. After Steve's birth, I wrote a letter telling Merck the exact date I wanted to return to work. I had the letter registered before I sent it. Sure enough, they brought me back the exact day I requested. They weren't messing around with me any more.

Chapter 23

By 1972, Greg was walking, talking, eating on his own, throwing a miniature football, and becoming a little boy. He liked to ride on Daddy's shoulders, hated going to bed, brushed his one tooth, and carried poor Aquarius around very roughly.

Doug was beginning to experience a little bit of "a woman's lot in life," as he called it, participating in childcare, changing diapers, feeding his son, and so on. He said he should be used to it all by the time Greg entered graduate school.

To keep up with everything, we tried to hire a cleaning lady. The first one we hired, however, was scared of our driveway and wouldn't come up it.

The next one we hired called on the appointed day of her first week, to say that she couldn't make it, because her kids were sick. The next week, she called to say she couldn't come, because her kids were out of school. The third week, she had another reason. The fourth week was Thanksgiving, so that was out, of course.

And the fifth week, she called to say her husband insisted she cut back, because she was working too much! So she couldn't come "any more." Well, at least she called.

Doug's work was taking us on a lot of trips, both large and small. We went to Princeton, Chicago, and Boston in the U.S. that year. We also took another trip to Paris, London, and Grenoble, France. Germaine Greer, the famous writer and feminist, was sitting in the seat in front of us on our return flight. I told her all about my case against Merck and she told me all about her latest South American "stud."

One other interesting story. In the fall of 1972, we were invited by EAT to an art opening in SoHo, which we went to. Princess Christina of Sweden was coming to New York for this opening. It was supposed to be formal, so Doug went out to rent a tuxedo.

Later, he was talking to one of his colleagues at Bell Labs, who was also invited. Doug said, "I'm renting a tuxedo for the opening. Are you wearing one?"

The guy said, "Oh, no, I'm just wearing a normal jacket, a blazer or something." So Doug canceled his tuxedo and went a little less formal. Guess what. All the other men were wearing tuxedos. He was a little embarrassed. Oh, well, scientists....

After the opening, we were also invited to Robert Rauschenberg's home for dinner. He had a three-story place in the East Village and put on a big spread. One floor was for the royalty, another floor was for artists, and another floor was for the rest of us commoners.

A lot of the food had been flown in from Sweden, like lox and so on. At the opening, we had had plum wine and hors d'oeuvres, but this was a feast. Andy Warhol was there in a red velvet suit. That was cool. The whole thing was covered on the front page of the New York Times.

One interesting thing, I went into Robert Rauschenberg's bathroom, to use it. While I was there, I saw his bathrobe hanging up on a hook behind the door. I thought, *Egads, if I had a party like this, I would put everything away. I wouldn't leave my bathrobe hanging around.* I guess he was a little more casual than me.

We lived in a pretty free and easy group of people though. Our Bell Labs friends were unusual by the standards we had grown up in. Most of them had very liberal attitudes. Most were also at least ten years older than us, so they had already had their children and were free of a lot of responsibilities.

We all hung out with each other and would go to some of the same parties. For example, Erhard and Britta, a Bell Labs German couple, would throw a Fasching party every year during February.

As I mentioned earlier, during this celebration in Germany, anyone could do anything. You could have sex with other people, your next-door neighbor, whatever. Anything. It was very open in Germany, but not so much in New Jersey.

Americans weren't quite as free as Germans, when it came to Fasching. People would flirt a lot at these parties. Maybe a man would kiss me. A guy might put his arm around a girl. That was acceptable. Maybe people had sex, but it wasn't supposed to happen, and it certainly didn't out in the open.

Still, casual sex was definitely part of the lifestyle at Bell Labs. All these guys fooled around somewhat, if they had a chance. I knew about it. We knew some of our friends were having affairs with other people in the group. They would get together every once in a while. This was the late 60s and early 70s, so people were pretty open to that kind of thing.

Doug and I were both considered very attractive people. Doug could really turn on the charisma when he wanted to. Maybe he did it with his eyes. If he was meeting someone, he would smile and his eyes would sparkle. There were definitely some extracurricular escapades for both Doug and me.

One time, Doug had gone by himself to a meeting in London. He was supposed to come back two days before the Fourth of July, because we were invited to a party up on a lake in New Jersey. Then I got a cablegram from him that he wasn't coming back on the plane he was scheduled for. And that was it. He didn't say why. I ended up going to the party by myself.

I didn't even know when to expect him back. I was upset, but I still had to go to work every day. I told one of my friends at work about it. He was a PhD, who I played tennis with a lot. He felt sorry for me, so he took me out to dinner that night.

I also told my next-door neighbor what I was going through. Her husband was away, so she said, "Well, why don't we have a drink. Just bring over whatever you like and we'll enjoy ourselves."

I went over there with some Canadian Club and stayed till about 3 am. Then I went home and guess what? Doug was there. I called in sick and didn't go to work that day. Besides a bit of a hangover, I had been up late, trying to find out what was going on.

Doug wouldn't talk about it. He just said he had decided to stay an extra two days. End of story. A few days later, I finally got it out of him. He had gotten involved with a woman over there. He told me he loved her...but he also loved me.

At this point in my life, I was just in my 30s. I couldn't accept that a person could have feelings for more than one other person. Well, now I know you can love 100 people. I was wrong.

But back then, I said, "You can't love two people. You have to choose, Doug, me or her." I guess he chose me.

Later Doug went to another meeting in California, which was where this woman was from. He saw her a second time and evidently it didn't go as well. When he came back, he said, "You don't have anything to worry about. I saw her again and it's just not the same."

All this fun and games came to a head when Doug and I went skiing at Gray Rocks in Canada, near Mont-Tremblant. We were in a ski class there with this fellow, Bud Huston, who was a dentist from Willoughby, Ohio.

Bud was by himself, so he hung out with us most of the time and we all became friends. Bud was a funny guy, so he was the one chosen to give a

100

talk our last night there, at a dinner with our ski instructor.

It was very creative what he did. He had a brown paper bag with a bunch of different items in it. He would pull something out and then make a risqué joke with it about each person in the class.

One girl had just had a baby, so he pulled out a milk bottle for her. He said this was what she used to feed her baby and that she also used it as a douche bag.

For Doug, he had a sexy book, *The Happy Hooker,* in which he had underlined all the dirtiest passages. He said that was Doug's favorite book. For me, he used this ski lock I used to wear around my neck. He had previously asked me what it was and I had told him it was my chastity belt, which was something I told everyone who asked. He made a hilarious joke about that.

His best one, however, was for this guy who came every year by himself to ski. He was married and had a bunch of kids. So Bud said in the evening when he went to bed, he would put out the "Do Not Disturb" sign on his door. Then in the morning, he would turn it over so it said, "Maid, Please Come In." Then when she did, he would have sex with her. That was the only way he could make it through the trip without his wife. It was pretty funny, funnier than I can tell it.

So, after he had pulled all the items out of the bag and talked about one for each person, he opened up the bag and said, "And finally, this is the amazing gift my last wife left me...an empty bag."

Obviously, Bud was a pretty sexual guy and he seemed to like me a lot. Maybe Doug got a little jealous that weekend, because as we were driving back home, he said, "You know, I think if we're going to stay married, we ought to open up our marriage somewhat."

He then went on to lay out a proposal for how we would do that. He had obviously thought it out. His idea was that when he traveled, which he did a lot, he would be free to do whatever he wanted. Likewise, I would be free to do whatever I wanted. The agreement also included the proviso that we wouldn't talk to each other about what we did.

I was a little surprised at Doug's idea, but not a lot. I like all kinds of things in life. I like trying different things. It made sense to me. We weren't real strict with anything anyway.

I had guys that would ask me out every so often and I had had a couple of flings before, but I never told Doug about them. I had to either sneak out to see these guys or just not go. Doug had had his flings too, but we generally never talked about those either. Now we were openly admitting what was going on.

At that time, I only had my first son, Greg. I was also still working, with an hour commute each day, each way. We had a babysitter, where Doug dropped Greg off and picked him up again every day. I was pretty busy and even busier when Doug was gone, so I didn't have much time to play around.

It didn't seem like such a good deal for me, but I had to face reality. This stuff was going to happen. We might as well deal with it responsibly. So I agreed to Doug's proposal. It sounded fine. We were free to do what we wanted, but we wouldn't bring it up to the other person.

That's how it worked. I would meet men at parties, and every so often one would ask me out. I would just say, "Well, I can go out when Doug goes away." It was easier that way.

We never talked about the specific details of what we did, because then there would be jealousy. For example, if Doug went on a trip and had a blast, while I was working, taking care of the kids, and not having a blast, I didn't want him to come home and tell me all about how much fun he had with someone else.

Likewise, if I told him I'd been with someone, he would be upset. So we had this agreement, but we couldn't talk about it. That was part of the agreement. Little did we know that this unusual arrangement would be so vital to helping us get through the difficult years ahead.

Chapter 24

In 1973, I got pregnant again. Everyone was looking forward to the new family member, who was due in February of 1974. Even Greg was excited about teaching the new baby how to walk immediately.

Our reliable old Volvo had a tragic death when it crashed into the side of the road after the front suspension gave out. Fortunately, no one was injured. We got a '74 Toyota Corona to replace her.

We also bought some land up in Canada in the Laurentian Mountains near Montreal as an investment, 110 acres with an ancient farmhouse on it. We paid $10,000, less than $100 an acre. In the process, we discovered the men of Montreal were still very sexist. When the real estate agent was drawing up the contract, he said he would only put Doug's name on it.

I said, "No way. This is my money too. We're not buying it unless I'm on the contract along with Doug." That was that. I was learning to stand up for myself.

As 1974 came along, our second son, Steven, did too. He was born on February 5. Right from the start, it was obvious he was different in personality from Greg. He was quieter, more contemplative, a little shy, more like Doug. Greg was constantly active, extroverted, and gregarious in the extreme, more like me. One thing Steve was not shy about, however, was food. He always let us know when he was hungry, also like dear old Dad.

We figured Greg would be something like an artist, athlete, politician, or physician. We saw Steve as becoming a philosopher, scientist, or some other academic type. We turned out to be right on both counts.

About two weeks after Steve was born, Doug went to New Orleans for a meeting. I was upset. I didn't want him to go, but he really wanted to, so I figured it was better if only one of us was depressed. I relented.

Still, I was crying as I drove him to Bell Labs. I didn't want him to leave me right after I had had a baby. Paul Green, his good friend and associate was going to be there, so he really wanted to go.

As far as work was concerned, as I said earlier, this time I got my maternity leave, with no problems. I also got my same job back the day I had requested. They held it just for me. Merck knew when they were beat.

On another note, one incident during this time shows the

complications we had adjusting to our new open relationship. It happened on a day when Doug and I were going to a Bell Labs wine tasting party. That same afternoon a strange letter came from a woman named Sandra. She used to go with her husband to some of the same parties we did. They lived about 40 minutes away from us then, but had moved and were now living in Pennsylvania.

The letter was addressed to me, so I opened it up. I was very surprised by what I read. She wrote, "Oh, I hope you're not angry with me," and went on and on in that vein. I had no idea what she was talking about or why she was sending me this letter.

A little perplexed, I went over to meet Doug at the wine appreciation party. There were about eight tables of people, with six to eight people per table. Typically at one of these parties, one table would go through six bottles of wine with bread and cheese. Doug and I were sitting together.

Toward the end, I couldn't contain my curiosity any longer, so I leaned over to Doug and said, "I got a letter today from Sandra. She acts like she's afraid that I'm angry at her. Why would I be angry?"

Doug leaned back over and whispered very casually to me, "Oh, I had an affair with her."

Nobody else could hear what he said, but if we hadn't been in a room full of people we knew, I would have just blown up right then and there. Instead, I just sat and simmered for a while. I was completely ambushed.

She had probably told Doug to tell me what had happened, but he never did. I don't know what he was thinking. Yes, we had agreed not to talk about our affairs, but if she might approach me about it, I deserved to be forewarned. That party was a terrible place to find out. I felt like a fool.

At the end of the wine tasting, I said to Doug, "I'm furious. I don't know if I'm coming home tonight. I'm going out."

Then I drove to this place on Route 22, where there was a cocktail lounge with music for dancing. I went to just think things over and maybe dance a little. I had to calm down.

Eventually I went home, but I was still flabbergasted. Sandra thought I already knew about their affair and she didn't want me to be mad at her. Well, that definitely backfired. Doug should have told her that we didn't discuss our flings with each other.

By the time I got home, I had had wine at the wine tasting and more drinks at the lounge. I was not in good shape. If they had been as strict on DUI then as they are now, I might have gotten in trouble that night.

In fact, that was one of the reasons Bell Labs stopped having wine appreciation parties. They didn't want the liability, if someone drank too much and got arrested going home. A lot of things have changed over the years.

For example, in New Jersey, a lot of those dance lounges that used to be so popular turned into sports bars. That never made any sense to me, if you want to prevent DUIs. With dancing, at least you burn off some of the alcohol. At a sports bar, you just drink and watch TV. Oh, well.

Navigating an open marriage can be tricky. Later on, I actually met the people who wrote the book *Open Marriage*, which helped popularize the whole idea. It was a bestseller, by Nena O'Neill and George O'Neill, published in 1972.

I met them at the home of a friend, Warren Farrell, who lived in the Village in New York. He was a famous writer and lecturer, who talked about male-female relationships, trading roles and so on.

Warren had this workshop, where he would completely reverse the gender roles, to help people understand the opposite sex. He would have a beauty contest, where the men had to get up in front of the audience in bathing suits and the women would choose the best looking and sexiest ones.

Another thing he did was to have the females each pick out a man they wanted to date and then ask him out. The guy could say no, just like women do, so women could learn to deal with rejection and men could learn to deal with waiting to be asked.

One time, during one of his workshops in an auditorium at Drew University in Madison, New Jersey, Warren chose me to play the male role in a typical scenario. I was supposed to ask a guy out and then try to seduce him. He told us to leave the auditorium for a few minutes, find some privacy, and then act out this situation.

So this guy and I went out into an office there and, as we were talking, I said, "How would you like to go out to a very nice French restaurant for dinner?"

"Oh, I'd love that," he said, all shy and sweet.

Then we pretended we had this lovely dinner together and afterwards, were walking down the street. Since I was the man, I was leading the action. I pretended we were passing this swingers' club called *Trapeze* and I said, "Oh, would you like to go into *Trapeze* with me?"

He said, "Yes, I would." Game over. I had been successful in seducing him. Of course, it's not really that hard for a woman to seduce a man.

But then, to make it even better, he said, "Hey, let's not go back into the workshop, let's just get out of here." That meant I really had seduced him in real life, as well as in our little scenario. Later, he did ask me out on a real date and we went out. True story.

Warren also taught workshops for couples on how to improve your marriage. He even offered a guarantee on it. If the workshop didn't help, he would give your money back. Nobody ever got their money back, because it always worked.

Doug and I never took that workshop, because it wasn't really relevant to our situation, but I've been to some of his others. He's still a good friend. I had a lot of Warren's books. He was actually the first male officer of NOW, the National Organization of Women. Talk about reversing gender roles!

When you look at Doug's and my upbringing in strict Baptist churches, it may seem strange that we could have an open marriage. Doug was raised religious by his mother, but he lost his religion.

He used to say that, while he was in college, he was sitting on the toilet one day and he just decided he didn't believe in all that stuff anymore, maybe not even in God. He never talked about God. I think he was an agnostic.

When his childhood friend, Hank Gran and his wife, would come to visit, Doug would often ask for some private time with Hank. Doug always wanted to know if Hank was still religious. Hank would say yes and Doug would ask, "Why do you still believe all that?"

I guess he was trying to figure out why Hank would stay the way he always was, while Doug would change. Hank was still a strict Southern Baptist. They had both gone to the same church together. Doug had even been youth pastor one summer, when he was a teenager.

Hank was an engineer, a scientific guy in his own right, though not on Doug's level, but he still believed in his religion. That was a mystery to Doug.

Doug's Catholic father had been disowned by his father for marrying a Baptist girl. Catholics back then were very strict about marrying non-Catholics. As far as I'm concerned, all these arguments and wars over religion are just crazy. Where's the love?

Generally speaking, most well educated people are pretty liberal in their attitudes. Most PhDs are definitely liberal. We brought our kids up in the Unitarian Fellowship, where they were taught about all the religions, so they could choose what to believe, as they grew older.

One more story before I close this chapter, just to show Doug's intellectual sense of humor. One night we were having dinner with a good friend of mine from the Asia Society, who's an MD. We were in a Spanish restaurant on 34th Street in Manhattan.

Doug was always very laid back and liked to joke around a lot. It was the end of the evening, so the waiter came up and said, "Is there anything else I can get you?"

I don't know why, but Doug looked up and said, "Oh, yes, I was thinking about getting a vasectomy."

The waiter was a little confused. Evidently he had no idea what Doug was talking about, because he said, very politely and sincerely, "I'm sorry, sir, but the bar is closed now." I guess he thought a vasectomy was some kind of mixed drink. So much for scientific humor.

Chapter 25

In 1975, Doug took a six-month sabbatical from Bell Labs to be an acting professor of psychology at the University of California in San Diego and Irvine. I didn't feel like being left alone to commute 10 hours a week, work 40 hours a week, and take care of two little boys in my spare time. So I went with him.

I resigned from Merck. Doug had been complaining for a while that it was too much for me to work and deal with two kids anyway, so that was the end of my career. I never went back to a professional position again.

We drove all the way out to California in our Toyota Corona, taking the southern route. On the way, we saw the Grand Canyon. I took the mule ride to the bottom, which was scary and really hard on certain portions of the anatomy.

Doug was too heavy for the mules. They wouldn't allow anyone over 200 pounds. The kids were too young, so I went alone. Steve stayed with a babysitter, while Doug and Greg flew over the Canyon in a small plane. It was spectacular, no matter how you looked at it.

In California, we lived in La Jolla, just north of San Diego. We rented a house on a hill, from which you could see the Pacific. This hill was even steeper than the one we had in New Jersey. Most people were afraid to rent something up there, but by now, we were used to it and we weren't afraid, since there was no snow or ice.

Then two days after we got to California, we got an emergency call from the university saying my father had disappeared. My girlfriend Elaine from grade school had called the university looking for me, since she didn't have our new number yet.

Daddy was now 76 and had been in poor health for a while. He had had a heart attack, two strokes, and other smaller incidents. He kept living at home though and driving his car, another Cadillac.

The night before we left for California, I had talked to him on the phone at his house. He was upset I was resigning from Merck to go to California with Doug. He thought I should keep my career going. That was the last time I spoke with him.

What had happened was that Elaine's mother had a friend who lived across the street from my father's house. This friend noticed that she hadn't seen Daddy in a while, so she called Elaine to let me know.

I decided to call my old prom date, Leighton Reynolds, who was now a police officer in Miami, to see if he could find out where my father was. He was able to discover that Daddy was in a hospital and why.

He had been going to a senior home every day for a few hours, but had stopped showing up there. The home called the police, who sent out a crisis intervention team. The team found him at home, lying on the floor under his dining room table.

They took him to a hospital, but nobody knew what was going on. Leighton was able to find him and then get him transferred to a nursing home. That's where Daddy was when I finally tracked him down.

I knew he hated nursing homes, because I had had to put him in one after his heart attack. Back then, he checked himself out after a couple of days, but he wasn't getting out this time.

The medical social worker assigned to his case said he couldn't live by himself any more. This was a problem, because we had no family in Miami and I was going to be in California for the next six months.

I went back and forth on the phone with the social worker for three weeks, trying to find a suitable situation for him, where there would be other people around to keep an eye on him.

Then I came home from grocery shopping about 5:30 one day and the phone rang. It was a health aide from the nursing home. She told me my father had expired...just like that...very blunt.

"Is this Sylvia Carroll? Your father died."

He was the last of my family. I was depressed about losing him. But I didn't have time to grieve. Now I had to deal with all the issues that come up after a death.

Doug was teaching. He couldn't be any help. Fortunately, I had already found a baby sitter I trusted, so I took the kids to her house and flew to Miami to take care of everything.

It was actually a blessing Doug couldn't go with me. Doug always wanted to procrastinate. I never would have gotten everything done with him around. I went there, arranged the funeral, and then went to work clearing everything else up.

The house my father had been living in was my grandmother's old Miami house. I stayed with Elaine and her husband at their nice home in North Miami Beach.

Daddy's house was a disaster. My friends Janet and Leighton came and helped me throw out all kinds of stuff that had to go. Then I put an ad in the paper, "House for Sale, As Is. Best offer."

There was a good response to the ad. These two young sharks from New York and an older man from Miami ended up bidding against each other. I liked the older man, so I told him, if he could close in five days, he could have the house, because I needed to get back to my family.

He did it. He paid cash. Daddy had borrowed money on the place, so Doug and I ended up paying off his mortgage, but it wasn't that much.

Then I had to deal with my father's Cadillac. I found out it was in his secretary's name and she was now dead. Somehow I got in touch with her grown kids. They met me and gave me the title, so I could sell it. A gay guy who lived in Coconut Grove bought it. My father would have keeled over dead, if he'd known that.

I got it all done in just three weeks. My husband never could have done what I did. He probably thought I was never coming back, but I knew, if I didn't do it then, it would be even worse later. I figured I might as well get it all taken care of in one trip.

I'm a worker. When I have a job, I don't stop. I just keeping going until I get it done. I've always been like that.

When it was all over, it was so nice to be back in La Jolla. We had fun there, with all the outdoor stuff to do. Doug took up scuba diving. I took sailing lessons. Tennis was year-round. Plus, there was the San Diego Zoo, amusement parks, the desert, mountains, skiing and more. I loved living in La Jolla. People said I looked like a Californian, even more than the people living there.

While we were there, we had some visitors, one expected, one unexpected. Doug's Aunt Betty from Miami came for a couple of weeks. She had never been to California before, so we invited her. While she was there, Bud, the funny dentist from our ski trip at Gray Rocks, showed up at our door.

He was such a character. We had remained friends and he had visited us before in New Jersey. He was very spontaneous. He never let us know when he was coming. He would always just show up and say, "Oh, hello! Do you know if there's a motel close by where I can stay?"

We would always say, "Oh, no, just come in. You can stay with us." We never made him stay at a hotel.

Except this time, we really didn't have any room for him. We had a three-bedroom house and Aunt Betty was in one of the three. My two sons were in another bedroom in bunk beds, while Doug and I had the last one.

When Bud showed up, Doug was teaching up at UC Irvine, which was 70 miles away, so he wasn't going to come home that night anyway. Bud took Aunt Betty and me out for a lovely dinner at a restaurant on a boat in San Diego. Then I had one of the boys come sleep with me, while Bud took one of the bunk beds. It all worked out.

One other thing happened in La Jolla that was not so much fun. My son Greg had a skull fracture. He was going to a Montessori school in San Diego. One day when I drove him to school, I was dressed in my tennis outfit, because I was going to play that day.

When we got there, Greg went out to play on a swing. The kid who had used the swing before him had adjusted the swing chain incorrectly. It had an "S" type link and the other kid didn't put it in all the way.

There was concrete on the ground under the swing, not grass or sand. So, when Greg started to swing, the chain came apart and he fell on his head, right on that concrete.

I had just gotten home from dropping Greg off and was getting ready to go to play tennis, when Doug told me the school had called him because Greg had fallen off the swing. They said he had cut his ear and wanted to know whether they should take him to a clinic. So I said I would go right back there and take care of him. Thank God, I did.

It turned out his ear wasn't cut. His skull was fractured. I took him to Scripps Memorial hospital, where they said he was bleeding internally and the blood was coming out of his ear canal. They admitted him because there was some concern he might contract meningitis. He also had a partial hearing loss in one ear.

This was all just before Greg's birthday. We were planning a party for him, but, after this injury, he couldn't run or play for about two months, so we had a quiet birthday. We had to keep him calm as best we could.

At first, the school told Doug they would pay all the medical bills, but later they said they wouldn't pay anything after all. Evidently their attorney told them, if they paid our bills, they'd be admitting fault.

Meanwhile, there was a Newcomers Club in La Jolla, which we belonged to. We went to one party they threw, where I met an attorney. I told him about Greg's accident and he said we needed to file a personal injury lawsuit. So, before we left California, we did.

That was the first of many.

Chapter 26

We moved back home to chilly New Jersey from sunny California in March of 1976. All four of us were packed into our little Toyota Corona. We had had a wonderful time out there and I would return to California many times to enjoy the peace and beauty we enjoyed there.

We made many friends in San Diego, especially people from the Unitarian Fellowship. We belonged to s group they called the Extended Family. We would all get together on Sundays for picnics after the service.

It turned out Greg's accident on the swing had caused some temporary brain damage, which he got over. It also caused partial hearing loss in one ear, which he didn't get over. It was due to nerve damage, so there was nothing that could be done to help it.

Greg learned to compensate well. We just had to make sure he was seated in the front of his classes, wasn't exposed to loud noises like rock bands, and, in general, was more protective of his remaining good ear.

Our first three months back in New Jersey, we couldn't live in our own home. We had to live in Berkeley Heights, because we had leased out our house in Bernardsville until the end of June. We rented a place from a guy at Bell Labs, who was in Germany.

I didn't particularly like the house. I liked modern and this was more old-fashioned. So that year, we lived in three different houses and Greg went to three different schools. There was a lot going on.

As fate would have it, Doug also went to Europe three times that year. On one trip, we went to a resort in Corsica, called La Chiappa. A French woman had told me we should. When we got to the airport in Corsica, there were two other couples also going to the resort. They had vouchers to get there, but we didn't.

So, we got into this station wagon with one of the couples. He was a physicist from London, while his wife was African. The other couple took a taxi. When we got to La Chiappa, there was a sign out front that said, "Please refrain from wearing clothes beyond these doors."

And that's when I found out it was a nudist resort! The French woman never told me. I booked it and didn't even know. But we had a great time. That was my first experience with a nudist resort, but certainly not my last. It became one of the favorite parts of my life.

In general, thanks to Doug's many business trips, our family got to lead a very interesting and active life. We did many things most people never could.

In 1977, we were all happy and healthy. Doug lost 15 pounds. Steve started Montessori school at age four, learning his numbers and the alphabet. He was also learning to play the piano.

One day, when I went to pick Steve up, his teacher told me he was already reading. He had been looking over the shoulder of a kindergarten student, whom she was teaching to read, when he just started reading it out loud on his own. He was very bright.

Greg had started first grade and was reading very prolifically. He did well in math and even enjoyed Spanish. His Spanish came in very handy later when he worked in Costa Rica and married his present wife, Maria, who was from there.

One weird thing happened when we went skiing at Mont-Tremblant in Canada. Doug got frostbite on his toe. Was that a warning? This was the same place he would later have his accident.

Since I had resigned from Merck when we went to California, I was now just a suburban housewife, with two children.

As Doug was getting more well-known in his career, however, people started to recognize his value. In 1978 he got an offer to take a position at the University of Illinois in Champagne-Urbana, heading up some psychology area. I didn't want to move there though. It's all farmland, and I'm a city girl. I didn't even like the suburbs of New Jersey

So for once, I put my foot down. Doug had a great position at Bell Labs. How much better could this be? I told him, "If this new job is more important to you than me, then just go…but I'm not going." Doug and I were both about to turn 40. I didn't feel like uprooting our life to go live in the Midwest.

The kicker, though, was they were also going to offer me a position in microbiology. Doug insisted that I had to go and at least look at it. So I did.

I had to get a baby sitter for the trip, but we went. Sure enough, they wined and dined us the best they could, but it still seemed like a very small town to me.

I also discovered a lot of the psychology people were having affairs with other psychology people. I guess there wasn't much else to do there. It reminded me of *Peyton Place*, which was a famous book and TV show at the time.

I just saw a good university surrounded by cornfields. If I wanted to even just go to Chicago, the closest big city, it would be a two-and-a-half hour train trip each way. I would have to hire a baby-sitter.

So when we came back, I said no way. I told Doug, "I moved out of New York when I didn't want to leave the Village. I'm not going to move out of New Jersey now. Enough is enough!" So we stayed put.

As 1979 rolled around, Doug and I prepared to both turn 40, a big milestone in anyone's life. Doug threw a party for me on my birthday, January 21ˢᵗ, 1979. That was just a few weeks before his skiing accident...on February 18ᵗʰ. This birthday just about marked the end of the first part of my life for sure.

I found the following in my diary for the big day: "It's my 40ᵗʰ birthday. We got up at 10 am. The Piersons arrived at 11 and we started on Bloody Mary's. They gave me a bottle of champagne. Then the Clarks arrived. They gave me chocolate. Then June gave me a disco dress. Barbara gave me bath oil. We had champagne and cheesecake, then went to see *Streetboys*, a play in New York, starring Geraldine Fitzgerald."

After the show, we all went to Windows on the World at the World Trade Center for their buffet. Of course, that's long gone now, but what a great birthday party we had...and it was all arranged by Doug.

The whole day was a wonderful surprise. I knew something was going to happen, because we went to New York and stayed at a friend's condo on Bleeker Street. His name was George Sperling and he was a colleague of Doug's. He's still a professor at UC Irvine.

Doug had been doing so well in his career that he was now president of the Psychometric Society. I guess this is as good a place as any to try to explain what psychometrics is. One standard definition is, "the branch of psychology dealing with the mental measurement and assessment of psychological trends." Still not clear, right?

It has to do with using statistical analysis to assess people's knowledge, abilities, attitudes, and personality traits. It's largely concerned with studying the differences between individuals. Doug's research and development of a technique called "multidimensional scaling" was very effective for analyzing data of all kinds.

People in marketing used his work a lot. For example, if someone were going to put out a new bar of soap, they had to decide: what size, what contour, what color, what fragrance, all these different variables and choices. Doug's techniques would process all these possibilities and determine what the product should be.

Doug was a theoretician. He worked a lot with high level mathematics, creating formulas and algorithms. He didn't do the practical application himself. He let other people use his work to analyze data.

His theory was also used in sociology, geology, and all kinds of sciences, wherever data needed to be analyzed and turned into conclusions.

Doug was at the very forefront of this new field, just as it was becoming popular. Even most of his colleagues didn't really understand a lot of what he did and developed.

As a part of his genius, my husband was fanatical about every detail being absolutely correct. For example, Doug always wore two watches. He was known for that. They weren't expensive watches, but they had to be one of each, digital and analog, one on each wrist.

An article about him from Rutgers University said, "One of the foremost authorities of Psychometrics in the World, talks about his two watches. The analog watch on his left wrist enables him to tell time with his right brain, which controls spatial and nonverbal concepts. The digital watch on his right wrist is for the calculation and language activity that is the domain of the left brain."

This was the man I married and loved. As intelligent as he was, he was about to make a huge mistake that would cost us both for the rest of our lives.

Chapter 27

Every year the Bell Labs ski club would take a bus trip to Mont-Tremblant, which is in Canada, one-and-a-half hours north of Montreal. It was usually a full busload of about 40 to 50 of our friends, enjoying four days of fun in the snow over the February holiday weekend.

In 1979, that holiday was still called Washington's Birthday. Now it's usually called President's Day. We loved that trip and never missed it. If only we had skipped that year….

I had hired a woman to take care of my sons over the long weekend. It was a long drive to get up there and back. We arrived on Friday and were supposed to return on Monday. We went skiing Friday, but the next day Doug and I went to see the local real estate agent from whom we had bought land up there several years earlier.

We had bought this property when Doug had a meeting up in Montreal. He saw it as a good real estate investment. I didn't really like it, but Doug was convinced we'd make a lot of money with it, so we bought it. Since we were up there now, we decided to go see the property.

I wanted to go on Sunday, but he insisted we go on Saturday. I don't remember how we got there. We either rented a car or the real estate agent picked us up. Anyway, we spent our Saturday poking around that place.

Years later, the deserted farmhouse that was on the property got vandalized and the town said we had to have it torn down. We didn't have to pay for the demolition though. We contracted someone who said they would do it for free, if we let them have the wood. Eventually we sold that property, because we were doing nothing with it, except paying taxes on it.

Sunday morning, Doug went to rent skis. Meanwhile, I hit the slopes with three other people in our group. There are two sides to the mountain there that you can ski on, the north and the south. I was on the south side, which was an expert slope called The Flying Mile. It wasn't too difficult in the morning, when I was out there.

After Doug got his skis, he saw me with these people, so he came over too. We went skiing down the left side of the slope for a while, then went in and had lunch.

After lunch, it was getting really cold, down to -26 degrees Fahrenheit. We were wearing facemasks as we took the chair lift up the

Flying Mile. It was so cold, I wanted to just quit skiing for the day.

They had a four-mile easy run, which I was going to take and then call it quits. Doug said, "No, I'm not ready to go in yet. I want to ski down the Flying Mile one more time."

I said, "Well, what time is it?" It was 2:00. After 3:00, I generally wouldn't ski anything I considered dangerous. They had already closed some of the other slopes, because the cold was making them too icy.

At most places in Vermont, 3:00 is when the snow turns into ice and you're smart not to ski on it. I usually just take an easy slope on my last run, to be sure I don't get hurt. But Doug was demanding that we take the Flying Mile one more time together before we stopped.

Finally I said, "Okay, but you go first."

Remember, Doug was 6'4" and about 230 pounds. If he slipped, he might kill little me as he fell. With two kids at home, I wasn't going to take that chance.

Doug started down the slope fine, with me following behind him. As we descended, however, we approached a treacherous area called The Waterfall. There was a sign there with an exclamation point on it (!), which meant "Danger" or "Caution."

You have to understand, at this point the Flying Mile had two sides you could go down. Doug chose to take the right side, which was steeper. That's where The Waterfall was. It was like a big hill. I had gone on the left side in the morning, which was easier. It didn't have The Waterfall.

To handle this steep area, Doug started trying to traverse. That's skiing back and forth, making short, sharp turns in opposite directions, as you go down the slope. You do that to slow yourself and stay in control. Otherwise, you'd just go straight down the slope, way too fast.

Instead of digging into the snow and turning, however, Doug's skis just slipped on the icy surface. He started sliding partially out of control. Somehow, he even got turned around, so he was going downhill, full speed and backwards, towards some woods that were next to the slope.

I saw Doug's skis slip into a "V" shape, with the backs wide apart and the fronts pointed together, which made him go even faster. Then he was sliding diagonally, off to the right, into a stand of trees. He just disappeared.

When I saw this happen, I knew Doug had taken the wrong side of the slope. This was not the side we had skied down in the morning. I immediately skied around to the other side of the slope, past The

Waterfall, to where I could see him again.

Doug was just lying in the snow, on his back in front of a tree. He wasn't moving. His head was right up against the tree. My first thought was, *Oh, my God, he's dead.*

As I tried to reach him, I started falling in the snow, so I took my skis off and started walking to him. Someone else got there before me. When I finally arrived, Doug was conscious. He just said, "It feels like my back is broken."

I just thought, *Gee, I can't even imagine how that feels.* I didn't know what to say or do, other than to wait for the ski patrol. I'm sure we talked a little, but I can't remember what we might have said.

Meanwhile, some guy from our trip was just then going by on the chairlift. He obviously didn't realize how serious our situation was, because he yelled out, "Sylvia, you need a drink!"

I thought, *That's the last thing in the world I need now. I have to keep my head together.*

We waited there a while, until the ski patrol came. Then the ski doctor came and he told me to just go down and stay in the clinic until they could get Doug down there. The clinic was a little further away than the lodge.

I skied down to the clinic and waited a while, but nothing was happening and nobody was there. Nobody came to tell me what was going on. I felt isolated. It was a French place and I was all alone. So I thought, *This is ridiculous. I'm just sitting here by myself. I'm going back outside.*

I went out to where I could see up the mountain, where they were still working on Doug. It was taking a long time. They had a rescue sled, which they used to carry people down the slope. They were slowly bringing Doug down the mountain on that sled.

I was so frustrated, that I went into the lodge and bought myself a pack of cigarettes. I didn't really even smoke, but I needed something to do, so I started up then. I waited two and a half hours before they finally got Doug down. Then it was another 15 or 20 minutes to get him into the ambulance, which had also been there waiting for a long time also.

Before we left, the ski doctor came up to me and said, "If he's your *anything*, take him to the Royal Victoria Hospital in Montreal."

Before Doug was loaded in the back of the ambulance, I said to the driver, "I want to go to Montreal."

"Oh, no, madame," he answered. "We don't go to Montreal. It is not in our district. We only go to the local community hospital, St. Agathe."

"You mean I don't have any choice?"

"No, madame, you have no choice."

So we had to go to the local hospital. We were there only about 20 minutes. Sure enough, there was nothing they could do for him there, except tell us he was badly injured. His back and neck might be broken and he needed more than they could do.

I never told Doug about this, but for some reason, they put tubing down his nostrils. I guess it was to help him breathe. It must have hurt, because he screamed like crazy. It was awful. I hope he didn't remember it. He lost all sense of smell after that. I think it was from that tubing.

The doctors there could see Doug's condition was very serious. He had severed his spinal cord and had no feeling in his legs. They couldn't handle it. I was trying to keep things together. I knew we had to get to the Royal Victoria Hospital in Montreal, but we needed another ambulance to take us there.

All I had on me in my ski clothes were three dollars in cash. Fortunately, Doug had a MasterCard in his pocket, because he had rented skis that morning. He had been planning on buying those skis at the end of the day, but, of course, that didn't happen. He never skied again.

Still, with his card, I was able to hire another ambulance with a nurse to take us to Montreal, about 80 miles away. That's how we got transferred from the ER at Saint Agathe to the Royal Victoria Hospital in Montreal.

We sped off into the gathering darkness, siren howling and lights flashing. Because it was an emergency, they opened all the gates on the throughway, so we didn't have to stop for tolls.

The nurse with me in the back of the ambulance kept taking Doug's blood pressure the whole way down to Montreal, but she refused to look me in the eye. I would look at her to get some indication of how Doug was doing and she wouldn't even glance back at me. That was scary. I didn't know, but I took it as a bad sign.

Meanwhile, St Agathe had notified the Royal Victoria that we were coming. There they had the neurological team, the orthopedic team and the accident team all waiting for us, ready to go, when we pulled in. They made me leave the ER while they worked on Doug.

119

Max Mathews, the director of Bell Labs, who had been on the ski trip with us, called while I was there waiting, which was very nice of him. Then the doctors came out and told me what a serious accident this was. They stressed that I could not, under any circumstances, leave for now.

I still had no idea what I was facing.

Chapter 28

Once I had Doug in Montreal under good medical care, my next priority was figuring out how to handle everything else in my life. I was still in my ski clothes. My purse and suitcase were back at the ski hotel. I was stranded in a strange city with nothing but a credit card.

Even during that long, nightmarish ride in the ambulance, I had started wracking my brain, *Who do I know in Montreal I can call for help?* We meet people from all over the world in our travels, so I figured there must be someone.

Then I thought of Al Bregman. He had been getting his doctorate in psychology at Yale when Doug and I were working there. We were all friends, so once the three medical teams at the hospital had taken Doug in, I called Al and told him what had happened. Then I asked if I could come stay with him.

He said, "Well, Sylvia, since I last saw you I have gotten married to a woman who already had five children, so it's pretty crowded here. We do have a little apartment down the street from where we live, which we use for a getaway though. You're very welcome to stay there."

I said, "Al, no, really I can't be by myself right now. I'd rather stay with you and your family, if there's any way I can."

So he very generously said, "Oh, okay. Well, then you can come and sleep on the floor of my study. That's the only place I can think of."

I said, "Fine. That will be great.

He responded, like a true friend, "Now I'm coming over there to the hospital to get you. I'll see you soon."

While I was waiting, a doctor came and gave me a couple of valium. I had never taken a tranquilizer in my life, but I started. Then Al showed up and the two of us went up to see Doug.

Doug had never lost consciousness. We stayed and talked for a while, before I left with Al. We went over to Al's house and I met his wife, who was also an academic. Her kids weren't that young. They ranged from 11 to 22.

As soon as I got there I asked for a drink. I remembered what that guy on the chair lift had said, about me needing a drink. Now it was finally true. I wanted to relax.

But Al said, "Oh, Sylvia, I'm sorry, we don't have any alcohol in the house."

I couldn't believe it. And I couldn't sleep at all. The valium hadn't done anything. In fact, for the next three nights, I didn't sleep at all.

The next day Al took me back to the hospital. I found out then that the doctors had not even expected Doug to live through the night. They said it was the worst accident they had ever encountered.

His back was so badly injured that, by the time we got to the hospital, he had a collapsed lung, his ribs were broken and he had a hematoma, which is a build-up of blood in the tissue. Doug had lost over a third of his body's blood from internal bleeding. You couldn't see it. There wasn't a scratch on his body. It was all internal damage.

By the second day they had pretty much told Doug that he was paraplegic. He wouldn't have the use of his legs again. He wasn't going to walk. He just closed his eyes and lay there, accepting it, probably pondering what would come next.

The prognosis was that Doug would eventually need to have surgery on his neck, because it was broken too, as well as his back. Fortunately, that break hadn't affected the spinal cord in his neck, or he would have been quadriplegic, without the use of his arms too.

Since Al didn't have any liquor in the house, I bought myself a bottle of vodka. I drank vodka and tonic in the evenings to stay calm. Al's wife had one son who was schizophrenic, so I'd sit in the room with this guy and have a couple of drinks, while trying find out what he was doing.

I went over to the hospital every day. Al's office was right next-door to the hospital, so he could drive me pretty easily at first. I would be there all day, then he'd bring me home for dinner and take me back to the hospital in the evening. He took me back and forth until I learned how to take the subway in Montreal.

I tried to get some sleep in a lounge area at the hospital when I could. I met a couple there, who saw me lying on the couch trying to rest and felt sorry for me. I was still in a state of shock. I was functioning, but I was traumatized

Meanwhile, Doug was in pretty good spirits, all things considered. He talked and responded to people.

At the ski lodge up at Mont-Tremblant, we had been sharing a bathroom with another couple. Fortunately, they had a car, so the next day they brought me our luggage and my purse. Now I had my phone book and I could start making calls, to let people know what had happened.

Since this was before cell phones, I had to use Al's home phone. I was making expensive, long-distance, international calls, so I offered to pay for them, but Al and his wife wouldn't let me. Such good people.

By the first morning, the news had already gotten back to New Jersey. The Bell Labs doctor called me at Al's house and other people started calling as well.

Then I phoned Doug's parents, who were living in Ft. Myers, Florida. I had wanted to tell them earlier, but their phone number was unlisted, and I didn't know it by heart.

When I reported the devastating news to them, Doug's father's only comment was, "Call us back when you have more information."

He was always very rigid and not terribly friendly, but his comment seemed so rude and short to me. I couldn't understand it. Then he just hung up. I heard my mother-in-law on the other phone, but she didn't say anything more. I thought my mother-in-law would say something like, "Well, Sylvia, where is he?" but she didn't say a word. She generally just followed along with whatever he wanted to do.

Maybe he was in shock at that moment and couldn't process what I was saying. Later he got worried, but he couldn't call me back, since he didn't know what hospital Doug was in or where I was staying.

Meanwhile, I certainly wasn't going to call him again with that kind of attitude. So he ended up phoning all the hospitals in Montreal, until he found his son. Doug's parents were shook up, because he was an only child, just like I was.

I asked friends to notify other people. Doug was supposed to be going to a meeting in Leipzig, Germany, the next month, in March. Obviously that wasn't going to happen now. We didn't know for sure what was going to happen. Everything had to be cancelled for the time being.

Believe it or not, one notification I made was because I had been planning to go skiing with a girlfriend the following week. I had somebody call to let her know I couldn't go and why. Later she told me she couldn't believe that, in all our tragedy, I would remember our date to go skiing. But I have that kind of memory. I keep a calendar. I don't like to break dates and I remember things coming up.

At this point, however, I wasn't even sure where my children were. I had left them with a French lady, who was a good babysitter and was taking care of them at her house. She had picked them up before we left on our trip. We were supposed to be back Monday night, of course, and I was supposed to pick them up Tuesday morning, when school started again.

Steve was in Montessori pre-school and Greg was in public school. I found out later that two different sets of parents, one from each school, took care of the boys separately for the first couple of nights. Unfortunately, at this most traumatic time, they were separated from each other. They had never been separated before. The director of Bell Labs eventually went and found Greg and took care of him.

Then, a dear friend and colleague, Tapas Sen, called my friend Lyndy, who used to work at Merck with me, and asked, "Have you heard about Doug Carroll?' She said no, so he told her all about the accident. She and her husband Walt volunteered to pick up both our sons and move them back into our house and take care of them there. This was a godsend for us and for the boys.

They located both kids and got everybody settled back in our home. Then we could all talk on the phone. Greg was old enough to know something really bad had happened. Steve had just turned five, so his attitude was, *Oh, Dad went away and broke a bone or something, but he'll be okay when he comes home from the hospital.*

Greg started doing poorly in school and having temper tantrums. Lyndy couldn't control Greg when he started a tantrum. He was always kind of hyper and rode his bike a lot, but he had been an A student before. Now he was just going crazy.

She would come home from her job at Merck, an hour commute each way, to find that he had gone off and left our house wide open. He wouldn't be there and she had no idea where he was. Lyndy would call me up in Montreal and have me talk to Greg, to try to calm him down. It was rough.

We were all just beginning to realize how much our lives would change.

Chapter 29

Two of Doug's colleagues lived up in Montreal. One was Jim Ramsey. They heard about the accident and Jim came over to visit Doug. When Jim came out of Doug's hospital room, he said to me, "Sylvia, he's gonna be okay. He's talking about his work."

Later, they invited me out for dinner one night and talked to me about the situation, reassuring me some more. Doug wasn't talking about this terrible tragedy that had happened to him. There was no self-pity, whining or complaining. That was important to me.

Most people would be thinking, *Oh, my God my life is over, why did this happen to me? Why, why?* Doug just wanted to get back to work. I admired that.

Doug loved his work. Another associate, Toshio, who was Japanese, also came over to visit. Same scenario. He and Doug just discussed work. That's how Doug was, right from the very beginning.

As for me, while Doug was in the hospital in Montreal, I had so much stress I was just burning up the calories like crazy. In three weeks, I lost 25 pounds. I didn't have a breakdown though. I kept it together. I was miserable, but I was functioning.

I could be in a coffee shop or someplace like that and I would hear people around me going on about typical mundane things in their lives. To me so much of that stuff was now just insignificant. My world had suddenly turned upside down. In a split second, I suddenly didn't have the life I had had before. Now I had serious things to deal with all the time.

There was never really any question of running away. I knew I had to stay with my husband, because I wasn't working at that time and I had two kids to raise. I'd be at the hospital during the day and sometimes in the afternoon I'd try to rest on the couch there.

I didn't break down crying or anything like that. I was under all this stress, trying to hold everything together, but I functioned. In fact, the only time I did cry was weeks later, after we got back and Tapas Sen and his wife Sondra had me over to their house. They started talking to me and I just broke down. They were so kind, asking me how I felt. They gave me the space to let it all out. That was the only time I cried about the situation.

I don't normally cry anyway. If I hear or see something really sentimental or touching, I might tear up a little, but all my life I felt I had to be strong. Growing up so independent helped that. My parents weren't the hovering type. They let me be on my own. They trusted me.

While Doug was there in the Royal Victoria Hospital, he was aware of everything the whole time. In fact, he insisted I go back up to Mont-Tremblant the next week with a photographer and take pictures of where he fell. So I did.

The two of us skied down to the spot of the accident, but by then it wasn't as bad. It was more like spring skiing. The photographer took pictures anyway and then we went down to the lodge to have lunch.

While we were there, he asked me if I would like to take an easy four-mile run before we left. I agreed to and I'm glad I did, as weird as that may sound. I think if I hadn't done that then and there, I might never have skied again. It was good. It was beautiful and easy. So I continued skiing after that and even took my kids skiing as well.

Supposedly, according to research by American Sports Data, the most dangerous sports, in order of risk, are: boxing, football, snowboarding, hockey, and then skiing. According to a study in New Zealand on "adventure sports," more people are injured by horseback riding, hiking, mountain biking, and surfing, than by skiing. Doug's accident was really a freak event.

Anyway, after three weeks at the hospital in Montreal, Doug's doctors felt he was stabilized. At that point, since Doug was an American citizen, their priority was to get him out of Canada and back to the U.S. They felt Doug's neck was so badly broken, that he would have to have surgery on it. They said his back was so bad that nothing could be done about it. He would have to just lie in bed and let it heal.

They decided to transfer Doug to New York City by ambulance. It was a 500-mile trip and they had to make sure his neck wouldn't move during the trip.

Doug had a bad break in his neck. If there was any movement, it could sever the spinal cord even higher up than it already was. So they gave him a halo ring. This is a metal ring around the patient's head. It's attached by adjustable metal bars to a vest, which fits snugly around the chest. It provides continuous stability to the cervical spine.

The halo holds the patient's head in position in the center of the ring with four titanium "pins." These are spaced around the halo ring and actually go into the skull. They had to do surgery to put the ring on with these pins.

They drilled a hole into either side of his forehead for the pins to go into. Those holes left scars on his forehead, which you could see for the rest of his life. Fortunately most patients don't experience significant pain from this process.

They sent us first to Bellevue in New York. That's a community hospital, geared to serving the poorer people who couldn't afford top health care. NYU was top-notch, but they couldn't get Doug into NYU right away, so that's why we went to Bellevue first.

We arrived with no disasters. A colleague and dear friend, Crawford Clark, met us at the Bellevue emergency room. I went home with him and spent the night in the city. What a great friend he was, to help us out like that. I was really impressed.

The next day, Doug's programmer at Bell Labs, Sandy Pruzansky, came into the city and took me back to Bernardsville. That's how I finally got home and reunited with my kids.

Doug stayed at Bellevue for a few days, before they transferred him to NYU. The doctors there had the reverse opinion from the doctors in Montreal. They said Doug should have a spinal fusion surgery on his back. They wanted to delay it though, because he was running a temperature. Later we found out that's normal with a spinal cord injury, but they thought he had an infection.

The doctor at Bell Labs was very helpful all this time. Without all our friends, I never would have made it through this whole ordeal. Never.

While Doug was waiting for his surgery, a lot of his colleagues brought him flowers when they came to visit. That's when he realized he had no sense of smell any more. He couldn't smell the flowers. He never recovered it, which was a shame.

Doug didn't finally have his surgery till May, over two months later. They gave him a spinal fusion and implantation with Harrington Rods, so he could sit up. Then he went to the Rusk Institute for rehab. It was right next-door, almost like a continuation of the same hospital.

While Doug was in New York, some of his colleagues came to visit. He was always talking with them about his work. Then he ran out of sick time with Bell Labs, so Mike, his department head went to the vice president to discuss it. They decided that with the work Doug did, he could do it in the hospital, just as long as he had a pencil, paper and telephone. So a presidential decision came down to keep Doug on the payroll.

He did do a lot of writing while he was there. I had dinner one night with Mike. He and his wife were good friends. He told me that Doug wrote a whole merit review from his hospital bed. He was impressed.

Now that Doug was back in New York and I was living at home with my sons, I'd take them into the city to see their father every so often. They were beginning to understand and adjust to what was happening.

The first weekend I was home, Doug and I had had plans to go to an opera with some friends from Maryland, my girlfriend, Priscilla, from the Rainbow Girls and her husband, Werner. I already had the four tickets, but I never told them what had happened. They came up and that's when I told them. I invited a woman friend of mine to go in Doug's place, so the four of us went together.

The reason I did that was because I wanted some company. I needed to get out. I needed to have someone around and I wanted to see the opera, so I just never canceled it. Boy, were they shocked when they found out.

That just shows how I was feeling. We had bought the tickets and they weren't cheap. I decided it would be healthy and worthwhile to have company for the weekend and start living life normally again. I could still have a good life. I wasn't going to let this stop me from being happy.

While Doug was in the hospital in New York, colleagues would come talk to him about work stuff as well. He just never quit. He probably got more involved in his work as life went on, because he was paralyzed. Otherwise, he never would have been as focused as he was.

Work was his main outlet. He definitely wasn't disabled in the brain. His brain was the same and it worked great. He would say, "I just need a new body."

Chapter 30

So many things we do every day we take completely for granted. Without thinking, we do them automatically, as if it's the most normal thing in the world. We don't realize what a gift all these little abilities are, until we lose them.

As the weeks and months went by after the accident, I began to understand all the changes that would be taking place in our lives, now that we were dealing with a major disability.

Doug's spinal cord was severed between the third and four thoracic vertebrae. That's just below the nipple line of the body. That meant three-fourths of his body was paralyzed, with no feeling and no control. He could use his arms, no problem, because they were above that line, but nothing worked below the injury point.

Doug had no control of his bladder, urinary tract, or bowels. We had to have regular medical routines to take care of all these things and keep him clean and healthy. This was part of what Doug and I learned as he went through rehab at the Rusk Institute. It was not pleasant.

He wore a catheter and a leg bag for urine control. The catheter had to be changed regularly. When he was in bed, the catheter tubing would be attached to a side bag on the bed. When he was up, in his wheelchair, he'd switch the tube over to a leg bag, which fit inside his pants, below the knee. He'd always wear long pants, so the bag was inside his pant leg. You couldn't see it.

Originally, Doug used a condom to attach the catheter to his penis. He had to use a certain kind of cement to hold it on. At Rusk, they taught him to put on the condom, then cement it onto his penis to be sure it was watertight. There was an opening at the end of the condom and tubing would connect to that for the urine to run out.

When he was changing that condom, he would have a few Chux pads under him, because otherwise he would get the bed wet and we'd have to change the sheets.

Chux are those blue, disposable, waterproof pads you see in hospitals. They're plastic on the outside, with white padding as a middle layer. If a person has an accident on a bed, Chux keep the bed clean. You can just throw them away after you use them. We used them all the time.

One problem with the condoms was that sometimes they'd leak. Then Doug's pants would get wet with urine. If he was out somewhere, that

129

was very embarrassing.

After a couple of years, he decided to get an operation to install a suprapubic catheter. That drains urine directly from the bladder. The catheter is inserted into the bladder through a small hole in the belly. Again, tubing is attached to the catheter, which leads into the bag where the urine is collected.

After the operation, Doug didn't have to go through cementing the condom on his penis every day. It had taken him at least an hour a day to do that and it had to be done every day. Doug was slow with that kind of stuff. It's not the kind of thing you can do fast anyway, but Doug never moved fast to start with...ever.

Between all the things he had to do and not being able to do them like most people, getting up and getting dressed took him three to four hours daily, just to get going.

When we went out and Doug's urine bag got full, if he couldn't get into a bathroom, I had to deal with it. This was before restrooms had to be wheelchair accessible, so it was no fun being disabled and out in public. We discovered first-hand why the American Disabilities Act (ADA) needed to be passed in 1990. But we were eleven years away from that when the accident happened.

New York has all these very old buildings. Most of the bathrooms are not on the first floor. A lot of them were in the basement or were very tiny. You had to walk down a number of just steps to get to them. They weren't even close to wheelchair accessible. But we had to cope.

We learned that when we wanted to meet people for dinner and a show, Doug would have to have his urinal in a backpack. After dinner, before we left for the theater, I would take it out. Being in a crowded restaurant in New York, with a lot of people sitting at small tables, no one hardly ever noticed. They were all busy doing their own thing.

The urinal looked like a quart plastic bottle. I would squat down near Doug's chair and get the urine out of his leg bag. Again, most people didn't know what I was doing down there. The friends we were eating with pretty much knew what I was doing, but they got used to all this with us.

Next, I'd take the urinal to the ladies' room, empty it, and rinse it out. Once that was done, I'd come back and return the urinal to Doug's backpack. No big deal, but it had to be done.

Doug's bowel routine was even more involved and unpleasant. It had to be done three times a week, to empty his bowels. It usually took a long time too, about three or four hours, and it smelled up the whole place.

To get the bowel cleared, you had to wear a glove and use your fingers to go up in there and dig the feces out. Doug couldn't feel anything, so it wasn't painful, but it was messy. I learned all about it in rehab.

As a little girl, about one year old, I remember watching my mother wash my soiled diapers in the toilet. I thought to myself, *Boy, I could never do that*. And then I ended up doing much worse than that.

If possible, Doug would do the bowel routine on his own. I couldn't be around because of the smell. I would just go out and come back to clean him up. If there was a toilet he could get to and sit on, he had a special toilet seat he'd put over the toilet and do it there.

If we were in a hotel room where he couldn't get his wheelchair into the bathroom, I'd have to put down a lot of Chux on the bed. So then he'd do it there and I'd clean him up there.

As you can imagine, there were a lot of adjustments we had to make in our relationship, in order to keep life running smoothly. For one thing, Doug couldn't have sex after the accident. I tried a few times to have oral sex with him, but it wasn't the same. It was very complicated and frustrating for both of us.

When Doug realized he couldn't have sex any more, he told me, if I wanted to, I could date and have sex with whomever I liked. The only thing he asked was that it not be with a colleague of his. Of course.

Doug was very frustrated by the fact he couldn't have sex. He had always been a very virile man and we had had a great sex life together. Years later, in 1989, Doug actually went into the hospital and his urologist gave him a penile implant so he could try to be sexual again, but it didn't work. The implant got infected, so he had to have it removed.

I started dating pretty soon after the accident. I am and always have been a people person, an extrovert. I need to connect with others, especially in difficult times. So, even when Doug was still in the hospital, I saw a couple of men.

What really saved our relationship and our family was that Doug realized I still had my own needs and, if he was going to keep me, he had to give me some freedom. He did. He never asked me who I was going with. He only asked when I would be home.

That first year after the accident, Doug and I talked. He told me all the women he had had sex with, even though we had previously agreed not to discuss it. There were maybe five or six of them, most of whom I knew. They were wives of friends of ours. Then Doug asked me to tell him the men I had slept with.

I said, "No, I'm not going to do that, because I am planning to continue seeing some of them and you don't want to know about it. I'd really rather not talk about it." So that's where we left it.

What I mainly did was go to a massage group. I met a couple of guys there I liked. One of them just called me recently, in fact. He's an attorney from Yale Law School. I dated him off and on for thirty years. He was originally married, with two kids the same age as mine, but then he got divorced.

I also met people on my own, at the beach, and so on. I had a lot of male friends, so that I could stay balanced and have some semblance of a normal life.

Our kids grew up understanding our situation. They knew I went out with other guys and they even knew some of them, who became friends of the family.

That gives you just a little sense of what we had to incorporate into our daily lives now, in order to keep going. It took me a few months, however, to realize we couldn't even continue living in our home.

An MD friend of ours from the Unitarian Fellowship came over to visit one day shortly after we were back and he said, "Sylvia, you know you're not going to be able to live here anymore."

I thought to myself, *The one thing I thought I still had left was my home and our neighbors*, but it was true. We needed a different house now.

Chapter 31

Here's how the whole rehab period of our lives played out while Doug was at the Rusk Institute. In July, 1979, Doug's parents came up from Fort Myers, Florida to spend a week and see him. While they were there, my father-in-law generally took the train with me to New York. Sometimes I drove both of them in. It was really a shock for them to see their son like this, but we were all starting to accept our new reality.

On July 28, the doctors let me bring Doug home for an overnight stay. It was just a temporary trial, to see how things would be. Our home was bi-level, so Doug had to sleep in one of the guest rooms downstairs. The bathroom was not wheelchair accessible. He couldn't get in there at all. So, even with a nurse to help, it took three hours the next morning for him to get a sponge bath, eat breakfast, brush his teeth, and get dressed.

My son Steve and I drove him back to the Institute that next day. By the time I got home, I was thoroughly exhausted. This was my first taste of what I would be dealing with for the rest of Doug's life. It was overwhelming.

One pleasant surprise was when one of our good friends showed up unexpectedly on August 2nd. It was Bud, the funny dentist, whom we had spent a ski week with at Grey Rocks, Canada, in 1972, when Doug first said he wanted to open up our marriage.

Bud drove all the way to New Jersey from Willoughby, Ohio, again without telling us he was coming. He had said he might come…and he did. He arrived late at night, so he slept in his car out on our driveway at the top of the hill, where there was a flat place you could park on.

The next day he knocked on the door, as usual, asking if there was a hotel around. He and I went to New York together, because he wanted to see Doug. He left August 5. He was a fun guy, like family. When he was visiting, if we were invited to a party or whatever, we would just take him with us.

August 11, I brought Doug home again. This time I wanted to try out a chair lift to take him up and down the stairs. It was impossible though. The back stairs were in two sections, with a landing where you had to turn around. You couldn't use a chair lift all the way up. So I took Doug back to the Institute the next day.

Doug couldn't come in the front door of our house at all. He couldn't access that. There was no real sidewalk to roll his wheelchair on. It was all grass, with stepping-stones to the front door.

Even if Doug could have gotten to the front door, he couldn't have gotten in the house. There were two steps to go up, one to get to the concrete slab, and then another to get into the foyer.

Once you got into the foyer, you had to go either up five stairs to the second floor, where we mostly lived, or down five stairs to the family room. Too many stairs!

It was totally impossible to give Doug access to the whole house. There was no way it could be modified or adapted. That's why we had to get health aides to help Doug while we were there. Everything was new to us.

August 13, Doug and I left for Washington, DC, for the American Statistical Association meeting. He had a temporary discharge from the Rusk Institute to attend it. The next day he was inducted as a Fellow.

That's the highest level of recognition the ASA can give. He also later became a Fellow of SMEP, the Society of Multivariate Experimental Psychology. This was the highest-ranking member you could be.

August 16, I took Doug back to Rusk. On the 31st, they finally discharged him. We went directly to the Waldorf Astoria Hotel for the American Psychological Association meeting there. We came back home on September 5 to our non-accessible home.

We had to live in that house in a makeshift fashion for about three months, until we could find another place to move into. Doug had to stay downstairs the whole time. He couldn't get upstairs at all, which was a real hassle.

On the upper level was most of the family space: kitchen, dining room, living room, three bedrooms, and two bathrooms. On the lower level, where Doug had to stay, were just the family room, utility room, two guest bedrooms, and a bathroom.

In his wheelchair, Doug had to enter through the garage, which was adjacent to the lower level of the house. From there it was a straight run, with no steps, to go into the family room and the two guest bedrooms.

That house in Bernardsville was on a steep hill and it was bi-level. It was not wheelchair accessible and couldn't be made so.

Doug had to have a health aide while we were still living there. One of his colleagues from Bell Labs would come and pick him up every weekday to go to work

I tried getting the house modified, but it was no use, so we started

134

looking for a one-story, ranch-style house. That was a whole other journey in itself. So many homes in our area had sunken living rooms. The real estate agents had no idea what we needed. It was ridiculous.

Finally, though, I found a house in Warren, New Jersey, which was really perfect. It was about eight miles away from where we had been living in Bernardsville. It also had a long driveway, like our first home, but it wasn't as steep.

It was a nice ranch house, all on one floor. It did have a basement, but Doug never had to go down there, because it was just for storage. The house had four bedrooms and three baths. The master bedroom was on one side of the house, along with a study and a bathroom. We were going to modify that area for wheelchair accessibility, so it would be Doug's wing.

On the other side of the house were a family room and three bedrooms. I slept in one and our two boys slept in the other two. In between, was a huge living room/dining room combined, with sliding glass doors leading out to the patio.

When you entered the house from the front door, you'd see a huge room in front of you, the living room/dining room. It had a big fireplace, which was nice. It was paneled in medium dark wood, nicely finished, which was very popular back then. The family room and the hallway from the foyer to the master bedroom were also paneled.

We closed on that house at the end of November, 1979, and moved right in. Now it was time to make it wheelchair accessible.

Chapter 32

There are many things in our homes that make life impossible for the wheelchair-bound. Most of these things we never think about or are aware of...until we have to deal with them.

Even though our new home in Warren was all on one floor, we still had to make a lot of modifications to get it wheelchair-accessible.

The master bedroom was going to be Doug's headquarters, so the doorway into it had to be widened, for Doug to get his wheelchair through it. The doorway from his bedroom to the master bath also had to be widened. We put a folding door in there.

There were two doors into the bathroom, one from the master bedroom and one from the hallway. That hall bathroom door had to be widened too.

Then we had to install a roll-in shower. Everything on the floor had to be flat, so Doug could use his shower commode chair to get in and out. He couldn't take his wheelchair into the shower, so he had a shower commode chair. He used it for two things, the shower and the toilet.

He could get on this chair and roll into the shower, to bathe himself. We installed a hand-held shower spray there, which he could use for washing, along with the overhead shower.

Then the toilet. We had to put in a new toilet, which was a little higher than the old one. Doug would position the shower commode chair over the toilet to do his bowel routine.

The vanity also had to be changed. Most vanities are closed below the sink, but Doug had to roll right up to the sink in his wheelchair or commode chair to use it, so there had to be open space under there for his knees to fit.

In the rest of the house, we had to build two ramps, one in the garage, from the house to the car, and one in the house, from the dining room out to the patio. The second ramp was a necessity as an alternate fire exit, in case there was a fire, which might make it impossible for Doug to leave the house through the garage.

The garage ramp was made of wood. We needed it, because there was a high step up, from the garage floor to the house, which you couldn't navigate in a wheelchair.

The patio ramp was concrete. Doug normally wouldn't go out there. He usually stayed inside or came and went through the garage in his car.

Still, he needed two different ways of getting out of the house.

If there were a fire in the garage, the rest of us could just walk out any door, but Doug couldn't. He wouldn't be able to get out of the house down the garage ramp. Instead, he could wheel himself through the dining room and out onto this concrete ramp to the patio.

We even built a wooden bridge outdoors, from our patio to our neighbor's driveway. The bridge crossed over a little stream of water, which ran between our house and the neighbors'. If there were such an emergency, Doug wouldn't be stranded on the patio. He could go over the bridge in his wheelchair to the neighbors' driveway and then go down it.

This planning was just another example of how Doug was so fastidious about everything being correct. Doug wanted to make sure he wasn't going to die in a fire, so he insisted we take every precaution. He even wore two watches. He wouldn't have been such a great scientist, if he weren't so concerned about little details.

Our garage was huge. It was a 2-car garage, with one big door for both cars. A lot of people would use a garage like that to store things in, like patio furniture, lawnmower, and so on. They can do that and still get one or two cars in there as well.

We didn't store anything in ours though. We needed all the space we had, to park the cars and to enable Doug to get his wheelchair in and out of his car and up the ramp.

Doug always parked inside the garage. When you live up north and there are three feet of snow on the ground, if a car is outside, a person in a wheelchair can't get to it.

Our house was on a hill, with trees near the driveway, but it wasn't as steep as at our first house. Still, when it snowed, the driveway always had to be plowed and sanded, for Doug to be able to drive on it.

Our new driveway was a lot longer than the old one, about three times as long. It went diagonally across the front of the house from right to left and up to our garage. We installed an automatic garage door opener, so we could use a remote from inside the car to raise the garage door and go in.

Doug kept his car on the left hand side of the garage, near the bottom of the ramp. I parked on the right hand side. Once Doug got his car inside the garage, he would maneuver from the car onto the ramp, then up the ramp and through the door into the dinette area of our kitchen.

The ramp was in front of where the cars parked. It went from the left side of the garage up to the house on the right side. There was enough space at the foot of it for Doug to turn his wheelchair and start up it.

The house was almost a foot higher than the garage floor. The ramp took him up to the level of the house. It had a raised edge on each side, so the wheelchair couldn't slip off it

There are ADA (Americans with Disabilities Act) regulations now that describe just how much of an incline a wheelchair ramp can be. It's so much per foot. If the ramp is too steep, someone might not be able to manage it and could actually fall over backwards.

Up next to the door into the house, there was a button to press. This would open and close the garage door remotely, so Doug could take care of that himself outside the car.

The door into the house had two doorknobs on the outside. People would always ask why. It was so Doug could close the door himself from his wheelchair, when he exited the house. He couldn't reach the regular doorknob very easily from the ramp. Inside the house, he only needed one doorknob.

When Doug went from the kitchen out to the garage, there was a button on the wall on the left, next to the ramp, to open and close the garage door. Doug would push that before he went out, to make sure the garage door would open properly.

That was important. He had to have the garage door open before he started the car, so he wouldn't risk being poisoned by carbon monoxide fumes. After he drove out, he would close the garage door from the car.

Doug didn't want to take a chance of getting in the car and then finding out the battery on the garage door opener was dead. If that happened, he would have to get out of the car again and go all the way back in the house. You have to think about these things when you're confined to a wheelchair...and he did.

Looking at the front of our new home, you couldn't tell it was now wheelchair-accessible. We had a big walkway and regular steps going up to the front door. That was unchanged. Doug only accessed the house from the garage.

Remember, Doug could never stand up again after his accident. He was always in a wheelchair or in bed. He did learn to drive, however, using hand controls. His first car was a Chevy Caprice. It had to be a two-door car, with a power driver's seat.

To enter the car, Doug would slide from his wheelchair onto the driver's seat, using a sliding board. This was a polished wooden board he could slide under himself and position from the wheelchair onto the driver's seat. Then he'd scoot across that into the car.

After he got into the driver's seat, he would pull the sliding board out form under him. His wheelchair was still there beside the car, so he had to fold that up from where he was sitting. Then he would move his car seat forward as far as it could go, to make room for the folded wheelchair to go behind him in the back, along with the sliding board and the Roho cushion he sat on in the chair.

Roho cushions are well-known accessories for wheelchair-bound people. They help relieve the pressure on the skin from constant sitting. Doug always had one wherever he was sitting in his wheelchair.

Next he had to put everything behind the driver's seat and finally he had to power the seat back again, to make room for his legs. He was a big guy, 6'4" with long legs, so, when he was driving, the seat had to be pretty far back. After all this, he could start the car and drive off, using hand controls, of course.

If you are able-bodied, just compare all that with your typical routine of walking out to your car and driving off. Quite a difference, right?

Reversing the process, when Doug wanted to get out of his car, he had to move his power driver's seat way forward again to make room to pull the wheelchair out from behind him. After he got the wheelchair out of the car, he had to move the power seat back again. Then he would unfold the wheelchair beside the car and put the Roho cushion back onto the seat, so he could transfer himself onto it with the sliding board.

Once he had transferred himself onto the wheelchair, if he was getting out of the car in the garage, then he would close the car door and roll straight ahead, turn, and start up that ramp.

All this effort just to accomplish something most people never even think about. This was in the earlier years after Doug's accident, when he was still able to drive a car. The whole idea was for him to be as independent as possible. And for a long time he was.

He drove himself to work and back, but he never came home early. Sometimes he'd get home at one in the morning. He loved his work. I'd just leave food out for him and he would heat it in the microwave. I had to go to bed, because I had to get up with the kids, make them breakfast and lunch, and then get them off to school.

That was our daily life.

139

Chapter 33

As Christmas, 1979, came around, our first Christmas after the accident, we broke our holiday tradition and didn't send out any cards or letters. The year had been too traumatic, both literally and figuratively, to try to talk about. It was the most difficult year of our lives.

The following year, however, 1980, we did send out a holiday letter and this is how Doug phrased his description of the accident:

"February 18, 1979, 2:10 pm, on the ski slopes of Mont-Tremblant, Doug had a drastic accident which created many extreme changes in home, lifestyle, and everything else. It was a ski accident, in which Doug hit a tree, broke his back and neck, and caused a spinal cord injury at thoracic 3 and 4. This resulted in paraplegia, complete paralysis, and loss of feeling from the waist down. He is now confined to a wheelchair."

It was still heartbreaking.

Doug went on to talk in that letter about how there had been no return of function after two years, so it was very unlikely he ever would have any. His only major hope was for some kind of breakthrough in spinal cord research, to regenerate or rebuild the injured area.

He talked about how there was, "considerable hope, if enough resources can be channeled into it. A bill is in Congress to fund research, but is moving slowly."

Even now, over 35 years later, there's been little progress on that front. I guess, instead, we just have to be grateful for the improvement paraplegics have had in their quality of life.

There's been a great deal of progress in that regard. Before the end of World War II, life expectancy for a paraplegic was about one year from the injury. Now it's essentially normal.

Our family continued adjusting to the new reality of our everyday life. We still owned our Bernardsville house, because we had gotten caught in a mortgage crunch, which led to a decline in real estate sales. We couldn't sell the place, so we were renting it out.

We had replaced our faithful old Toyota Corona though, with the big Chevy Caprice, which was necessary for Doug. His office at Bell Labs had also been redone for wheelchair accessibility. They were very helpful and positive there about our situation. They did everything possible to help Doug work there.

They even had him on fulltime payroll while he was in rehab at the

Rusk Institute. So that was the one part of Doug's life that hadn't changed. He continued working, doing research, writing papers, and becoming even more productive. He often worked late afternoons, evenings, and weekends. He also went to a lot of professional meetings.

The meetings were an important part of Doug's work in psychometrics. They were mainly for educational purposes. Doug would exchange ideas with other colleagues in his field from all over the world.

People would give talks about their work, their research, and so on. This kept everybody up to date on the latest developments. Many of these meetings were in the summer, because most academics were teaching the rest of the year.

After the accident, however, there was always risk in our traveling to these meetings. We were constantly facing unknown environments and unforeseen situations. They could often be difficult or even dangerous.

Our first trip abroad after Doug's accident was really strange, a perfect example of what I'm talking about. We were going to Holland. When we showed up at the airport, we found ourselves in a line of 100 other people, waiting to board the same plane, all in wheelchairs. Yes, we were on a plane of over 100 paraplegics.

This was the Wheelchair Olympics team. They were going to Holland for some games that would be going on while we were there. As if that wasn't strange enough, the airline lost Doug's suitcase and couldn't find it. So he had no suitcase when we arrived.

Fortunately, Doug had packed enough medical supplies in his backpack to survive for the nine days we were there. The airline never did find his suitcase, so he had to buy clothes. That wasn't easy.

Being in a wheelchair, he couldn't stand up to try things on, so he couldn't be sure how things would fit. His colleagues took him out to get the clothes. They did the best they could, just guessing at sizes.

Doug took his first solo trip, without me along to help, in 1980, to Ft. Worth, Texas. It seemed that he could handle a short two- or three-day trip on his own by then.

My first solo vacation after our traumatic year of 1979 was to Club Med in Martinique. Doug's parents came to help take care of him and the two boys while I was gone. This was in January, 1980. It was going to be the first time in eleven months I had gone anywhere by myself, with nothing to worry about except having a good time.

I had been seeing a female psychologist at Bell Labs for some therapy.

There had been such a drastic change in my life, that they offered me free counseling with one of their psychologists and I took it. Anything to help me get through this ordeal seemed like a good idea.

Before I left for Martinique, I told my therapist this was probably going to be my last vacation...ever. When I arranged the trip, I really believed that. I couldn't see how I would ever be able to get free again. Thank goodness, it wasn't so. There were many more vacations to come. But at the time, my dread was overwhelming.

Greg and Steve were getting used to our new community and to their new schools. Greg was playing soccer, while Steve was playing tennis and doing judo. Greg also played the flute, while Steve played piano. Each boy had a hamster, which was very fascinating to Aquarius, our cat, who continued to thrive in our new home.

Steve's only complaint about school was that he was being taught subjects that he had already learned the previous year at his old school. His complaint earned him placement in a gifted child program. The previous Bernardsville school system probably was more advanced, but he was very bright anyway, so he liked new challenges.

Even though we were now only eight miles from our old house, I didn't like our new community as much as the old one. Warren was more rural and required more chauffeuring of the kids.

By 1981, we were still renting out our house in Bernardsville and having the typical problems with tenants. Being a landlord was neither fun nor profitable and it all fell on me.

Our trips continued, however, and that I enjoyed, despite the complications. What happened that year in Europe gives you an idea of how difficult our travel could be.

We were going to Vienna. One of Doug's colleagues had checked out our hotel ahead of time, but if you don't have someone in a wheelchair actually trying to do things, you don't realize where the problems might be.

Paul Green, Doug's collaborator, was there a week or so earlier than us, giving lectures. He inspected the room to make sure it was accessible. Doug had given him the dimensions for his wheelchair, so Paul measured everything to be sure. It turned out the room was fine, but neither Paul nor Doug had thought about the elevator.

It was too small. Doug couldn't get his wheelchair into it. The men actually had to carry him up 60 steps. That was terrible. Don't forget. At

142

6'4", 230 pounds, Doug was not a small man.

The next day, Doug gave me an assignment, "Sylvia, please, go find a wheelchair-accessible hotel."

I went with one of his colleagues to look for a truly accessible hotel in Vienna. I finally found one, but that trip was a real learning experience. We had been assured ahead of time everything was okay. As I was to discover, however, over and over again, it never was easy.

No matter where we went, the rooms usually had to be rearranged. Maybe another mattress had to be added to the bed, to make it higher, so Doug could transfer himself from his chair to the bed. Maybe the phone had to be moved. Furniture might be in the way and have to be moved for the chair to get around. There was always something to be adjusted.

When we got to Paris, I had to find a suitable hotel there as well. When I did, the hotel only had eight rooms that were accessible, so we kept the name and address of the place written down for future reference, so we could be sure to get one.

Sometimes it seemed like we were on a crusade to raise the consciousness of European hotels about wheelchair-accessibility. We were pioneers in a wilderness of insensitivity.

In spite of all that, Doug got even more ambitious about increasing the number and extent of his solo trips in 1981. His most ambitious was to Vancouver, British Columbia for five days, completely solo, with no friends or colleagues on the same flight.

At home, many people were very helpful in making our lives richer and easier. For example, Crawford Clark, who met us at Bellevue when Doug was transferred from Montreal, sent me the key to his cabin at Mastic, Long Island. He said we could use it any time we wanted on weekdays. He and his wife only used it on weekends. I and the two boys used to go to the beach there, Smith Point, in the summer for a few days during the week.

Paul Green, Doug's collaborator on many books and papers, was great too. He taught at Wharton and held the S.S. Kresge chair there. Paul always considered my husband as #1 and himself as #2 in their work together. Doug would do the theory; Paul would do the application.

Paul was the nicest guy. He would let us stay at his and his wife's vacation home in the Poconos whenever we wanted. I would take the boys there and we would ski nearby.

Doug and I tried going together to the Caribbean, but it only frustrated him to be near a swimming pool or a beach. Someone did help him once to get into a pool, but it wasn't easy. We went to two islands and then he said he didn't want to go any more. He just wanted to take work vacations, going to meetings.

His friends and colleagues would be at the meetings, which picked him up. They were extremely supportive and admiring. Doug actually became president of every professional organization he ever belonged to.

Towards the end of his life, he even received a Lifetime Achievement Award from the Psychometric Society. That was the highest honor they could give, a really big deal. When I heard about it, I rushed over to the hospital where Doug was a patient, to tell him. By then, I never knew if he would come out alive or not.

One of the guys he grew up with in Jacksonville once asked me, "Sylvia, do you think Doug would have been as successful as he was if he hadn't had that accident?"

I never thought about it before, but it was true. Doug couldn't take vacations or do fun stuff as easily as he used to before the accident. Work became his greatest pleasure.

Chapter 34

Back in the 1980s, there was a self-help seminar that was popular with a lot of people. It was called EST, which stood for Erhard Seminars Training. It was founded by Werner Erhard in 1971 and stayed in business until 1984.

EST was a two-weekend (60-hour) course that was supposed to "transform one's ability to experience living." The main thrust was getting you to recognize you were in charge of your life, no one else.

The whole experience was rough and confrontational, from what I heard. During the training sessions, they wouldn't let you pee or eat or even speak without permission. The peeing part was not a problem for Doug, because he wore a catheter and leg bag, but it was a problem for some people.

Doug went to EST, to see if it would help with his mental outlook after the accident. We were both trying to adjust to our new situation, which was totally different from our previous life.

Doug liked the first weekend, but the second weekend not so much. I don't know exactly why or if it helped him or not. It seemed to me EST was very abusive and difficult. That certainly wasn't what I was looking for.

I wanted something gentle and loving. So a week or two after Doug's experience, I signed up for Living Love, another seminar. It was run by Key Keyes, who was a quadriplegic. That means he had no use of his arms or legs. He was paralyzed from the neck down. His wife, or girlfriend's, name was Penny.

The seminar was held in downtown New York, from Friday night to Sunday afternoon, on one weekend a month. The organizers promised to find a place for us to sleep overnight at someone's house, if we wished,.

I didn't want to commute back and forth, because I felt going home to my regular life every night would break the flow of the workshop. If I dropped back into my everyday reality, I would lose my train of thought on what I was trying to accomplish.

I ended up at someone's house in New Jersey, but at least it wasn't my house. Some people I knew were already in Living Love, so I felt comfortable. One was a man who worked at Bell Labs, Frank Ackerman. There was also a woman named Jane Verloup and some other people. They had all read Ken Keyes' book, *Handbook to Higher Consciousness*.

I forget the exact subject matter of our sessions, but we would meet about once a month at someone's place and just talk together. The basic theme was to realize that your choices don't have to feel like you're subject to some kind of addiction. You don't want to feel like you *have* to do something.

Instead, your choices should feel more like a preference, feeling that you can choose what you like. If you feel you *should* do something, it's like being addicted. You have to do it. But if you feel something would just be nice to do, then that's a preference.

They didn't like the word "should," as in, "I should go to the doctor." They said that, if you feel your decisions are being dictated by some force outside yourself, it's hard to feel happy and free about what you choose.

As an example, instead of saying, "I have to get a hair cut next week," you are better off saying, "I prefer to get a hair cut next week." After all, you do prefer doing that, rather than letting your hair get too long, right?

So it was all about realizing everything is a choice. They thought of it as addiction vs. preference. Some people are addicted to thinking they have no choice in life.

Living Love was a support group. I don't know why these other people were in it, because they didn't have any serious problems that I knew of, certainly not like my challenges. Frank had been divorced, but had a new girlfriend. Jane was divorced and had a daughter and a son. I guess a lot of people were just looking for a way to make their lives better and more fulfilling

Anyway, that year Jane decided to throw a Christmas party. She invited some people from the support group and also some other people from outside the group. I met a guy there who I started dating. He didn't know Doug, but he liked me and asked me to come over to his place a couple of times.

Doug was at Jane's Christmas party with me and was talking to her. I overheard him saying, "I really messed up Sylvia's life. I feel very bad about it." He probably didn't know I heard him. I was sorry he felt that way. After all, I was choosing to stay in my life, right? It was my preference.

I met another man, Bill Wallace, at Living Love, who became a good friend, almost like a family member. He was a lot older than me and there were no romantic feelings on my part. Later I realized there were on his.

Before we moved into our new house, I had always invited people over for Christmas dinner and I continued the tradition afterwards. The second year we were in our new house, we had two couples and Bill Wallace as guests. I was busy preparing the dinner, so I asked someone to start a fire in the fireplace.

The fireplace was in the living room, which adjoined the dining room. It was at the end of the room in the same wall as the sliding glass doors to the patio. So as I was trying to get the food on the table and keep everything warm, all of a sudden the whole room filled up with smoke. Evidently, the flue was closed. It was terrible.

The two couples who were there just started analyzing and discussing how this could have possibly happened. It was ridiculous. They were just sitting there talking about it and not doing anything.

Bill and I had to go outside, get a ladder, and go up on the roof to look at the chimney. We couldn't see anything. I finally called one of my neighbors to help. He came over with metal garbage cans and took the wood and ashes out of our fireplace. What a disaster…but I appreciated Bill.

He remained a friend of the family for five or six years. He had divorced his first wife, and kind of adopted us. My kids just loved him He'd take us to New York at Christmastime, take the boys ice-skating at Rockefeller Center, have dinner in a nice restaurant, and so on.

He'd been in the navy and had six kids, all grown, but he would sometimes act like my sons were his. One time we were walking to Rockefeller Center, when Greg had to go to the bathroom. So Greg went into a restaurant to use the bathroom. He didn't come out for a while, so Bill went in to find him.

The hostess in the restaurant said, "Can I help you?" and Bill said, "Oh, yes, I'm looking for my son." That didn't sit right with me.

I never had sex with Bill, but he was in love with me. He'd send me the most beautiful arrangements of flowers. He gave me presents, like a bottle of perfume, for no reason. I never saw such generous, unconditional love as he had for the kids and me.

He would go to the hospital in New York with me sometimes when Doug had to go. Once, Steve had to go to a doctor and Bill went with us. Sometimes he would even take care of the kids for us, when Doug had a meeting out of town.

One time he took me to Lutece, a famous French restaurant in New York. Another time he took the kids and me to a show by the two magicians, Penn and Teller. Steve was sitting in the audience right next to

Jackson Browne, the famous rock musician. When they asked for a volunteer, Steve got right up on stage. It was quite a night.

The only problem was Bill became possessive. I was going out with other guys, but he didn't know about it. I invited a friend, Bob, from my massage group for Christmas dinner one year when Bill was also there. I liked Bob a lot. Bill picked up on the vibes between us, even though Doug never did.

So Bill took me to brunch that Sunday, plying me with champagne to get me to open up about Bob. He even took me into the bar for more drinks after we ate. He was asking me things like, "So, did you ever go to Bob's house?"

I said, "No"

"Did he give you a Christmas present?"

"No...."

All these things were actually, "Yes," but I wasn't going to tell him that. The next day I decided I couldn't do this any more. Even my own husband wasn't like that with me. So I called Bill and told him, "You have to find yourself a girlfriend." That was it.

I couldn't be his girlfriend. He was more like a father to me. I wasn't interested in him sexually at all. He was in love with me, but it wasn't happening vice versa.

When Doug heard that I had broken up with him, he said, "Oh, I'm going to miss those good leftovers you brought home from all those fancy restaurants." Doug was funny.

Here's another funny thing. Many years after I broke it off with Bill, one Thanksgiving, we were all sitting down to our family dinner. My sons were grown, with one married. There were even a couple of grandkids there.

I had just laid the food out on the table, when the phone rang. It was Bill, calling all the way from Oregon. He talked to each of us, even to my daughter-in-law.

When he spoke to me, he made a point of saying, "Sylvia, you are the best thing that ever happened to me." In spite of the fact I broke up with him, he still felt that way. That was really nice to hear.

Chapter 35

In 1981, AT&T was preparing to divest itself of its subsidiary companies due to an antitrust suit by the Federal government. Bell Labs was going to be split off. It was a big deal, because nobody knew how it would all work out. Doug said we were living in "interesting times," as the Chinese say in their famous curse.

Our biggest trip that year was to Europe. For a little while we were treated like royalty, with a private car and chauffeur, lots of wining and dining, and even a party in our honor.

We stayed at a spa in Germany for one meeting. While we were there, Doug didn't feel so royal. He couldn't use the bathroom in our hotel room, because it wasn't set up for wheelchairs. He had to use a bathroom in the spa area instead.

Meanwhile, back home, our old house still hadn't sold, but we were getting better at being landlords. I was the one who had to do everything, of course. I really didn't like owning that place, because it was so much work. Whenever a tenant left, I had to go clean it up and get it ready for the next one. Once we even had to take tenants to court, to get them out of there.

Still, Doug didn't want to sell the house, even when a buyer finally came along. I put my foot down. I had too many other things to do to be running that place too. I was dealing with Doug and all the meetings, getting a babysitter when we left, speaking to the kids' counselors at school, going to their athletic events, managing the house and a million other things. One small example, every Saturday morning, I would take Steve to judo, 17 miles away, wait for him there, and then bring him back again.

Yeah, it was a hassle being me.

Still we had lots of good times. Doug and I both always loved parties. Before the accident, we often got invited to parties at people's houses. After it, we didn't get invited as much as before.

It was difficult to get Doug into homes that weren't wheelchair-accessible. At some places, for example, where there was just one couple or where there were a lot of steps, it was impossible for one man and two women to carry Doug into the house in his wheelchair. That put a crimp in our social life.

We did socialize a lot through the International Club. I belonged to it for over 30 years. It was a club for women from foreign countries. They invited me to join, even though I was an American. Since I had lived in Germany for a year, I was eligible.

My first exposure to the International Club was when I was on maternity leave from Merck with my first son. One of my female friends from Denmark invited me to a coffee they were holding. They liked me so much, that after that first meeting, they invited me to join.

There was another woman who came to the coffee the same day. She really wanted to join. I, on the other hand, never planned to, because I was set on going back to work. I didn't expect them to invite me, but they did. Unfortunately, they didn't like the other lady that much. She was upset when she heard about it.

The club was run by a woman from Belgium. There are a lot of people from all over the world. They don't know anyone. Their husbands get transferred to the U.S. and they are here all alone. This was a way they could meet other people in the same situation. Most were from Europe, but there were also women from Chile, the Philippines, China, Japan and more.

We had a token membership of five or six Americans, but only those who had lived abroad, so it was a very cosmopolitan group. The people were lovely, including the husbands. They had great parties.

There were many women there who liked Doug. They would always tell me, "Oh, Sylvia your husband is so charming." Of course, men had always liked me too, so we were a popular couple.

Every year they had a big Christmas party. The International Club was just for women, but for the Christmas party, we'd invite the husbands too. We went to a lot of those parties, because they made a special effort to include Doug. A bunch of men would carry him in his wheelchair up the stairs into the party. They were very nice and happy to do that.

The first two years we lived in Warren, in 1979 and 1980, we had the Christmas party at our house. Originally we were supposed to have 78 people the first year, but three couples called me at the last minute and asked if they could come too. They were friends of ours, so I said to Doug, "What do you think?"

And he said, "Oh, six people won't make any difference," so we said okay. We crammed 84 people into our ranch-style house. People were sitting all over, on the floor and wherever they could. It was wall-to-wall bodies. This was a dinner party, but I didn't have to prepare it. I just offered my house.

People have much bigger homes now. Ours was four bedrooms. It wasn't small, but for 84 people eating dinner, it was. The next year, it was 70 degrees outside, even though it was December, so we had a lot of people out on the patio. It wasn't quite as crowded, but after that second party, the club limited all gatherings to 60 people.

We would throw another party in April, when I would invite 100 people and 80 would come. I always said, if all 100 show up, I'm leaving. Everybody loved our parties. People made the party. It was always very academic, scientific, interesting people, local friends, and so on. I didn't do anything special.

When I was throwing a big party, I just had liquor, wine, and beer, with mixers and club soda on a table in the dinette area. Some people didn't drink, but they would always ask me to have club soda. Then I would have many different hors d'oeuvres on the dining room table, like cold cuts, cheese, dips, things like that. When it was over, I just cleaned up the whole thing.

We also used to belong to a Newcomers Club in Bernardsville before Doug's accident. We went to a lot of parties with that group, so we joined the Newcomer's Club in Warren too. Doug was in a wheelchair, but we still went.

Every town had its own Newcomer's Club. Back in 1979, they would come and drop off a little basket at your house with samples of local products and coupons for local businesses when you moved in. They don't do that any more.

After we got established in Warren, if somebody new moved in on our street, I'd go over and introduce myself. I don't think anyone else did that, but I was that kind of person, so I did. After awhile, though, I even stopped that. Times change.

Before Doug's accident, we had a lot of pool parties and cookouts. We once invited his mentor from Princeton University to dinner with his wife. I remembered that he loved Glenlivet scotch, so Doug bought a bottle. Of course, the wife didn't like him drinking it that much, but whenever he came, we would always have it there and give him a glass.

Sometimes I might throw a dinner party for about eight people. Doug would usually want to invite some of his colleagues. They invited us to their homes, so we reciprocated.

For example, I usually had Christmas dinner at our home every year. We'd invite two or three couples, and sometimes their children. That was a lot of work. For even a small dinner party, I had to worry about planning and preparing a whole dinner. Then, I had to get the house cleaned, buy the food, cook, set the table, and clean it all up. Dinner parties were as much work as throwing a big shindig with 80 people.

If we had 80 people at the house for three or four hours, they could just entertain each other. I always enjoyed those parties the most. It was a lot of work, but it was great seeing all our friends.

Both Doug and I looked forward to that. Some friends were from Bell Labs, some from Merck, some from New York, neighbors…it was everyone we liked.

I always felt good after I got to see all my friends. Once everything was going on, talking to people I hadn't seen for a while, entertaining people, it was fun. We were famous for our parties. Afterwards, everyone would say, "Oh, when are you having your party again?"

We usually just did it in April. When we lived in Bernardsville, nobody could get up our steep driveway in wintertime, with the ice and snow. Even in Warren, if there was snow on the ground, people couldn't get up our driveway. It wasn't as steep, but it could be difficult. By April, snow wasn't a problem, so the party was on!

Chapter 36

In 1982, Doug and I took our first real vacation together since the accident. No meetings, no work, just trying to have fun. We went to Santo Domingo in the Dominican Republic. Another couple, Jacqueline and Willem, who were friends and colleagues from the Netherlands, joined us. They were both spending that year working with Doug at Bell Labs, in the office right next-door to his.

We also had another friend living down there, who invited us to hang out after he heard we were coming. He had a PhD in political science and drove a little VW bug. It was a small car, but, believe it or not, he actually squeezed Doug into the front seat of that thing. Doug was amazed. They even got the wheelchair in back too. We never thought it would be possible.

Doug spent a lot of time talking with Willem and Jacqueline. Willem actually wrote the seven-page "In Memoriam" profile about Doug after he died almost 30 years later. It was a very thorough and beautiful piece, which appeared in the Psychometrika professional journal.

It included a nice tribute to me at the end. I was gratified. Both he and I knew that, without me, Doug never could have gone to most of the meetings he went to, served as president of all these organizations and so on.

In February I took a trip by myself to California. I went from San Diego to San Francisco, with a stop at Esalen. That was my favorite place to go. Two psychologists I knew from the American Psychological meetings, whom I was very friendly with, recommended I should go there. They said I would like it.

They were right. At Esalen, I always feel at peace, emotionally, psychologically and intellectually. It's the only place in the world I've ever had that feeling. I've been there 20 times in my life and taken 18 workshops.

Esalen is right on the Pacific Ocean. I love how the waves come crashing in, the beautiful Monarch butterflies you see everywhere, and, of course, all the workshops. People are very caring and interesting there. The sun can be beating down or the stars out overhead, but people are very open all the time.

It's a spiritual kind of place and still my favorite place to go. When I have to leave Esalen, I never want to.

I also love is the baths they have, made out of stone, which overlook the ocean. People sit in them in the nude. You're not allowed to wear a bathing suit in the baths. It's the only part of Esalen where you have to be nude. Oh, and they give massages in the nude, outdoors if you like. Otherwise, everything is clothed. It's so relaxing.

The first time I went, I took a massage workshop, which was great. I got hooked on it. I was under stress most of the time in my home life. At Esalen, I didn't have any. There were no phones and no pressure from the outside world.

Two Stanford graduates, Michael Murphy and Richard Price, founded Esalen in 1962. They didn't know each other when they were both students at Stanford, but they met later in San Francisco. Michael's parents owned this wonderful property in Big Sur, right on the Pacific Ocean, and that's where they built it.

Together they created this institute to explore new ideas and techniques in spirituality and psychology. They have very famous people from all over the world teaching and giving workshops. There are many wonderful programs.

In July of '82, Doug and I took Steve with us to meetings in France. Steve and I had even taken French lessons to prepare for the trip. He enjoyed practicing. I thoroughly enjoyed seeing Paris again through Steve's eyes, including all the standard tourist spots.

After the meetings, the three of us went to the French Riviera for a week. We enjoyed spending time in Nice, Cannes, Monaco, and St. Tropez. We soaked up the sun on the beaches and at the pools.

One real highlight was when Steve and I went parasailing on the beach in Cannes. I had never even seen parasailing before. Steve was real excited when we saw them doing it and asked if he could too, so I went over to find out if we could go up together. They said, "No, only one at a time."

I told Steve, "Okay, I'll go first and see if it's safe. If it is, then you can go too."

The view from up there was spectacular. It was actually the most beautiful parasailing I ever did, just great. I went four more times in my life, but the first time was the best. Of course, Steve got to go too.

In fact, as he was applying to college, he wrote an essay about the experience. He said that he knew, if he just nudged his mother the right way, I would let him go. I'm glad I did.

Meanwhile, Greg had preferred to stay in the States. He had a great time with Bert and Mary Ella Zippel, friends of ours, at their vacation home in the Poconos. Evidently, Greg and Bert spent hours arguing the relative merits of the Yankees versus the Mets.

Greg also helped in both the preparation and consumption of Mary Ella's lavish meals. I didn't know he enjoyed cooking so much. He was looking forward to spending time with them again the following summer.

Our final trip of 1982 was to Denver for a meeting of SMET, Society of Multi-Variant Experimental Psychology. As usual, Doug was president. Meanwhile, I got to visit some friends.

One of the friends I saw had a son, Eric Riley, who was in a rehab center there. He was a quadriplegic as a result of a recent accident, when he fell off the roof of his house. Doug was only paraplegic, with full use of his hands and arms. Eric was quadriplegic, without the use of his arms. Some people who are quadriplegic may have a little range of motion in their arms, but not much.

Eric had just fallen not long before. He was in a coma for two or three weeks. They didn't even know if he would come out of it. Now he was conscious and adjusting to his new reality. I was able to give them a little insight on what to expect, based on my experience after Doug's accident.

While he was comatose, Eric was at a hospital in New Brunswick, New Jersey. When he finally got out, they flew him to the Craig Institute in Denver, which was the rehab that had been recommended to them. I don't know why they didn't just go to the Rusk Institute in New York, or the Kessler, which was right there in New Jersey.

When I first learned about the accident, it was just a day or two before we were leaving for Paris. I was at a travel agency in Basking Ridge, asking a question about our travel arrangements. While I was there, I heard that Eric had fallen from the roof of his house and was in a coma in the hospital.

We were very friendly with the Riley's. We would spend Thanksgiving dinner with them every year. The father was a psychologist and knew of Doug's work. They lived in Basking Ridge, just four or five miles from us.

We were going to a gourmet dinner put on by the Newcomers Club in Bernardsville, when we met them. We walked up and introduced ourselves. Then Dick Riley realized who Doug was, since he was so well-known among psychologists.

155

"Oh, you're Doug Carroll?" he said. He couldn't believe it. So we became good friends. And now this had happened to their son.

As soon as I heard about it, I called and found out what hospital Eric was in. It was about 5:30 at night, but I left the travel agency and drove straight down to the hospital. I knew how devastating something like this was for the family.

His parents and his grandmother were there. It was a tragic, heart-rending story. He was just thirteen and their only child. He had stolen some liquor from somebody's house with some other kids, so his parents had disciplined him by sending him up to his room, as part of his punishment.

Later his parents went up to his room, but he wasn't there. He had climbed out the window. They went downstairs to see where he had gone to and then he fell…right in front of them onto the driveway. He broke his neck. Terrible.

When Doug had his meeting in Denver, I knew Eric and his mother would be there. His father was still in New Jersey, because he was on the faculty at Stevens Institute in Hoboken. I went over to the rehab facility to support them.

I used to send her "care packages" while she was out there. She liked a certain kind of Entenmann's pastries, which she couldn't get in Colorado, so I would send them to her.

After the accident, when we had Thanksgiving dinners with them, my sons would be very nice to Eric. They understood his situation, from living with Doug. People at Eric's school weren't so nice to him, though. They didn't understand what he was going through. He died years later at age 25. He had gone to live in a home in Michigan, had a seizure, and passed away. A very sad story.

It reminds me of another friend I had, a very famous physicist. He helped me after Doug's accident and then he ended up a quadriplegic himself. He fell down the stairs in his house in the middle of the night and broke his neck. He's dead now also.

Over the years, we often gave money to the Keck Center at Rutgers, which was doing research on spinal cord injuries. Even though at first we had high hopes for that research, in over 30 years, no one has been able to find a way to repair spinal cords.

I remember when Christopher Reeve was alive, he was at Washington University in St. Louis participating in a study. He was in a pool walking

156

with the help of aides holding his upper body. I remember seeing that, which represented progress for him, but nobody's ever recovered totally.

Some people who have an accident where the cord is just bruised, not severed, can recover, but if the cord is severed, it doesn't re-grow. I've never heard of a miracle like that.

There was a story on CNN about four men who were paralyzed from the chest down, but, with electrical stimulators surgically implanted in their spines, were able to get out of their wheelchairs and stand up on their own.

They are still working on regaining the ability to walk, but the men said this new technology has allowed them to have sex again and significantly improved their bowel and bladder control.

The Christopher and Dana Reeve Foundation is raising $15 million to do this procedure on dozens more patients. More than 4,000 people have already signed up to take part. Any help is appreciated.

Chapter 37

In 1984, Doug started having serious problems with decubitus ulcers. This is what eventually killed him. Decubitus ulcers are also known as bed sores, pressure ulcers, or pressure sores. They are open wounds on the skin, usually over bony areas.

What happens is the skin breaks down from continuous pressure on the same spot for too long, which creates an open wound. It's a common problem for people who are bedridden or wheelchair-bound. It's serious for people who are paralyzed. The ulcers can become infected, septic, and even fatal.

Most of Doug's decubitus ulcers occurred on his buttocks, because he was always sitting or lying on the same area. He suffered from these ulcers all the time. Sometimes we had to cancel trips because of them.

Doug had to spend long periods lying on his side in 1984, because he was recovering from a surgery for a lingering ulcer, as well as from a surgery for his back. They had wanted to do the back surgery earlier, but the M.D. at Bell Labs, who had been monitoring Doug's decubitus ulcer, thought we could cure two birds with one stone by doing both surgeries at the same time.

The idea was he could recuperate from both the skin surgery and the back surgery simultaneously, by lying on his side to stay off the affected areas. Doug was going to get the back surgery at the NYU teaching hospital.

It was to remove the two Harrington rods that had been inserted in the months after the accident. They had become dislodged after he fell on a faulty wheelchair ramp at a local hotel.

Doug was attending a professional meeting in New Jersey at a Holiday Inn. When he went to leave their restaurant, he was going down the wheelchair ramp, but it wasn't properly built, so he ended up falling on his back. We had to sue them to recover our damages, which included removing the rods in his back.

They were now causing problems because they were loose and moving around. Fortunately, we were able to get the same doctor who had originally put them in and had done the spinal fusion. The surgery went well and eventually Doug's ulcer healed up too.

That same year, Steve got his purple judo belt. He even came in third for his age and weight in the New Jersey Junior Olympics. Greg continued in his sports, playing racket ball in a men's league, as well as baseball all-star, basketball all-star, tennis, and more.

We also took a family trip to California. One of the reasons we went out there was to do a deposition for Greg's lawsuit in San Diego, from when he was injured at the Montessori school.

While we were there, we rented a two-door car with hand controls, so Doug could drive. We got his wheel chair in back, but it was tight for all four of us. After our deposition, we drove north from San Diego, along the coast to Santa Barbara, where Doug had a meeting.

After that, we continued up the Pacific Coast Highway, which is spectacular...and scary. It included a hair-raising drive through Big Sur, where the two-lane highway curves back and forth, hugging the mountainside. We thought Doug was going to kill us.

Greg said, "Dad, we thought you were a good driver!"

It's not easy for a paraplegic to drive a car with hand controls, especially on a winding road, next to all these cliffs overlooking a churning ocean.

Finally, I couldn't take it anymore. I just said, "Okay, I'm driving."

I was very familiar with that drive. I took a lot of vacations to California on my own. After Doug's sabbatical in California, I had started going out there every year. For about ten years, every February I would go to California for ten days. I'd usually spend a week in the San Diego or Los Angeles area and a weekend at Esalen.

After Doug and I had agreed to have an open marriage in 1972, I was dating other guys pretty regularly. I had male friends and went with different ones, as the occasion permitted.

Sometimes in the summer I liked to go to the beach near home. When I could, I'd take my sons to Long Island, to our friend Crawford's cabin during the week.

One day I was there at the beach, but I was bored. There were a lot of families, with noisy boom-boxes and so on. It wasn't very nice for me, so I asked a woman to keep an eye on my blanket, while I took a walk. My kids were in the water and there was a lifeguard watching, so I wasn't too worried about them.

I walked west and ran into a fisherman, throwing his line out into the surf. I asked him what was further down the way I was walking. He said, "Oh, I think there's a nude beach down there."

That sounded good to me, so I kept going and, sure enough, soon

159

there were naked people all over the beach. I loved it. I stayed about two hours, then walked back.

The woman I had asked to keep an eye on my blanket had already left. Before she did, she asked my two sons where I was. I guess she thought I must have drowned, because she said to them, "Is your mother a good swimmer?" They both assured her I was.

After that, when I took the boys to that beach, I would usually just walk on down to the clothing-optional area. I didn't want to stay at the regular beach, totally bored by myself, with all these families there. The families weren't really friendly to strangers. Nudists were a different breed. They were very friendly.

My boys knew my lifestyle and how much I liked nude beaches. They were never interested in any of that themselves, but they accepted that I was. When they would run out of money for the snack bar or need me for something, they would come down to the nude beach to see me, no problem.

One of the other things I really enjoyed doing was working out at the YMCA about three times a week. I had started that in 1976, before Doug's accident, when we came back from La Jolla. I was always taking body-shaping classes and exercise classes.

After Doug's accident, I really needed to focus even more on staying in shape. I had to be fit and strong to do all I had to with him. I couldn't be a weakling. If something happened to me, it would be bad news for our family.

In the three weeks right after Doug's accident, I had lost 25 pounds from all the stress. When I went back to exercise classes, everyone commented on how skinny my legs had become. I put the weight back on as muscle though.

As part of being an independent woman, I had my own friends. I would go to New York when I could, sometimes by myself, to the Asia Society to hear a lecture, or to art openings. I went to movies, plays, and other cultural events. Sometimes I'd do things with one or both of my sons.

I also played tennis with a girlfriend once a week, took care of the house, belonged to several clubs and organizations, and did the million things any mother has to do.

Doug and I would often go out for dinner. We always celebrated our anniversary, which was January 2nd and his birthday, which was the next day, January 3rd. We'd celebrate them together.

Sometimes for his birthday, I would surprise Doug and make arrangements to go to New York. We'd meet another couple in the city for dinner and a play. My birthday was the same month as his, so sometimes he would do that for me as well.

We had a regular kind of life, but it was made so much more difficult and complicated by all the extra things we had to do for Doug's disability.

One time there was something on TV about how much people got paid for doing different jobs. I couldn't keep quiet when I saw that.

I turned to Doug and said, "Doug, from what I see, I'm doing the work of seven people around here: household administrator, treasurer, labor mediator, supervisor of teenagers, chef, social coordinator, and occasional nurse.

"You could never afford to pay me, if you had to."

Chapter 38

1985 was an eventful year, as our family progressed through life together. Greg graduated from middle school and started high school, which was a big transition, but he was doing well.

He excelled in sports, started windsurfing that year, and had a nice growth spurt. That was good for his basketball game, which had become his favorite sport.

Greg still didn't know what he wanted to be when he grew up, but at that point he was leaning toward business or law. The one thing he was sure of was he wanted to be in a field where he could help people.

Steve was now in middle school, which, conveniently, was just a couple of blocks from our house, so he could walk.

He still loved judo. He had originally started taking it at age seven, in order to defend himself from his big brother, a common problem for younger brothers. At age 11, he was already a 12th degree purple belt, the highest he could reach before age 14. That year he entered a state tournament and came in third in his age class.

Steve was also still playing piano, like his mother, and was the lead in a school play that year. He was already interested in computers, even though they were still very new. He was proficient in programming, using the Apple II we had bought the previous year. Sure enough, he did eventually become a computer scientist.

Doug continued working full speed ahead at Bell Labs. He never stopped working in the over 32½ years he was paraplegic. He kept going right up until the day he died. The accident had no effect on his career, except to make it more difficult to get around.

People would frequently call from all over the world to consult with him about multidimensional scaling. He was one of the top authorities in the world in his field, which was why he was always being invited to address big international meetings.

Doug and I took Steve with us to Europe when we went to two meetings that year, in Karlsruhe, Germany and in Cambridge, England. We stopped in London first to enjoy a few days there. We were staying at a hotel, which had a special section especially equipped for wheelchair access.

This was a new thing then. The hotel had been designed in cooperation with the British Paraplegic Society, so it had all kinds of special equipment. Virtually everything could be controlled from the bed: lights, TV, intercom, even opening the door.

While we were there, I took Steve to all the typical tourist sights. We even went to see *Starlight Express*, a musical where the cast was all on roller skates, which was a fad then.

From London, we flew to Frankfurt, Germany, where we visited with our good friends, the Sesslers. Steve actually stayed there with them for two weeks. He went to school every day with their son, Gunther. He learned some German and, of course, he starred in English class. He was able to give the teacher some expert, if unsolicited, advice.

Meanwhile, Doug and I went to a three-day meeting of the Classification Society in Karlsruhe. Joe Cocker, the famous rock musician, happened to be staying at our hotel while we were there. We didn't know it at first, but we found out very quickly.

As our driver was dropping us off in front of the hotel, Doug was in the front seat of the car, on the passenger side. He had a beard, as usual. Once he grew that beard back at Yale, he never shaved it off, even when he had surgery.

So anyway, all of a sudden, a crowd of teenage girls came swarming up to mob our car. They thought Doug was Joe Cocker. Joe also had a beard at the time, so I guess there was some resemblance...enough for the girls, anyway. When they found out Doug wasn't Joe, they were a disappointed.

We finally got to check in and learned that, sure enough, Joe was staying there. Later one night, he was down in the lounge with his entourage. I met his guitar player, John Troy. He was a very nice guy. Joe himself was a real lush though. He was taking a lot of stuff at the time, mixing valium and liquor, and so on. He was out of it most of the time, but I did get friendly with John.

On the day we were leaving, I was checking out, paying the bill at the front desk. I saw Joe in the lounge across the lobby, so I walked over to tell him goodbye. I had on a sexy, black jumpsuit and, because of that, Joe called me "Satan." He was funny.

After I got back to the States, I told some of my beach friends about my encounter with Joe. About two or three months later, one friend informed me, "Hey, you know, Joe Cocker will be performing at the Beacon Theater in New York. Would you like me to get tickets?"

So I said, "Sure, I'd like to go."

My friend took me and it was fun. After the concert, I ran up to the stage to see Joe before he left. I think I was the only one who did. We had seen each other just a few months before, so I asked him straight out, "Do you remember me?'

He said, "I certainly do!" I don't know if he really did or not. I do know he didn't call me Satan again…maybe because I wasn't wearing that jumpsuit.

So that's my Joe Cocker story. Tina Turner was also in Karlsruhe, while we were there, and I saw her perform at a stadium. Then, just a few weeks later, we shared a hotel with her too, when we were in Newfoundland. I met all these interesting people when I went to meetings with Doug.

After Germany, we returned to England, where we rented a car, to drive to Cambridge for the next meeting. The day before, back in Germany, Doug had asked one of his colleagues if there was anything important on the meeting schedule for the next day, when we were arriving.

He said, "Oh, no, nothing important tomorrow."

So the next day I was driving to the meeting and Doug was reading over the program for the day. Suddenly, as we were going through a traffic roundabout, he said, "Oh, no, I don't believe it. The program says I'm supposed to give a talk just ten minutes from now!"

Evidently, his colleague had been sarcastically joking and didn't expect Doug to take him seriously. Needless to say, we didn't make it in time for Doug's talk.

When we arrived, we found out a colleague of Doug's had given a synopsis of his work instead. The people in charge wanted to know if Doug still wanted to give his presentation, but he said no. Everything was fine. The rest of the meeting went smoothly, as Doug participated with other delegates from the Classification Society.

After that, we drove to Heathrow Airport, where we were to meet Steve, who was flying in from Frankfurt, to depart with us back to the States. As we approached the gate, Steve was already there in line, waiting to board our plane. He heard my unmistakable laugh and called out to us. No problems.

Three days later, Doug and I took off on another trip and there were lots of problems on this one. It was to St. John's, Newfoundland. Thanks to confusion by the Bell Labs travel agent, it was a comedy of errors. By

164

mistake, they booked us to St. John, New Brunswick, not St. John's, Newfoundland. That little "'S" at the end of "St. John's" made all the difference. I wonder how often that happens!

We discovered we were headed to the wrong place, when we got to Newark Airport to leave from New Jersey. We were told we could still make the right connection in Boston, where we had a layover the next day.

St. John, the wrong destination, was closer to the States than St. John's, where we were supposed to go. Our original ticket was only about $300. In fact, when one of Doug's colleagues had heard the price of our ticket before we left, he said, "How did you get such a low price?"

Little did we know....

Bell Labs always paid for Doug's trips, but not for mine. We always had to pay for my ticket ourselves, even though I had to go with him to help him get around.

So we got a flight from Newark to Boston. They put us up there overnight, because we had to connect the following day, to get to St. John's. We stayed at a Marriott Hotel, went out to dinner, and tried to relax. There was nothing more we could do.

The next day, our flight wasn't leaving till 4:00 in the afternoon, so we just went out to the airport after we checked out of the hotel. There was a lot of construction going on there. It was terrible.

Doug was sitting in his wheelchair at a payphone there, talking to the Bell Labs travel agent for over an hour, demanding they pay the difference in his ticket. It was no small matter, probably about $150. I couldn't believe they didn't just agree.

He was on the phone with them forever, it seemed, before they finally realized they had made a mistake and said they would make it right. It was only reasonable. We weren't asking them to pay for my ticket too.

After that, we left on our flight to Halifax, Nova Scotia. We had a layover there, before we got to St. John's. While we were in Halifax, I got a Molson Ale, which wasn't really well-known in the U.S. I loved it, when I tasted it.

After we were back on the plane, they said they had a mechanical problem. I thought, *Oh, no, we're never going to get to this meeting. Now we'll be stuck here overnight, with the nearest hotel 23 miles away from the airport.*

They finally got the problem fixed, though, while we were still on the plane, and we made it to the meeting, two days late. Our long-awaited destination was a picturesque, little fishing town, one of the most northern and eastern locations in North America

We were staying at the Newfoundland Hotel. When we arrived, we found out we were sharing the hotel with Tina Turner, another great rock musician, and her whole crew. As I said, I had seen her in concert in Karlsruhe, Germany, just a few months before. While we were in St. John's, we never actually saw Tina around the hotel, but we did see a lot of her people there.

Anyway, after we checked in, I couldn't wait to taste another Molson Ale. We went up to our room, got settled, and I said, "Let's go down to the lounge and get a nice, cold Molson Ale."

When we ordered that frosty beverage, we found out there was a big beer strike going on, and we couldn't get any Canadian beer at all, including Molson's. Whoever heard of a beer strike?

All we could buy was Lone Star beer, from Texas. That was one of the worst beers I ever tasted. Sorry, Texas! I never drank Lone Star again, even when I visited the state. It was awful.

I was exhausted anyway. It took me a day to recover from getting there, especially with no Molson's to help. I just went to the pool the next morning, to swim and relax. We did drive around the island on Sunday afternoon with another couple, but that was it.

Couldn't wait to get home!

My mother, as a demure young woman

My father as a dashing young man

Me as an infant, held by my mother

Here are four generations, from my great-grandmother to me

Doug as a boy

Me as a Rainbow Girl

Doug and myself on our honeymoon

Our family, Christmas, 1978, just before Doug's accident

Our second house in New Jersey

Me at Christmas in 1980, at age 41

Doug in 1989, for the Distinguished
Scientific Contribution Award from the
American Psychological Association

J. Douglas Carroll, Ph.D.
14 Forest Drive
Warren, NJ 07059-5802

Four Wishes
c/o Al Roker
30 Rockefeller Plaza
New York, NY 10112

Dear Al,

I am a 53 year old paraplegic who has become increasingly "cerebral"
and less and less involved in physical activity since suffering
a spinal cord injury about a month and a half after my 40th birthday.
My wish is to experience some physical activities which I know are
possible, even though they would be very difficult for me to undertake
without a great deal of help, and even some special training. Many of
these are experiences I enjoyed tremendously before I broke my back and
became paralyzed, and some are some new experiences I've never had, but would
really love to have before I shuffle off this mortal coil for good! Since
I have not figured out yet how to reverse time's arrow, I figure I better
do these things soon, or give up on them forevermore!! It's literally
"now or never" for me on these activities, I fear!

The list of activities I would particularly like to experience includes:

(1) Riding the rollercoasters at places like Great Adventure, Disneyland and
Disney World-- especially those new super-duper 360 degree jobs that
take you literally around a full loop-the-loop at close to the speed of light
(or of sound, anyhow)! Riding rollercoasters used to be one of my favorite
things to do at amusement parks, but the one time I went to Disneyland
since being in a wheelchair I discovered just how impossible it is to
get on almost any of their rides without massive help. (Unfortunately,
I'm 6'5" tall, and not the lightest person in the world). I'm sure it's
totally IMPOSSIBLE for me to experience a rollercoaster ride without all sorts
of prior special arrangements. My two sons (now 18 and 21 respectively)
would like to accompany me on this adventure, and could both assist in the
logistical details. I suspect my wife would prefer just to watch, however!

(2) Going skiing. Since I became paraplegic in the first place due
to a ski accident, I have been particularly reluctant to risk this
activity again. I've heard great things, though, about skiing
for paraplegics and other people with disabilities (using a specially
designed ski on which you sit instead of standing). This occurs at places
like Winter Park in Colorado-- and more recently I believe at much closer
spots, such as Vernon Valley right here in New Jersey! I feel it would be
not only extremely exhilirating, but psychologically very therapeutic for
me to get over the fear of tackling a ski slope, even in this modified way,
after my last extremely traumatic experience on one back in Februray 1979!

(3) Going scuba diving. I was certified in scuba diving shortly before

Doug's wish list, sent to Al Roker of the *Today Show*

Doug's installation as President of the Classification Society

Doug's 60th birthday

Doug and myself in Costa Rica, 2002

Family Thanksgiving, 2008

Chapter 39

It was always an adventure taking those international trips with Doug. I never knew what might happen. I should have seen our first major trip after Doug's ski accident as a sign. Our plane had been full of paraplegics going to the Paralympics Games…and the airline lost Doug's suitcase.

You can imagine my stress when that happened. What a way to be introduced to traveling with a paraplegic.

It was interesting. Those men and women athletes, mostly men, were very able. Doug never was. They would crawl down the aisle, to go to the bathroom on their own, rather than be assisted.

One thing we did learn on that trip was to always keep all of Doug's medical essentials in his backpack. Paraplegics have to carry all kinds of medical equipment and items, to keep them healthy and comfortable. That backpack prevented a medical emergency.

On that same first trip, when we were leaving London to come back home, we got to the airport three hours early, just to be safe. We were relaxing, having a beer, while we waited. Then, all of sudden, we heard the announcement they were closing the doors for our flight.

We hadn't heard any of the other announcements for boarding before that. Normally wheelchair passengers go on first, because they need help and take longer to do it. We had to run like crazy, just to make the plane at all. Then they weren't going to let us on, but I went over to the gate and really lost my temper. I made a scene, but I got us on the plane.

Turning to another challenge we overcame, in 1985, after six years of life in landlord hell, we finally sold our old house in Bernardsville. What a relief to no longer be dealing with tenants. We had had to rent the place out, because the interest rate in 1979, when we moved, was up to 19% and 20%. Nobody had been buying.

Funny thing, with the house we bought in Warren that same year, we got a mortgage of just 10.5%. That was unheard of. We were lucky. Our real estate agent was so eager to get to the bank and lock in that rate, that she got a speeding ticket on the way!

Finally the interest rates came down and the market improved. Our last tenants were about to retire and already had a home in Maryland, so they let our Realtor show the home, and we got it sold. That was nice.

The holidays started out on a sour note though. Steve got his skull fractured on Christmas Eve, right at the end of '85. He was at a pinata party at the Unitarian Fellowship, when another kid hit him in the head with an aluminum baseball bat.

Evidently, the blindfolded kid with the bat didn't realize he had already broken the pinata. Steve bent over to pick up a piece of candy, which had fallen out, and, as he stood up, the kid swung again and nailed Steve in the head. He was out of action for a month. Lots of plans had to be cancelled, but he recovered completely and was back to normal.

It was tough that it happened on Christmas Eve though, because we had invited company over for Christmas dinner the next day. Steve was in the hospital overnight and I had to go pick him up Christmas morning. It made the day pretty tight...but memorable.

Steve didn't eat pizza for five or six years after that accident. Pizza was the last thing he had eaten before he got hit in the head. Somehow he lost his taste for it.

One sad series of events, which happened in 1986, began with a phone call from Doug's parents about 6:30 one morning. That's never good to get a call that early. They were phoning to announce that Doug's Aunt Betty, the sister of his father, had been diagnosed with terminal cancer of the lungs. There was no way to know how long she had.

When a patient is diagnosed as terminal, it means they're definitely going to die...soon. There's nothing anyone can do about it. When my mother was diagnosed terminal, they estimated it would be three months. After she came home, she was gone in 14 days.

Betty was living in Miami and she needed help...now. She had to go into a nursing home, get her affairs in order, and prepare for the end, which could come any time.

Betty had been single all her life. She had been engaged to a man who was killed in the Second World War. She was very attractive, with a great personality, but after she lost her future husband, she just never found another.

Even though Doug's father was Betty's brother and lived in Fort Myers, just two hours away from her, he didn't want to go to Miami to help. Doug's father supposedly had a nervous stomach. He actually had been discharged from the service because of it.

So now Doug's parents were asking me to leave my paraplegic husband, along with my two young children, in order to fly down to Miami and handle everything for them.

When my mother-in-law spoke to Doug, she actually said, "Sylvia's

168

going to have to go down to Miami and help Aunt Betty, because your father's stomach is bothering him." '

When I heard that, I thought, *What? How is this my problem?*

Doug tried to protect me. He said, "This is going to be really difficult for Sylvia. Her mother died of cancer and she was taking care of her when she did."

It was true. It had been very hard staying with my mother up till the end, when she passed away. It was still vivid in my memory, difficult to even think about. Now I was going to have to do it all over again, with someone I wasn't even related to.

Doug's protestations didn't do any good. So, yes, Sylvia, the workhorse of the family, gritted her teeth and got on a plane to Miami, to do what nobody else could...or would.

It turned out Betty was making Doug and me the executors of her estate. In Florida, they call it "personal representative" instead of "executor." Doug couldn't do much physically, of course, so I had to do it all anyway.

When I went down there, I had to have her put me on her Certificates of Deposit, so I could pay her bills. Since Betty was single, she was leaving most everything she had to Doug.

While she was in the nursing home, I had to ask her what kind of funeral she wanted, so I could arrange it. She was Catholic and wanted a Low Mass, which means the priest just reads the words and doesn't sing them. They also don't use incense. So it's kind of the simple version of the ceremony. I took care of the details before I left.

I also had to go pick out a casket for Aunt Betty all by myself. So there I was, spending my Saturday morning in a funeral home, trying to decide how to bury this sweet woman. It was very sad.

She was my husband's aunt. She was dying. So I did it. I didn't get a real expensive casket, of course. Why waste money on that?

I left the funeral home feeling depressed and went straight over to the nursing home to visit her. As soon as she saw me, she asked for a Carlton cigarette. That's what she smoked and that's what killed her. She was already terminal, so she might as well enjoy her last few days, right?

Betty was a lovely lady, a very attractive and upbeat kind of person. Believe it or not, she cheered me up that morning. I didn't tell her what I had just been doing, but, after I gave her that cigarette, we talked for a while. She kind of put it all in perspective. She made me feel better, just by being herself.

Once all the arrangements were made, I couldn't stay there with her, to wait until she passed. I had a disabled husband and two little boys to take care of back in New Jersey, so I flew back.

A couple of weeks later, she was gone. Doug and I were at an APA meeting in Washington, DC. We had only been there two or three days, when the call came that Aunt Betty had passed. We left the meeting early, went back to New Jersey, and I jumped on a flight to Miami.

Doug wanted to go with me but he really couldn't. He even argued with me about it. I knew it wasn't feasible. Her house wasn't wheelchair-accessible and there was a lot to be done down there. I needed to be free to focus on handling all the affairs of the estate. I put my foot down and Doug stayed.

I had that Low Mass funeral for her and took care of wrapping everything up in Miami. I inherited her Certificates of Deposit, while Doug inherited her house, which I eventually sold.

Good-bye, Aunt Betty. You were a peach.

Chapter 40

As I said earlier, I went to Esalen every year in Northern California, to refresh and rejuvenate myself. With all the stress and responsibility I had in my life, these little solo vacations I took every year were really essential to keep me going.

I had so many great experiences at Esalen, that I just have to share a few. The first story shows how difficult it was for me to escape the worries of my everyday life, even there. They didn't have phones anywhere, except in the main office. If somebody called for you, the office would leave you a message on a bulletin board in the community area.

So one Sunday, after I had taken a workshop, I was feeling just great, like a ten on a scale of one to ten. Then, as I went by that bulletin board, I saw a notice up there for me. It said, "Call your son Steve."

Immediately, my outlook dropped from a ten to a two. My first thought was, *Oh, my God, Doug died. That's why Steve is calling me.*

I was so upset, that it took me 45 minutes before I got up the nerve to call Steve back. Instead, I was talking to other people, telling them, "I'm so worried that something has happened to my husband. I really don't want to hear any bad news right now."

Finally, I pulled it together, went into the office, and called Steve back. I was on pins and needles, as the phone was ringing. It turned out, Steve just wanted to know if he could have a German exchange student come and stay with us for a month. He had asked his father about it, but Doug had said, very wisely, "Well, you'll have to check with your mother about that."

Another year, I had gone to Esalen to take a workshop in Gestalt psychology. That's the branch of psychology that studies the human mind as a holistic entity. They say that, in trying to understand reality, our minds perceive things not as separate items, but as part of a greater whole or system.

One of the famous Gestalt demonstrations you've probably seen is those pictures where, depending on how you look at it, the meaning completely changes, like a cube going in two different directions.

It's all about what you focus on. They say this is something we can use in our daily lives. We can change the picture by focusing on something different.

171

Anyway, I had gotten to the workshop a little late, because I gotten lost looking for it, as I came from breakfast in the dining room. I was talking there with a guy about going to Tibet.

This was a wonderful lostness though. It was magical. Esalen is somewhat hilly, so you're always going up or down. There was also a stream there, so I crossed over a bridge.

I walked further than I probably should have and then, all of a sudden, I came upon a flock of beautiful Monarch butterflies. It was incredible. It was the only time in my life, that I ever got lost and had such a great time doing it.

I ended up going to the office, to ask where the workshop was. It was back in the direction from where I had come. But I still remember that sweet feeling of being lost and not caring. It was great.

Anyway, this workshop was limited to ten people. The woman running it was named Debbie. Everybody had to have a partner, so Debbie assigned me to this man who was having a weird problem. He said he felt like he was making love to the body of his mistress, but to the head of his wife.

So I said, "Wait a minute. Does your wife know you have a mistress?" He said, "Yes."

I said, "And does your mistress know you have a wife?"

"Yes."

So, I said, "Well, it all makes sense to me. You like the way your wife thinks, but you like your mistress's body better."

It was funny he hadn't seen that himself, because he was a psychiatrist from Berne, Switzerland. We actually became friends there and he kept in touch with me for some time afterwards.

There was another guy in the workshop, who had a schizophrenic son about 23 years old. The man had divorced his son's mother and was now married to his second wife, who was a psychologist. Debbie, the workshop leader, was working with this man. Let's call him Gene. She was having Gene talk to his son, as if his son was actually there.

This was all taking place in a meeting room. Debbie had two straight chairs, which she would use to stage an imaginary dialogue between a group member and whoever they needed to talk with. The chairs would face each other.

So Gene was sitting in one chair facing the other chair, where his son supposedly was. Gene had to speak both sides of the conversation. After he said his piece, when he responded as the son, he had to actually go sit in the other chair. This was pretty effective, because it gave the experience of speaking from the other person's point of view. It helped a lot of people.

Debbie started the whole thing off by saying, "Gene, tell your son what you want him to know. Then have your son tell you what you think he wants you to know."

So he would talk and switch back and forth. I thought he got pretty deep with what Debbie was doing, but I guess I was wrong.

In between workshop sessions, I spent a lot of time with Gene, just sitting in the baths and talking. I told him a lot about my situation with my husband and how I was dealing with it.

Then, the last day of the workshop, at the end we were supposed to go around the circle and tell the group three things we had gotten out of our experience in the workshop. People generally said things like love, caring, healing, wisdom, compassion, whatever.

For each thing you said you received, you were supposed to look at one person in the room and give that quality to that person. So we were all doing that.

When it came to Gene's turn, he said, "I didn't really get anything out of the workshop itself. What I did get, though, which was very valuable, was from talking to Sylvia outside the workshop."

What a gift. That felt like the nicest gift I ever got in my life, the nicest thing anyone ever said about me. It was wonderful. These things don't happen in the outside world...only at Esalen.

Another time, I was sitting in one of those natural baths, relaxing. There were two men there with me, a fellow from my workshop, who was a professor from Tufts, and another man I didn't know, who was sitting on solid stones.

The second one suddenly up and said to us, "I just killed my son."

I said, "Excuse me?"

He repeated, "I just killed my three-year-old son."

I asked, "What happened."

He said, "I was going through a car wash in my truck. My son was in the truck with me, but he got out, and I didn't realize it. I accidentally rolled over him."

How horrible. What a tragedy.

He told me that he and his wife had separated after this happened. A

173

lot of couples break up after the death of a child. So I asked him, "Well, what about her...where is she?"

He said, "She's here with me." They were trying to find some way to heal and understand and go on with life.

I was so upset hearing this story, that I couldn't go back to my own workshop until much later. The professor and I spent a lot of time talking to that poor man, trying to help him.

Amazing things like that were always happening there at Esalen.

Chapter 41

In 1987, Steve took the SAT exam early, as part of a special program for gifted teenagers. As a result, e received a Certificate of Distinction for New Jersey in a special awards ceremony. This was sponsored by Johns Hopkins University, where he also ended up working years later. Amazing.

That same year we also took a trip to Germany, Belgium and the Netherlands, taking Steve with us again. While we were in Europe, Greg stayed at our house. We left his friend and basketball coach with him, just to make sure everything was safe and sound.

Greg was a sophomore now and towered over me, at 6'1". He was starring at school in basketball, and also playing on the junior varsity soccer team. He had saved up money to buy a car, which he finally did that year. It was a 1978 Pontiac Gran Prix, a beautiful muscle car, with just 45,000 miles on it.

Steve, age 12, was now teaching judo, since he couldn't achieve a higher rank as a student, until he was 14. With all those years of hauling him back and forth to class, I became friendly with his instructor, and still am, in fact.

My dear, sweet, cat Aquarius passed away at age 17 that year. We missed her, but then Steve wanted to get a kitten, so we went to the pound in Sterling. There we chose a little sweetheart, a long-haired kitty with lots of fur, all grey and white, and a little black.

She was very cute and only weighed a pound. She was premature, but delightful. We had to feed her with a doll's baby bottle. At first we named her Mittens, but that changed later to Macavity, which was the name of one of the cats in the musical *Cats*.

One story I have to tell also took place in 1987, when we had a meeting in Rome. A dear colleague, Michael Greenacre, was there. Michael is South African and a statistician. He is one of my favorite people.

He is a wonderful pianist. Michael would play at parties and had a great personality. He had been in the States, which is where we met him. He and his wife had split and he was living in Spain at the time of our trip.

Before we even got to Rome, Michael had contacted Doug to let me know that Joe Cocker was going to be performing while we were there. He knew I was a big fan of Joe, from hearing my stories about him. Michael said he would be willing to take me to the concert, if I could get the tickets. That sounded like fun.

So one afternoon in Rome, I was on my way to get the tickets, walking along the sidewalk, when I happened to meet this 25-year old student. He was very friendly and spoke English well.

This was not surprising. Roman men are very forward, especially towards me. The first time I was in Rome, at age 21, I was very innocently walking around the Coliseum, when a policeman came up behind me and pinched me on the butt. They do that there.

I was always meeting people randomly anyway, almost every time I went out. So this student started talking to me in English.

He asked, "What are you doing here?"

I told him I was going to buy tickets for Joe Cocker, and he said, "Oh, I'd like to go."

So I told him that I was already going with a friend. He said, "Well, if your friend doesn't show up, I'll go with you."

I said, "Well, he'd better call me soon, because the show is tonight. If he doesn't come through, you can go with me." Little did I think that would actually happen.

This was before cell phones, so I told the student to call my hotel room later, to see what was going on. It turned out that Michael didn't call. I don't remember his reason now, but I was at my wit's end about what to do.

Meanwhile, Doug was having cocktails with five of his colleagues. They all knew about my plans with Michael, so I went in there and said, "I don't know where Michael is and he hasn't called. This is weird, but I don't think it's going to look very good for him to stand up Doug Carroll's wife."

That got a laugh. We all knew he would never do that. He wasn't that type of guy. I figured something had gotten confused.

Meanwhile, the student called and then showed up at my hotel right on time, so I told him, "Okay, I never heard from my friend, so you can come with me."

We went together and it was a good thing. I didn't know how to get to the concert, so he led the way. We took a bus to the outskirts of Rome. We had a great time and then he brought me back to the hotel.

Later, I told him I was 50 years old, but he didn't seem to mind. In fact, he asked if I had any other girlfriends who were like me and were coming to Rome too. I was flattered.

People compliment me all the time like that, even still today. That's just the way it is. People like the way I handle myself. They tell me I'm a woman of class, independent, and all kinds of nice things. Maybe some others say bad things too, I don't know. I wouldn't pay attention anyway.

The next day, it had gotten back to Michael that he had stood up his colleague's wife. He protested that he did call later, but it was too late.

I don't think I ever told him that I went with someone else. The next day, though, I did see him and he said, to make up for his lapse, he would take me out to dinner that night and then, the next day, take me to Assisi, the city where St. Francis was from.

So we went out to dinner and it was lovely. The next morning, we met early and took the train three hours up to Assisi. It was very quaint. I ended up buying three little monk figurines, which I still have in my condo.

We had lunch, walked around, saw the sights, and then took the train back again, arriving home about 10 pm. It was an all-day excursion and a lot of fun. So that's how Michael made it up to me.

Two days after returning to the U.S. from that trip, Doug was working late at Bell Labs, trying to catch up on everything. Suddenly, he started having chest pains, numbness in the arms, shortness of breath and so on. He thought it was just a stress reaction to all the travel and jet lag, so he stopped working and sat quietly trying to relax.

The symptoms continued, though, so he called the guard at the reception desk. Soon he was on his way to Overlook Hospital in an ambulance. It seemed he might have been having a heart attack, so he spent five days in the hospital and got lots of test. His heart was finally pronounced in good shape and he was discharged.

Next they checked to see if it had been something gastro-intestinal. Sure enough, it turned out he had a duodenal ulcer and a hiatal hernia. So he had to go on ulcer medication, with dietary restrictions.

Doug was doing a lot of work that year. In addition to his fulltime position at Bell Labs, he started teaching as the Proctor & Gamble Adjunct Professor of Marketing at the Wharton School of Business in Philadelphia. Wharton is generally considered the best business school in the U.S.

Doug was giving a PhD-level course in quantitative methodology, multi-dimensional scaling, and so on. He taught one night a week. I'd go with him and we'd stay overnight at the Sheraton Hotel.

Doug had an office mate at Wharton named Terry Oliel, who was on the faculty at Rutgers. Terry never got tenure at Rutgers, which you have to do to stay at a college permanently. He was teaching at Rutgers temporarily, as well as at Wharton.

So one night while Doug was in with his class, I was in the office with Terry. He made a point of asking me what Doug was going to do after he retired from Bell Labs. I said, as far as I knew, he wanted to go into academia. So Terry immediately went to Rutgers and told them that Doug was willing to go into academia and they should snatch him up. This was like some undercover surveillance!

So, while Doug was still at Bell Labs, before he was ready to retire, Rutgers came forward and offered him an incredible position: Board of Governors Chair in Marketing with a joint appointment in Psychology. That was a big deal.

It involved teaching PhD students just three classes every two years in quantitative methods. The rest of the time Doug would do research and writing.

Rutgers wanted to get Doug first. They wanted him on the faculty because of his world-wide reputation in psychometrics. His work in multidimensional scaling was very effective and much admired.

Rutgers offered Doug more money than he was making at Bell Labs. He would also have a fulltime secretary and a teaching assistant, plus a $20,000/year research fund, which he could use for travel, office equipment, computers, or whatever.

His department head at Bell Labs told him, "Doug, you just won the lottery."

Doug already had 25 years at Bell Labs, so he could retire officially. He accepted the offer and the rest is history. He stayed at Rutgers the rest of his life.

All this happened just because I told Terry that Doug wanted to be an academic. I've always been a big talker and promoter anyway, especially where my loved ones are concerned. This time it really paid off.

Doug and I were a team. He had his role and I had mine. That was how we achieved so much, despite all the challenges that arose in our lives.

Chapter 42

In 1988, Greg was 18 years old and so was our track record of writing a long holiday letter to our friends and family every year. For some reason, we decided to end the letters.

Doug announced in our last holiday letter, which came out that year, "We've concluded we should end our tradition of writing this letter, since it has, along with Greg, reached adulthood after 18 years. This is our last one."

It was a lot of work doing those letters, believe me. Doug used to write them and I would edit them. Once Doug wrote 34 pages, double-spaced, in longhand. He was a very prolific writer. Steve and I had to get it down to two pages.

Here are all the steps that were involved to get that letter out. After Doug wrote the first draft, I had to edit it, type it up, make 100 copies, fold them, put them in envelopes along with a photograph, address them, and finally mail them...with a big sigh of relief.

Sometimes it took me four days to do all that. It was a tremendous job, but I wanted to keep in touch with our friends and family, so it was worth it for those 18 years.

As it turned out, we didn't really end our holiday letters for good after all. We got many responses from people over the next few years, saying we had always written the most interesting letters and they were missed.

So we started up again in 1996. Steve helped me, which was nice. Then it got to the point Doug didn't want to even write the first draft any longer, so I became the author as well as the publisher.

I still do a holiday letter, though I only send out about 50 now. I try to get a photo of my family with everyone together each year, to make a holiday greeting card. Then I do a one page, hand-written letter to each person, saying what I've done over the year.

I don't like it when people just send a card and don't say anything about what they're doing. Why even bother sending it?

We didn't want to miss anybody. Most of our friends were academics, so in the old days, they wrote a mimeographed letter. Now, of course, it's computers and copy machines.

Some of my girlfriends back then would even write in longhand. One girlfriend, who now lives in Colorado Springs, still writes one every year. She's a lot older than me, so she's not a young cookie, but she writes beautifully.

One more funny thing about holiday letters. An old friend, who knew Doug even before I did and taught in New Jersey for a few years, now lives in Naples, Florida. He called me about ten years ago to explain why I wouldn't be getting a holiday letter from him any more.

He said, "Sylvia, I'm an atheist now, so we don't send out holiday letters any more." Still, he and his wife did invite me over for Christmas Eve dinner one year. Go figure.

Our big trip of 1988 had been when Doug and I went to China on a 19-day, wheelchair-accessible tour with Wings on Wheels. There were eight people in wheelchairs and eight able-bodied people. We saw all the highlights and enjoyed many luxurious hotels and lots of delicious Chinese food. It was very ambitious and a great trip.

They even got the disabled people up on the Great Wall. They pushed the wheelchairs up there as far as they could, in an area close to the beginning of the Wall.

Unfortunately though, all the hotel bathrooms were not wheelchair-accessible. So the tour wasn't 100% accessible in my mind. Doug couldn't get into any of the hotel bathrooms over there, but we managed.

When Doug had told me he wanted to go to China, I told him I wanted to go to Tibet. He said if I went to China with him on this tour, then I could go to Tibet later by myself. I agreed, but after that tour, I lost interest in Tibet, until just about two years ago, when I finally did go.

When we were on these trips, Doug couldn't take his shower commode chair, so he had to do his bowel routine on a bed. I'd put down all the Chux that he needed and then I'd go out for two hours. It would take him that long and the place would really get stinky. He was lucky he didn't have a sense of smell.

When I came back, I had to ask the hotel for a lot more clean towels to clean him up. Doug would have to set aside half a day, three days a week for his bowel routine, no matter what.

These were all the unpleasant things I never told anyone about. It was just part of what we had to do, in order to travel.

When Doug had to get up early for a morning meeting, I'd have to help him get going, then I'd usually fall back into bed. He hardly got any sleep when we went to these meetings. He'd wheel into the room late at night. Then it would take him a while to get into bed. I don't know how he did it.

180

At one point, back home, one of Doug's health aides talked him into getting a colostomy, because his bowel routines were getting to be too much work and taking too long. As you get older, you slow down. You can't do things as quickly as you used to

The day before he went in for the colostomy, Doug had to take all this liquid stuff to clean out his colon. We hired this health aide to come over and help. Poor Doug was up all night with that. It must have been terrible.

Meanwhile, Doug was now teaching at Rutgers and on a whole new routine. He would normally drive himself into his office, which was in Newark and drive himself back at night. No problem.

Then one morning I got up and looked in the garage. His car wasn't there. I checked in his bedroom and he wasn't there either. I didn't know what to think, so I called his secretary and said, "Do you know where Doug is?"

She said, "Oh, sure, he's sitting right here, next to me." He had stayed there all night, because he was too tired to drive home and didn't bother letting me know. Later he told me, he didn't want to wake me up.

I guess he just slept in his wheel chair over there. He was definitely not supposed to do that. To help prevent decubitus ulcers, wheelchair patients shouldn't stay sitting in the same position.

They're supposed to shift their weight frequently, like at least every 20 minutes. You don't shift your weight when you're asleep in your wheelchair.

If they have the strength, wheelchair patients are also supposed to do wheelchair pushups–pushing down on the arms of the chair to raise the body up off the seat and relieve the pressure. My son Greg was always after Doug to do his chair pushups at least every 20 minutes. Doug didn't pay much attention to all that.

I was a little upset with my husband about his overnight disappearance, but I let it go. Then the next day I got up to get the kids off to school and he wasn't there again! I called the office.

"Do you know where Doug is today?'

"Oh, yes, Sylvia, he's right here next to me."

So he stayed there two nights in a row, working at his office, sleeping in his chair. Doug was always more into his mind than his body.

It was understandable that he didn't want to make the effort to come home. It was a half hour drive from Rutgers, plus the time it took to get himself in the car, transfer his wheelchair in back, drive home, reverse the whole process, get inside and get ready for bed.

When he was tired, I guess he figured it just wasn't worth the effort, so he just stayed. I don't know what he ate there – probably just his trusty granola bars. There was no food in his office.

This just shows how deeply involved he got in his work…and how much stress I was under. I got up and he wasn't home, the car wasn't in the garage, so I had no idea where he was or what might have happened to him. Since he never called, I didn't know.

Then, sure enough, one evening, when he was driving home from Rutgers, he did have an accident. Someone ran into him. It wasn't his fault and fortunately nothing serious happened, but he was very shook up over it.

Our financial advisor came over the morning after the accident. Even he could see how upset Doug was, which was pretty unusual, because Doug was pretty imperturbable.

In 1989, Doug had turned 50. I threw him a surprise birthday party in the hospital, where he was getting a procedure done. I had champagne and a cake for him. There were about ten people there, all told. Our old friend Crawford Clark helped put the party together and we had some other friends from New York who made it.

Doug really enjoyed it. He was definitely surprised. In fact, in my diary I wrote, "He was stunned."

Now that Doug and I were both 50, our financial advisor had some advice for us. He saw that Doug traveled a lot and nothing seemed to keep him down or hold him back. He felt we should get long-term insurance for home healthcare and nursing home care, mainly for Doug's sake.

He pointed out that Doug might get worse as time went on, and we might need it. So we bought it.

Can you believe, ten years after his terrible accident, confined to a wheelchair, Doug was actually able to get long-term coverage…even though he was already paraplegic. I don't know anyone else who's done that.

Actually, that long-term coverage came in very handy. It paid for the health aides and live-ins we had to hire as Doug's life went on and his health began to decline. His last six years, we had to have a live-in 24/7 and the insurance paid for that.

Originally Doug didn't buy the home care, just the nursing home care, but I got both. Doug's premium was $600 a year and mine was $800.

Then one day the company offered him home health in lieu of nursing home and he took it. Thank God, because he never went into a nursing home, but he sure used those home health aides.

Doug wouldn't have been able to work in a nursing home and he wanted to work till the day he died. That was my goal too, to keep him working and happy right up to the end, no matter what...and we succeeded.

Chapter 43

As I mentioned earlier, even at our second house, our driveway could be difficult at times. I guess we just lived in a hilly area of New Jersey. In 1990, my son Steve and I had a serious problem with that driveway.

Steve was in high school then and had a learner's permit to drive. One day he called me from school and asked if I could pick him up. When I did, he asked if he could drive home. So I said yes.

When we arrived, as we were going up the driveway, I said, "Steve, you don't have to put the car in the garage. I'm going out again in a couple of hours."

So he parked out on the driveway, in front of a shed we had there. There was a bit of an incline and the car was a stick shift, so he put the emergency brake on. I didn't tell him to also leave it in first gear, so he left the car in neutral.

He was just learning to drive and didn't know any better. It was my responsibility to supervise him. At the time, I knew he hadn't left the car in gear, but I thought, *Well, the emergency brake is on, so that should be enough.*

We went on into the house and then I came out again two hours later. There was no car to be seen...anywhere. I went back in the house and asked Steve, "Do you know where the car is?

He said, "I don't know, Mom, I parked it outside with you."

Well, by this time it was pretty dark, so he came out with me to try to figure out what happened. Finally, we saw the car had rolled all the way down the driveway to where some trees were by the septic system. It had hit one tree, bounced off it, and hit another before stopping.

The car was all banged up, with about $5600 worth of damage. Of course, it was my fault. I should have known better. I didn't blame Steve. I just got the car fixed and life went on...but that's how dangerous our driveway was!

What made the whole thing even worse was that I had just removed the collision coverage from my car insurance, so I ended up paying for all that damage out of my own pocket.

For some crazy reason, since the car wasn't brand new, I didn't think I needed that much insurance any more. Can you imagine, no collision coverage, with a teenage driver in the house? What was I thinking? Well, that's how we learn.

Turning to happier thoughts, one great escape from all the troubles on the home front was always going to meetings with Doug. In spite of all the logistical difficulties, I still loved traveling and reconnecting with people.

I liked all the meetings, but my favorites were for the American Psychological Association. Their activities were very diverse. Doug would go for the mathematical side of it and I would go for the clinical side. Later I also got involved in humanistic psychology.

One APA meeting we went to early on was in Miami Beach. At the time, I was five months pregnant with Greg, but that certainly didn't stop me.

Doug had his mathematical meeting to go to and I was looking for something to do. One of my clinical psychologist friends told me the Society for Humanistic Psychology meeting was going on at the same time.

He said, "Why don't you go to that? I think you'll enjoy it."

So that's how I found out about Humanistic Psychology. Before that, I didn't know anything about it, but I really got into it. I had minored in Psychology in college.

In fact, back then, I had thought about becoming a clinical psychologist. I liked dealing with people and their problems, but I didn't want to stay in school to get a PhD. Still, I was interested in psychology all my life.

Humanistic Psychology was always a fun weekend, so I would go to their meetings whenever I could. Later, they separated the mathematical from the clinical, but that was many years after.

Sometimes I went to more meetings than Doug did. I just enjoyed learning things. Gloria Steinem would be at some of these meetings too and I always admired her. They'd also have a dance and I always loved dancing. My two friends, Dick Carrera, from Miami, and George Lawrence, from Washington, DC, were usually there too.

Doug enjoyed meeting people at these meetings as well. I think he had a few female admirers there, along with some from his work at Rutgers. One time Doug asked me if he could have the house for the weekend. He wanted to entertain a female colleague from Washington, DC.

He was planning to take her to New York for dinner and then to the Metropolitan Opera. So I had to figure out a place to stay. I probably stayed with one of my boyfriends for two nights.

The understanding that Doug and I had, along with our willingness to accommodate each other, was essential to our relationship. I think that's a big part of how we were able to endure as a couple for our whole lives, in the face of so many challenges.

We weren't living a romantic fairy tale. We had to deal with a tough reality and make it work.

One year Doug was going to be in the hospital on Father's Day. When I asked him what he would like for a gift, he told me he wanted a Playboy magazine. So I bought him one and took it in to him.

He had fun showing that magazine to everyone who would look at it, "Hey, look, this is what my wife gave me for Father's Day!" It was hilarious.

That's the way he was. He kept his sense of humor his entire life. He never got bitter...although he would sometimes get depressed. But who wouldn't?

We also went to a lot of plays together. We both loved going to shows. The Schubert Theater in New York gave discounts to people in wheelchairs and to their attendants, so we went there a lot.

The theater did this because wheelchairs could only get to an orchestra seat on the lower level. They couldn't go up the steps to the cheaper sections. That discount made it possible for wheelchair people like us to afford to attend.

John Hockenberry, the famous paraplegic reporter for the TV show, *Dateline NBC,* and the author of the book *Moving Violations*, helped make all that possible. In 1992 he was denied access to a Broadway theater, after he paid $60 for a ticket to the musical *Jelly's Last Jam*.

He had been assured by the box office that the house manager would seat him. Instead, on the night of the show, the manager told Hockenberry, "I'm sorry, sir, we are not allowed to touch you."

This led to a heated argument in the theater lobby, during which Hockenberry grabbed the manager's shirt. When it was over, Hockenberry was out on the sidewalk with his worthless ticket and a very bad taste in his mouth.

He promptly sued the theater's owners, and under the terms of a settlement, the theater installed a lift to allow wheelchair access from then on. Meanwhile, other Broadway theaters started figuring out how they could better accommodate the disabled as well.

It's been a long, slow grind, believe me.

Chapter 44

Every time Doug and I traveled together, we had to be ultra-careful about everything. The worst possible scenario was that Doug would get sick or injured when we were overseas. Still, as careful as we tried to be, it happened anyway.

A good example is when Doug broke his leg in Scotland. He had a meeting there in Edinburgh. While he was at the meeting, his colleagues and he decided to take an excursion to an island for a day off. I went along. We were all taking a bus, so his colleagues carried Doug onto it and off of it, since it wasn't wheelchair-accessible.

We made it around the island with no problem, but when we came back, tragedy struck. We were just walking down a sidewalk. A student from Estonia, who was there for the meeting, was pushing Doug in his wheelchair, to give me a break.

I was right behind them, so I saw it happen. All of a sudden, the chair ran into a piece of metal that was sticking up about five or six inches out of the sidewalk. It was a terrible hazard. The footrest of Doug's chair hit that thing and his left leg got dragged right under the wheelchair. It was horrible.

I screamed, but when we looked at Doug's leg, it seemed like he hadn't been seriously injured. Of course, Doug had no feeling in his leg, so he couldn't tell us if there was any pain or not.

I don't know if this had anything to do with the accident, but that night, Doug told me he thought he might have a urinary tract infection. He sent me to a hospital to get sterile saline solution to irrigate his catheter. He stayed in the hotel room while I was gone.

The next day, we flew back to Newark. Everything seemed to be all right. Doug was at home in bed, working from there. He did a lot of his writing and research in his bed.

Meanwhile, I was looking forward to going to our next meeting, which was in just four more days. We were scheduled for the American Psychological Association meeting in San Francisco. I went to meetings to help Doug, but I also went for my own interests. I loved those APA meetings, since I had so many friends there and I enjoyed the clinical talks.

On our second day back, though, Doug called me into his room and showed me his left leg, the one that had gotten dragged under the chair. It was all swollen and looked awful.

I phoned our primary physician and he said to call 911 and get Doug to the hospital right away. It turned out he had a spiral fracture on that leg. A spiral fracture is when a bone breaks from being twisted so far and so hard it has to give way.

Believe it or not, this injury kept Doug in the hospital, in traction, for five months. Traction is no fun. His secretary had to come there to work with him. He was planning to teach his class from his hospital bed, but fortunately he didn't have to.

Even though his contract said he had to teach three classes to graduate students every two years, he was able to get out of teaching for that time. His students came to visit him anyway, just because they missed him.

I was very disappointed. It was terrible that Doug had to be in the hospital for so long over something that seemed so small when it happened. He missed out on his home life, his school life, and, of course, the meetings we couldn't go to.

Every time Doug and I went out of the country, I was happy to get him back safely. If we had gotten stuck overseas after that accident, I wouldn't have been able to stay there for five months to be with him. Somebody had to be at home, to take care of the kids, the pets, the house, the bills, and everything else.

So traveling with Doug could be stressful, even though I enjoyed it. Of course, I also took a lot of vacations on my own...to California, Florida, the islands, and so on.

I had my male friends I went out with or sometimes traveled with or traveled to. The guys I went out with were my own friends, although sometimes Doug and the boys would meet them and get friendly with them too.

Sometimes I might go away by myself or with a guy for a weekend or something. It was okay with Doug, as long as it was no one he worked with. Still he did have some jealousy and insecurity too. Doug really preferred it when I took Greg or Steve on a trip with me.

I'd take the boys to Long Island in the summer, to the beach, the movies, a school play, to New York to see the Christmas tree, whatever. They didn't have to be big trips. Whenever I was going to do something like that, Doug was all positive about it, but he wasn't quite so positive about me going away with a friend.

I'd always have to make sure everything was taken care of while I was gone. One year, after the boys were out of the house, I went to Russia by myself for a week. The only way I could do that was because my son Steve offered to come and stay with his father while I was gone.

When I was there in St. Petersburg, I saw a really nice chess set, so I bought it for Steve, as a little thank-you. Both my sons and Doug all played chess. I knew Steve would like it.

From St. Petersburg, I took the train to Moscow. The subway system there is fantastic. It's clean and beautiful, like an art gallery. I was only in Moscow for two nights, so I didn't even unpack my big suitcase. Then I flew home.

When I got home, I went to give Steve this beautiful chess set, but it wasn't in my suitcase. I was so upset. I couldn't imagine what happened. I bought him another one, an Italian one, but it wasn't the same.

I didn't find out what had happened until months later, when I was skiing with one of my male friends in Vermont. When we got to the hotel, he put my suitcase up on a stand for me to open. I looked at it and saw there was an L-shaped slit in the back.

My guess is they did that at the Moscow airport. The chess set was in a wooden box. They probably felt the box inside the suitcase through the fabric, thought it was a jewelry box, and made a discreet slit to pull it out. I wonder if they ever played chess with it.

My solo trips were also really good to help relieve the pressure that built up at home over time. From the very beginning, Doug could sometimes get negative with me, even though I was doing so much to help him. This was understandable, of course, because he would feel very negative about life at times, and it would spill over onto whomever was around.

When he was at the Rusk Institute in 1979, rehabbing from the accident, he knew two other men there, who were in the same situation he was. They had girlfriends, who were spending a lot of time with them at the Institute. So Doug was complaining to me that I wasn't as devoted as these other girls were.

What he was forgetting was that those girls did not have children...or as many responsibilities as I did. I had two small children and lived 35 miles away from the Institute.

Bottom line: Later on, Doug told me both those girls left their disabled boyfriends. I never left Doug. That's what matters.

189

At that time, right after the accident, I was also going to New York to take classes on how to deal with this new situation, especially concerning sex. I don't remember exactly what the classes covered, but I do remember they showed films on sex with people who had spinal cord injuries. It turned out quadriplegics were more likely to get an erection than paraplegics, because their injury was higher up, in the cervical area.

At one point, years after the accident, Doug actually got a penile implant. He was still interested in sex and trying to have it, even though he wasn't able to feel anything down there. He went to his urologist in New York to get it done, but it didn't work. So he finally had to have it removed after about six months. Too bad.

They told us in these classes the most important thing was to treat the disabled person just as you would anyone else. It's a psychological thing. They're not weird. They're normal people, sitting in a wheelchair. They're still your husband, your friend, the father of your kids, whatever.

You have fights. You have good times. You just keep going. That was the basis, the essence of Doug's and my relationship. We were still the same people. We still loved each other. We just couldn't do some of the things we had done before…one of which was sex.

Chapter 45

Along the way in my dating life, I did feel like I fell in love with two different guys at different times. I even thought of leaving my husband for each of those guys, but I didn't do it. I'm glad I didn't.

Early in our relationship after the accident, Doug and I had discussed, on more than one occasion, what we would do, if that situation ever arose. Whenever we talked about it, Doug was very philosophical. He just said, "Well, Sylvia, if you ever leave me, you have to take the boys with you."

He knew he couldn't raise them by himself. I didn't want to deprive him of his sons and I didn't have a job, so on a practical level, it made good sense for us to stay together. Besides, we really loved and enjoyed each other as people.

When I fell in love with these two other guys, I never told Doug about it. I would never tell him anything like that. He knew I dated people, but I didn't go into detail, as per our agreement. There were other men I dated, whom I liked a lot, but I never thought about leaving Doug for any of them.

In both of the situations where I did think about leaving, I realize now it wouldn't have worked out anyway. One fellow, whose name I can't even remember, I met in New Jersey at a Marriott Hotel. I had stopped in there for a drink and we happened to start talking.

Sometimes I would go to a hotel near me on a Saturday night to have a couple of drinks and hopefully talk to someone. This guy worked for AT&T and was staying there. He lived in Pennsylvania.

He told me he was getting divorced and going through mediation. We started seeing each other and I ended up falling for him.

This was within the first six years of Doug's accident, when we still owned both houses. I really liked this guy and, since he was getting divorced, I started thinking maybe I should get divorced too.

I even started calculating in my head, *Doug could stay at our house in Warren, since it's wheelchair-accessible. I could take the house in Bernardsville, and that way we'd still be close to each other.*

It seemed like an easy way out for me at the time. All this went through my mind, but that relationship just ended somehow. Maybe the man realized it wasn't a good thing, which it wasn't, or maybe I realized it. It was just something that happened, not too serious.

The other situation happened later on, with a fellow named Bob. He was in my massage group, which is where we met. He was single and lived about 20 minutes away from me. I fell in love with him too.

I think I was very vulnerable at the time. I was in this situation with a paralyzed husband and loads of stress every day. My kids could tell what I was going through. They would even buy me books on how to reduce stress in your life.

So I fell in love with Bob. I never did anything to follow through on making it permanent. He was a little younger than me and the whole thing was so complicated, that I never actually pushed anything about leaving.

I just thought about it. Again, probably just another imaginary escape. It was tempting to want a normal kind of life, like I used to have, like other people had. I was in my early 40s and everything had just happened. It was probably part of the whole process of accepting my fate.

There's some story about a princess, who can't get out of a garden. I remember hearing it a long time ago. It's a famous story. She's trapped. At times, I thought I was in a similar situation. I felt like that princess. I couldn't get out of my life. I was stuck in this situation, with no escape. My only escape was going out with different guys, going to the beach, attending cultural events, and traveling.

At first, right after Doug's accident, when I got back to New Jersey, I was desperate to escape. I was still dealing with the trauma of what had happened.

I would wait till my kids went to bed and then I would sit in the living room by myself. I would have vodka and tonic and listen to music. That was my escape.

At first, I drank a lot to forget this crushing new reality I was dealing with. I felt like I did when my mother died. I just wanted to run away and forget. I remember going to a lot of movies too.

Fortunately, my husband understood and gave me a lot of freedom. The fact that he let me date and have discreet sex made all the difference in making an unbearable situation bearable.

Doug drank a lot too. His doctor at the Rusk Institute had told him he could, so many nights he would sit in his wheelchair in his room, drinking beer.

We both tried not to show any weakness to our children and that also helped get me by. I had to be strong and display strength, especially for the kids' sake. Whenever Doug was in the hospital, I would take them to see their father, so they would know he was alive and okay.

It may sound strange to say, but I was glad both my parents were deceased. I was happy they never knew about the accident. If they had known, they would have been very disturbed.

Just ask yourself, *What if you had a daughter and she got married to a really intelligent, successful guy, and then a few years later, he became paralyzed and your daughter had to take care of him for the rest of his life?*

How would you feel if you were parents in that situation?

If something like that happened to one of my sons, I would be devastated. I know my parents always wanted the best for me. My father wanted to make me a member of La Gorce Country Club, so I could marry a surgeon or someone successful.

Doug was a great catch, as far as I was concerned, but if they had known Doug had this accident, they would have been very, very unhappy. I was glad my parents never had to see my situation. That shows you a lot about what I was going through.

Yet, somehow, I realized along the way, this was not a dress rehearsal for something else. This was it. This was my life. I thought about that all the time, *I'm never going to get these years back, so I'm going to enjoy them as much as I can.*

That whole time, all those years, I knew I had to do what I wanted and what I enjoyed, while I could. I had to do it right then, because I wasn't going to get that time back. That's what I call grabbing life by the horns and riding it till it drops.

When I had a bad day, I'd be talking and complaining to my son Steve and he would always say, "Well, Mom, this IS your life." No whining allowed. He was very much like his father, very perceptive.

He would remind me, this was it. This was all I got. No do-overs. And complaining didn't help. So I ended up traveling more than the typical wife, who didn't have the kinds of problems I did. And I had experiences all over the world most people will never have.

I had women come over to my house, health aides or whatever, and they would say, "Oh, I don't know how you do all this." People were always saying things like that. One nurse came in and was amazed. She just couldn't believe it.

Our friends helped get me by and helped my husband. They were so supportive. I remember one social worker at Rusk who liked me. Once, when I was feeling doubtful, he told me, "Oh, you're going to do just fine."

People always told me that. Maybe it helped inspire me to do fine. It wasn't until years later that I realized I had made the right choice by not leaving Doug for another man. Yes, at times I was very frustrated and felt trapped like that princess, but I know now I did the right thing staying with him and keeping our family together.

I felt it was what I had to do. The situation we lived in was not what either one of us had asked for, but it was what we had. We were a team. I really felt we worked that way.

I was practical and he was intellectual. He was diplomatic with people and I was direct. Together, we could handle most anything. And we did.

Chapter 46

I've never spent a lot of time philosophizing and pondering about the meaning of life. I've always been more of a doer, not a thinker like Doug was. For me, life is to be lived. That's what it's all about.

Still, one experience really did set me thinking...so much so that I wrote about it afterwards in an essay for our Unitarian Fellowship concerning what they called the "Search for Meaning."

Doug and I were long-time friends with a couple in New York, Bert and Mary Ella Zippel. In fact, Bert was Doug's best friend from Princeton. Unfortunately, Bert died of cancer while our kids were still young.

Bert, like Doug, had earned his doctorate at Princeton. He ended up teaching at Hunter University. His first wife died of cancer. Then he got remarried to another woman, Mary Ella.

The four of us all used to go out to dinner and then to the Metropolitan Opera. We enjoyed each other. As I wrote earlier, one summer my son Greg even stayed with them in the Poconos, when the rest of us went to Europe.

Bert and Mary Ella were good people and good friends, the kind that would pick you up at the airport. In fact, when I went to Club Med that first year after Doug's accident, Bert and Mary Ella did pick me up on my return. I even stayed with them overnight in Queens. They were always very helpful.

Then, lo and behold, out of nowhere, Bert came down with cancer of the colon. It hit him hard. Soon he was dying in the hospital. Mary Ella told us if we wanted to see him we should get there soon.

It was a Friday night that we decided to go in to the city to see Bert. Doug and I drove, but we got caught in some terrible traffic. It was so bad, I wanted to just give up and go back home.

Doug insisted we keep going though. He said, "No, I started this and I want to see Bert. Whatever it takes, I'm determined to get there."

He was very firm. So we stayed the course and finally got to the hospital. Bert definitely looked like he was not long for this earth. He was a dying man.

It was a revelation to me. This was the first time, since Doug's accident, that I looked at my husband and realized, even though he was disabled, he still had his health. This was very significant to me. It was like a light went on in my head. I kept thinking about that.

At the Unitarian Fellowship, which was the only church we ever went to, one of their theme principles is the search for meaning in life. Sometimes during a program or a service, someone would get up and share something they had written about their own personal search.

If you did this, the experience you described was supposed to be something significant that had happened, something meaningful that helped you understand life in a new way.

So I wrote about this incident and how it had changed my perception of Doug's condition, which also changed my perception of my whole life. Here's some of what I wrote:

"I am not describing my search for meaning just for myself and my husband Doug, but in memory of our dear friend, Bert Zippel. It was only in his terminal illness of cancer that he taught me to re-evaluate my life.

"After my husband's accident, which left him paralyzed, I thought death would be easier to deal with than the continual difficulty of paraplegia. I even wished for my own death. I thought that then Doug could go on with his work and raise our two sons.

"Doug and I left on a Friday night to visit Bert for the last time. The traffic was atrocious and I wanted to give up, but Doug said he was going to do what he came to do. Finally, we got to the hospital three hours later.

"Bert's wife had warned me that he had grown older and thinner. Nevertheless, I was shocked when I first saw him. Bert's response to us was happy though. He said, 'We did all get together again!'

"I looked at him and I saw a dead man. I looked at my husband and I saw a healthy man. For the first time in six and a half years, I felt that Doug and I had put our energies together, to make it to this final visit with Bert.

"Doug and I had been through so much pain, both together and individually. Now, for the first time, I found strength in my husband. Doug and I realized that we had come a long way together already. Possibly for the first time for me, death wasn't a better alternative any more."

That was my story...and I'm sticking to it.

After Bert died, there was a memorial service at All Souls Unitarian Church in New York. We took both Greg and Steve to it with us. Doug was asked to be a speaker at the service. I think he was the only speaker, other than the minister.

He talked about how he and Bert were best friends. We had a lot of friends, and before that, I had never realized that Doug felt Bert was his best male friend.

Doug's talk reinforced my change of perspective. I realized now that he wasn't so bad off after all. He was alive and healthy, while his best friend was already dead.

After Bert died, Mary Ella used a lawyer whom they had known from All Souls Church, to help her settle the estate. Then, lo and behold, she ended up marrying him!

His name was Guy Quinlan. He had gone to Harvard and never married before. He had some kind of peripheral vision problem, which caused him to be a little disabled, but he worked for a well-known firm in the city. He and Mary Ella are still married.

Life is strange. You never know what might happen. One day Doug was able-bodied, the next day he was stuck in a wheelchair for the rest of his life. It was very frustrating and difficult for all of us.

Doug wasn't religious. His mother had a brother out in Southern California, though, who was a religious fanatic. After the accident happened, this guy actually wrote Doug a letter, saying that it happened because Doug didn't believe in his religion. What an awful, ignorant thing to say. Very un-Christian, if you ask me.

There's so much more to life than the simplistic beliefs people have. You have to live life, to understand it. What has helped me most has not been church, but socializing with my friends, going places, and doing things with my sons.

People are amazed that, even today, I am still out and about every single night. I go out by myself a lot. I'm not afraid to. I've done it all my life. It's nothing new. Most people my age have never lived the way I have. They can't believe my energy and zest for life.

I know that I need to be out of the house and doing things, in order to feel right. I'm a people person, but I'm also disciplined. Every morning, I write in my diary, which I've kept it since I was 11 years old. Every morning I also teach a water aerobics class at my condo.

One time up north, a psychiatrist I was seeing was listening to me talking about my husband being paraplegic. After a while, she said, "You know, you suffer from depression." Funny, I just thought I was in a depressing situation.

Anyway, she suggested I try taking an anti-depressant, Wellbutrin. Since she prescribed it, I now take it every morning when I wake up. It gives you a lot of extra serotonin, so it's really good and it doesn't have any bad side effects that I've seen.

I'm sure I could live without it now that I'm here in sunny Florida, but when I was living up north, stuck at home all winter in the cold, wet and darkness...well, it was nice to have.

Chapter 47

Once I went to New York to have dinner with a lawyer friend of mine, whom I was dating there. The next day, I took Steve, who was 15 at the time, out for lunch. As we were eating, I asked him, "Steve, what do you think of my lifestyle?'

His response was typical of his contemplative nature. He said, "Mom, under the circumstances, I don't know what else you could do."

He understood and always sympathized with me. My son Greg was another story. He was very demanding and had a temper. It was his way or the highway. If he got angry, he would throw something.

When the boys were younger, every morning I would get up to see them off to school. I would usually also make them a lunch to take. One morning Greg was eating a bowl of cereal at the dinette table, while I was doing my mother stuff. For some reason, he got mad at me and actually threw his whole bowl of cereal all over me and the big picture window behind me.

It was a mess…and it scared me. He was getting bigger then, bigger than me. If Greg had wanted to, he could have come over and started shaking me or something.

Another time, he was so angry, he broke the bathroom door. I realized I had to be concerned about protecting myself, because Doug couldn't do anything to help, if the situation arose. Steve had started taking judo for the very reason, that we never knew what Greg might do.

A couple of weeks after Doug and I saw Bert Zippel in the hospital, I had two teenage girls babysitting the boys at the house. While we were gone, I heard later, the boys were wrestling in the family room, where there was wall-to-wall carpeting. Just typical roughhousing, you would think.

The next day we took them to Bert's funeral in New York. As we were out, I noticed Steve's shoulder was all slumped down and he was in pain. The next day, I took him to an orthopedic surgeon. It turned out he had a broken clavicle…just from wrestling with Greg.

After that, I decided I wasn't going to hire a baby sitter any more. It didn't do any good anyway. I figured, *These boys are either going to learn to live together or kill each other.* That was my attitude. I couldn't stop them.

Greg was nine years old at that time and Steve was six. I researched it and found that only three states have a legal age to say when you can leave a child alone, without a baby-sitter. It ranges from 8 to 14. There was nothing at all like that back then. So I was okay leaving them alone. Somehow they worked it out. Maybe Steve's judo helped.

As the years went by, I started thinking I should get some help in dealing with my two boys. At first, I asked a counselor from their school to come over and talk to us. He did a couple of times, but then he said he really couldn't help us. I guess our situation was a little too complex for him.

However, he said he did know a psychologist we could hire, who he thought might help. The other guy's name was Joe. We hired Joe because of Greg, but it turned out he really helped Steve more than Greg.

The first time Joe came over, our whole family was all in the living room. Joe knew nothing about our background or relationships, except that we were a family. So he was feeling things out, asking us general questions.

Greg brought up that he was upset, because he felt his father didn't control his mother enough. He thought his father should rein me in. He saw the situation very differently than Doug and Steve did.

Doug spoke up in my defense and said, "Greg, your mother is a totally free person. If she wants to get on a plane tonight and go to Timbuktu, she can do that. I can't stop her. She's a free person and neither you nor I have any control over her. She stays here of her own free will."

That was Doug's attitude and it was beautiful. Yes, I went out a lot. I was very independent. Unfortunately Greg couldn't understand that. I really liked that Doug didn't try to control me.

Doug wasn't jealous, like Bill Wallace was. I could never live with a guy who was possessive. I'm faithful to my partner in my heart, but if I want to do something, I need to be free to do it. He has to trust me and trust our love.

After Greg said his piece, Joe turned to Steve and asked him about something. Steve responded that what was bothering him was something that had happened when Doug and he and I were in Paris on a trip together.

Steve had been nine years old. We were staying in the Left Bank and Doug had to do his bowel routine in the bathroom that night. It usually took a long time, like three or four hours, and it smelled up the whole room.

I wanted to go out. Sometimes I had to help Doug, especially when he was doing it in the bed because he couldn't get in the bathroom. That night, however, he could use the bathroom. We had a routine. After I helped him get set up, I'd go out for a couple of hours, and then come back to clean him up.

We were in Paris a lot, so I was familiar with the city. There was a London-style pub a few blocks away, which I knew had really good jazz. So I went out to hear some music and then came back.

Steve had to stay in the room with Doug, because he was just nine at the time. I never knew anything had happened while I was gone, until we had this conversation later with the whole family.

Steve said that, while his father was in the bathroom that night, he kept saying, "Oh, nobody loves me, nobody loves me."

That sounded strange to me, because I had never heard Doug say anything like that before. He certainly never told me he felt that way. He knew how much I loved him, to stay with him through all that we enduring.

Doug said a lot of things when he got angry, but never that no one loved him. Steve had kept this from me all that time. If I hadn't hired Joe, I never would have known anything about it. Evidently the experience really hit Steve hard.

Doug shouldn't have been saying that stuff with his young son around, but he did. Steve had been holding it in for about two years. I knew nothing. He just kept it hidden.

Joe didn't know what to make of this family. He was there for an hour, then he told us he wanted to talk to just Doug and me separately the next time we met.

It wasn't until the second time that he found out we had an open marriage. We told him then about our whole lifestyle. We explained that we believed, in a marriage, the two people involved make the rules. Nobody else. Whatever they say is okay for them and their relationship…is definitely okay.

After that, Joe could better understand where my kids were coming from, especially Greg. From then on, he would spend half an hour with Greg and then half an hour with Steve.

Of course, Greg didn't like Joe. He didn't like anyone telling him what to do. Evidently, he felt like Joe was trying to. Psychologists don't really tell you what to do, they just listen to you, but I'm sure Greg didn't enjoy having to reflect on himself. That was more Steve's style.

Chapter 48

In talking about Doug's life, he accomplished so much in his professional career and overcame so much in his personal life, that it's easy to overlook the fact that he was a great, proud father. He loved his two sons.

Besides that, he was a great husband, as I've tried to express already. Strangely enough, it was when Doug was in the hospital for the procedures he had to have, and I would visit him, that we had our best conversations.

We would talk about the boys, of course, and our life together, as most couples do, but Doug would also discuss all kinds of interesting ideas and tell stories about things that happened to him when he was growing up.

One time, when Steve came to the hospital with me, Doug made us laugh a lot talking about his life. For some reason, when he was in the hospital, he was even more fun to be with than usual. Somehow, it brought out his lighter side.

When we went to dinner with friends, Doug was always on top of things, with intellectual conversation and interesting tidbits to share. When he was just with me at home, we'd generally talk more about practical things in our everyday life. Not so much fun.

Some of my fondest memories with my husband were when we traveled together and he received professional awards. He won many awards for his work. I still have all the certificates. There were so many, that I had to take them out of their frames when I moved to Miami. There were too many to keep up on the wall.

One thing Doug always wanted us to do was go on a cruise. He felt that it would be an easy way for him to travel. So he and I went on two cruises together, one to Alaska on the Star Princess in 1994 and one to the Mediterranean, in 1995, after a meeting in Europe.

Because Doug wanted to go on a cruise, I became an outside travel agent, working from home, so that I could arrange a wheelchair-accessible tour to Alaska for him.

To start our trip, first we went to Vancouver, where we spent three or four days. We rented a car and I drove us over to Victoria Island, which he wanted to see. We came back that same day, which was a lot of driving for me.

Another day, while Doug was doing his medical stuff in the room, I went to Wreck Beach, which was a clothing-optional beach in Vancouver.

Then we boarded the Princess cruise ship to sail the inside passage, which is a coastal route through a network of seaways between the islands on the Northwest Pacific coast.

We went to Glacier Bay, which was very beautiful, as well as to Juneau, Skagway, and Ketchikan. In Skagway, Doug was determined to take a helicopter up to see the glaciers there. They really didn't want to take him, because he was such a big person in a wheelchair, but he was so insistent, they finally agreed.

So we went up in a helicopter and saw this whole remote area, with rugged mountains, beautiful valleys, and massive glaciers. I got to get out on the glacier for a little, but, of course, Doug couldn't. Still, he really enjoyed it.

Our second cruise came when Doug had a meeting of the Psychometric Society in Leiden, the Netherlands in 1995. His colleagues, Willem Heiser and his wife, Jacqueline Meulman, were there. They taught at the University of Leiden.

The meeting went on for three days. At the end, there was a big banquet in a cathedral, which was really neat. All of Doug's colleagues, mostly psychologists and statisticians, were very cool and they knew how to party.

Nobody in Doug's field was uptight. They were all open to just about anything you could think of...affairs, pot, drinking, whatever. I never hung around with rigid people in my life, never.

In the Netherlands it was legal to smoke pot, so after the banquet two of the guys at the meeting asked me if I wanted to go to a coffee house and try it out.

Always up for an adventure, I tagged along. They bought a marijuana cigarette there and I had one puff. It was interesting, but nothing special, as far as I was concerned.

After the meeting, we flew to Genoa and boarded the *Costa Romantica* for seven days. We departed from Genoa and ended up back there. Every day was a different port, with seven ports of call in all. The first was Sicily, then Tunis, Ibiza, Barcelona, Pompeii, and back to Genoa.

At Sicily we went on a nice tour of the island, so that was good. We didn't do much in Tunis, though, because Doug's wheelchair got a flat tire. We spent the whole time there getting it repaired. While he was waiting, Doug had to sit on a hard straight-backed wooden chair, which he's not supposed to do.

We put his Roho cushion under him, but he still had to endure that hard surface, while his chair was repaired. Not good.

The only souvenir I got in Tunis was a copper plate with camels on it, which I found and picked out in the bazaar. I still have it in my condo. After our repair ordeal, we just got back on the ship.

Most everything else was a lot of fun, except for Ibiza, which was a bit of a disappointment. Doug couldn't get off the ship there, because the boat couldn't go in to the dock. They only had little dinghies to take you to land. With his wheelchair, Doug couldn't ride in one of those dinghies. So he had to just stay aboard.

I still managed to have a good time there though and even a bit of an adventure. I saw the walled city, which was built in the 16th century on a site that's been occupied since before the Romans. It was fascinating.

Then I got a taxi with two strangers, to go to a clothing-optional beach, where I took a bunch of photographs. I was going to take a taxi back to the ship, but, when it was time to leave, I discovered there were none. I had to wait for a bus to get back.

I would have missed the last dinghy to the ship without the help of a young Swiss male nurse, who was on the bus with me. I told him how upset I was, that I might not get back in time for the last dinghy. If I missed it, I would have to fly to the next port of call and meet the ship the next day.

I was worried about Doug, not about me. He would be on the boat all by himself, not knowing where I was. Without me to help him, he would have a hard time taking care of himself.

Maybe this male nurse understood what a serious situation it was to leave a disabled person stranded, because he offered to help me catch the dinghy by carrying my big, heavy purse down to the dock for me.

When we got to the dock, we both ran as fast as we could. Thank God and the helper he sent me, I just barely caught that last dinghy. Without that guy's help, I would have been stuck there overnight for sure.

The rest of that cruise went pretty smoothly, all things considered. Those were the only two cruises Doug and I went on.

Later, Steve offered to take Doug on a cruise, but it really wouldn't have been possible at that point. By then, Doug's health had declined so much, he would have had to also take his live-in health aide along. to help with his medical routines.

I told Steve, "It's nice of you to offer, but without a health aide or me, it just wouldn't work."

Doug's ski accident made a drastic change in our lives...a permanent one, which continued to affect us more and more as the years went by. Even though at first I wished that either he or I had died, eventually things worked themselves out. We learned to adjust to our situation and make the best of it.

Chapter 49

In 1995, Steve graduated college with a BA in pure Mathematics, after just three years at UC Berkeley. Doug and I were there for the ceremony and there's a story to be told about that. It shows how wrapped up in his work Doug really was, even though he loved his family.

When Steve was still in high school, the summer before his senior year, Doug and I were at a meeting in Belgium. Doug was with a colleague from Ghent, discussing another meeting, which was scheduled for the next June. I realized the date they were talking about was exactly when Steve would be graduating from high school. I just blew up.

I confronted Doug and said, "You have to go to your son's graduation."

"Oh, no," he said, "Steve won't mind if I don't go."

"Doug, you have to go."

We ended up getting in a big fight about it, but I made sure Doug went.

The ironic part is that three years later, when Steve was graduating from Berkeley, Doug wanted desperately to go, but he was having medical problems and wasn't sure if he could travel. Fortunately, he made it.

Doug had done his graduate work at Princeton, so he used to give the school money, thinking his son would apply there and easily get accepted. When the time came for Steve to choose a college, however, he didn't want to go to Princeton, because he didn't want to stay in New Jersey.

Steve didn't get accepted at Princeton anyway, in spite of all the money Doug had given them. Doug got really angry. He never gave them another penny.

Steve did get accepted at Berkeley, however, which was considered the best public university in America. Recently I was flying on a plane next to a man, who had a list of all the top colleges, including the Ivy League. It said the number one school overall in the country was Pomona College in California, if you can believe it. That's a very small private college. The number one public, state school was Berkeley.

So when Steve got accepted there, he decided that was where he wanted to be. He had applied to about nine schools, but Berkeley was it. When Steve started college, he already had 23 Advanced Placement credits from high school. His counselor told him, if he majored in math, he could graduate in three years, which he did.

Greg, on the other hand, took four and a half years to graduate. He was taking mostly psychology courses and other electives. Greg had applied to eleven schools and been accepted by six. Then, after he started school, he kept moving around to different universities.

He started out at the University of Florida, Doug's and my alma mater. He went in August, to the orientation for out of state students. It was so hot and humid, he decided he couldn't tolerate it.

It's true. Gainesville is in the middle of Florida, away from the coastal breezes, and the humidity there is awful. I never spent a summer in Gainesville myself. I couldn't have.

But Greg actually threatened us to get his way about where he wanted to go instead of Florida. He told us that, if he couldn't go to the University of Colorado, he wouldn't go to college at all. We couldn't stop him. It was his choice completely where he went to school, because he was paying for it with his own money.

Remember the accident Greg had at the Montessori school in San Diego, when the swing chain came apart and he fell on the concrete?

Well, Greg had gotten a large sum of money from the lawsuit over that incident. It was the money Greg was using to pay for college. The total award had been $140,000, of which the lawyer got $30,000. It took about seven years to settle, but Greg received about $110,000 at the end.

That money had been in a CD out in California, because that's where the case had been tried. It had to stay there till Greg turned 18. It was a legal thing. So, the money was never ours, it was Greg's.

I even had a financial guy come over to advise Greg on how to invest the money when he got it. To hand a boy $110,000 all at once on his 18th birthday is a lot to deal with.

After Doug's accident, we hadn't been sure what our financial situation might be in the future, so we had decided to set that settlement money aside for Greg's college fund. Life had shown us you never knew what might happen. You have to plan for the unexpected.

While the money was sitting in the CD, every year we would ask our attorney to go to court and release some, so we could pay the income tax on it. The attorney didn't like that. He said we were the most responsible clients he had ever encountered in his life. I guess most people got away without paying the tax, but we thought it was the right thing to do.

Greg had been accepted to the University of Colorado. He was also accepted to the University of Wisconsin, which was a better school academically, but he didn't want to go there. He was looking for the total experience, social life, recreation, the whole thing, and he felt Colorado had more to offer than Wisconsin.

I went out to Boulder with Greg for five days, when he went to school. It was beautiful, no doubt. He's an avid skier, so I thought for sure he would love it. Then, lo and behold, after a month, he called me and said he wanted to transfer again in January, at mid-term. Now he wanted to go to Rutgers. Go figure.

I had been helping Greg through this whole process of applying to college and making his choices, but at this point I told him, "I'm not going to help you any more." I was done.

I had hired a tutor to help him prepare for the SATs. I had hired a private counselor to help him with college application. If he wanted to call the shots like this, he'd have to take the hits on his own, if they came.

Later I spoke to one of Greg's high school teachers and he told me he had asked Greg why he left Colorado. He said Greg told him, "It was too hedonistic. There were just too many drugs."

I never asked Greg why he left. I was just so sick of the whole thing, that I didn't care. You have to understand, Greg was very anti-drug. He has never done a drug in his life. Never even smoked a cigarette.

Right after Doug's accident, I had started smoking and drank a lot. I smoked Carltons, which were the weakest cigarettes you could buy, even though they killed Aunt Betty.

When we moved to Warren, I'd be fixing dinner and having a vodka and tonic with a cigarette. Steve would get upset. He'd say, "Mom why don't you quit smoking?" I did quit eventually, but I had smoked because of all the stress.

Getting back to Greg, a big part of the reason he chose Rutgers was because it would be tuition-free, since his father was on the faculty. Everyone said he would never get in though. Even the private college admissions counselor I had hired said Greg wouldn't get accepted at Rutgers at mid-term...but he did.

Greg handled the whole transfer application process on his own. I did help him with one question, which he couldn't answer. The rest he did by himself.

Lo and behold, one day in December, a letter came to our house addressed to Greg Carroll. It said he was accepted in mid-term after all.

He started there that January!

Greg always had an uncanny knack for doing things you didn't think he could do. Another example, after he graduated from Rutgers, Greg was accepted into a graduate program in biopsychology there.

It was very difficult to get into. Everyone said he'd never do it, but he did. Of course, I'm sure Doug's position on the faculty at Rutgers helped more than a little.

Later on, Greg found out he would have to dissect rats in that program. He didn't want to do that, so he was going to quit. When he called his father to tell him, Doug was so embarrassed, he told Greg he had to finish the semester at least.

Greg did finish that semester, but he quit after it. Eventually, of course, he became a chiropractor, which involves dissecting human cadavers to learn anatomy. I guess he got over his distaste for dissection.

Still, it took him a long time to figure out what he wanted to do.

Chapter 50

In 1996, due to popular demand from our friends, we re-started our tradition of sending out a holiday letter at the end of each year. Reading those letters now helps me remember everything that happened. Some things I wish I didn't have to remember.

That year started with a bang. We were overwhelmed by what they called "The Blizzard of the Century." It was a severe nor'easter that paralyzed the U.S. East Coast with up to four feet of snow, which fell January 6 through January 8. That storm was one of just two blizzards in our area that ever got the top rating of 5, "Extreme," on the Snowfall Impact Scale.

As if that wasn't enough, later that year Doug had another accident overseas. This one would affect him for the rest of his life. We were going to Japan for a meeting of the International Federation of Classification Society when it happened.

I had told Doug that, with him in a wheelchair, I didn't think we should go. As usual, he didn't listen to me. Instead, he said, "I have to go. I'm the President."

We flew to San Francisco and then on to Osaka, Japan. Whenever we traveled, we and the other disabled people always had to be the first ones on the plane and the last ones off. I always watched carefully, to be sure the crew people didn't screw up…because they often did.

When we landed in Osaka, this colleague of Doug's got off before we did, with the other passengers. When it was finally our turn to leave, a male Japanese attendant transferred Doug from his airplane seat onto what they call an "aisle chair," to roll him down the aisle.

Since most planes have narrow aisles, it's impossible for a wheelchair to maneuver down them. So they use an aisle chair, which they keep on the plane. It has three wheels – one in front and two in back – and is very narrow and kind of flimsy. They strap wheelchair people into that, so they can get them up and down the aisles, when they're boarding or disembarking.

So this small Japanese man was wheeling 6'4", 230 pound Doug off the plane on one of these aisle chairs. There were three flight attendants standing in a row, by the front three seats before you reached the door, waiting for us to leave.

All of a sudden, for some reason, the little Japanese guy reached for something and let go of the chair for a moment. Because the aisle chair only has three wheels, if someone doesn't keep a tight grip on it, it can easily tip over. He did let go of the chair. Sure enough, it started to tip and fall.

In trying to break the fall and save himself, Doug put out his left hand and touched the floor. It was scary to watch, but, as far as we could tell at the time, Doug was okay.

We continued on out, but we knew from the incident in Edinburgh, when Doug's leg was fractured, that something might show up later. He might have broken his leg or God knows what. We couldn't be sure, because he had no feeling down there.

When we went inside, we reported there had been an accident on the plane. It happened right in front of the flight attendants, so we had witnesses. Still, we had to fill out a whole form. It's good we did, because days later we found out Doug had been seriously injured in that fall.

From the airport, we went to our hotel in Kobe, a very famous place, The Osaka. We couldn't stay at the hotel where our meeting was, because their guest rooms weren't wheelchair-accessible. The meeting rooms in their conference center were, but not the guest rooms.

So every morning some students would come pick Doug up in a Lexus and take him over to the meeting. Then they'd stay with him, pushing him around all day in his wheelchair to wherever he had to go.

One bright spot was the last night of the meeting. They had a banquet, where the mayor of Kobe presented Doug with a beautiful, small screen, which had a map of the world on it. Since Doug was the president, he received the honor and got to keep the screen. I still have it here in my living room today.

After our three-day meeting in Kobe, we took the bullet train up to Tokyo for a three-day tutorial. We stayed in The Osaka hotel there too. Again, some Japanese students pushed Doug around to all his meetings.

When we finished in Tokyo, we took a wheelchair-accessible taxi to the airport, to fly to Honolulu. It cost $450 for that taxi. Everything in Japan is expensive. I remember I had a continental breakfast and it was $16, back in 1996. This was a business trip, so we got reimbursed for the taxi, but still....

We were stopping in Honolulu for two days. When Doug and I had disagreed about whether to take this trip, I had said I wouldn't go, unless we stopped in Hawaii on the way home to relax.

When we got to the Tokyo airport, Doug started pushing himself in his wheelchair again. This was the first time he had, since Japan. That's when he started feeling pain in his left arm up near his shoulder.

When we got to Honolulu and checked into the hotel, Doug was exhausted. He slept the whole first day. He hardly gets any sleep when he's at meetings, so, while he recovered, I went to the beach.

The next evening Doug wanted to go to a musical show they were having at the hotel next door. We took a taxi over there, but by now Doug was in a lot of pain. All we had was some extra-strength Tylenol and the Mai Tai's he was drinking, but they didn't help much.

When we got back to our room that night, he was in even more pain. The next morning, it was so bad, he couldn't get out of bed. Our flight back to Newark was scheduled for that day, so I had to call a doctor to come see Doug in our room.

He gave Doug an injection of narcotics in his left arm, so we could make it out to the airport. There, the person at the airline desk said, "Oh, I see you had an accident in Osaka on your flight with us to Japan. Please, let me see if we can make you comfortable on your way home."

So they upgraded us to first class from Honolulu to Newark. That helped, but the next day, Doug was still in severe pain, so I took him to a neurologist. He diagnosed Doug with a brachial plexus injury and put him in the hospital for five days.

"Brachial plexus" refers to a group of nerves that come out of the spinal cord in the neck and go down the arm. They control muscles and provide feeling for the shoulder, elbow, wrist, and hand.

Some brachial plexus injuries are minor and people completely recover in a few weeks. Others are so severe they cause a permanent disability in the arm. That's what happened to Doug. He lost partial use of his left arm for the rest of his life.

We got into a lawsuit over the whole incident. It was a special lawsuit, because we were the first people who had ever sued over a situation like that. One of my good friends is a lawyer and he looked it up. He said we were famous in the legal community.

It had to be a federal lawsuit, since it took place in Japan. We had to sue: United Air Lines; the little Japanese guy, who worked for a separate company hired by United; and some other party I can't remember.

Of course, these lawsuits all take forever, usually about seven years on the average, to settle. We always settled, we never went to jury trial. We

212

ended up getting $75,000 in the end. That was very little for all the pain and trouble that accident caused over the years.

Chapter 51

Greg started chiropractic school in Atlanta, Georgia in 1997. He really liked it. He was finding his place in the world. My place was all over the place. My adventures continued....

I've actually been to two bachelor parties in my life. Not as a stripper, but as a guest! Bachelor parties are generally just men, so not too many women can say that. Both of my invitations kind of happened on the spur of the moment.

The first one was when I went to Atlanta, to visit Greg for Mother's Day weekend, while he was in chiropractic school there. I only got to visit him there twice, which was less than I wanted. Doug never wanted me to go at all.

Actually, he never wanted me to go anywhere, but I did anyway. I felt I had to travel to stay sane, so I did. When I started talking about this trip, Doug said, "Oh, you don't have to go see Greg."

I responded, "Well, I am going anyway." So I went.

My plane was a little late leaving Newark. As we were all sitting there in the plane, waiting to take off, I noticed three guys sitting across from me, in their late 20's. They were chugging beer like crazy.

Meanwhile, the guy sitting on my right, totally unrelated to the other guys, was telling me that he was going to Atlanta to have a rendezvous with a woman he'd met on an airplane a week earlier.

Then, for some reason – I swear I don't know how it happened – I started to show my seatmate some photographs of me at the beach...in the nude. I guess I figured, if he could have a rendezvous with some woman he just met on the plane, he could understand me being a nudist.

Then one of the three young guys, Steve Goldberg, asked me why I was going to Atlanta. I told him about visiting my son and he said, "Oh, we're going for a bachelor's party. It's going to be at the Gold Club. That's a really famous gentlemen's club. Would you like to come?"

I have no idea why he asked me. I hadn't shown him any pictures! So I just said, very demurely, "Oh, no, thank you. I don't think so."

Then the guy on my right chimed in, "Oh, you should go. It is a really nice club."

Well that got me to thinking, *Why not?* So then I said to Steve, "Okay, I'll come. What time is the party?"

He said, "It's tonight at 8:00." I don't think he really believed I was

214

going to come, even though I said I would. As we walked off the plane together, he said, "Now are you sure you're going to be there, Sylvia?"

I said, "Hey, if I tell you I'm gonna come, I'm gonna come." That's me. That's the way I am.

I rented a car and went over to my hotel, the Drury. They had some balloons all over the lobby for a real estate meeting. My son and his roommate came over to greet me and they brought me in one of those balloons as a little welcome gift.

As we were talking, I told my son, "Hey, Greg, I got invited to a bachelor's party tonight. It's down in Buckhead." Everybody knew that was the chic, upscale part of downtown Atlanta.

Then I added, saving the best for last, "It's at the Gold Club."

Greg came right back with, "Oh, well, there's an even nicer club..." and he mentioned someplace else. Nothing fazed him.

But I said, "Well, this party is at the Gold Club and that's where I'm going."

Greg was always very accepting and supportive of me, as he got older. Maybe those counseling sessions with Joe helped after all. Anyway, he just said, "Oh, okay, that's cool." That's just the way Greg is. I don't know what his roommate thought of all this.

So, I went down to Buckhead and stopped somewhere to eat. I was sitting at the bar, drinking wine and eating calamari, when I told the bartender, "I'm on my way to a party at the Gold Club."

"Oh, you'll never get into the Gold Club," he said.

"Well, I was invited."

"Sorry, you'll never get in."

Undeterred, I went down, parked my car, and walked right in the front door of the club. No problem. I don't know what that guy was talking about. Inside, I saw my new friend Steve and he came right over.

"Oh, hey, Sylvia, I'm glad you made it. Can I get you something to drink?"

I had a drink with him there in the lobby area and we just sat there talking and looking around. There were a couple of girls doing lap dances and so on, but I didn't see anybody stripping. I did meet the groom. I probably only stayed about 20 minutes altogether.

It was no big deal for me. I had been to gentlemen's clubs before with a guy I used to date. He was a professor at Princeton. Those professors can be pretty crazy. They're a lot of fun. He liked to take me to strip clubs, but he was the only other guy I ever went to one with. So that was my first bachelor party.

The second bachelor party was in the Netherlands, so it was a bit wilder. I was in Amsterdam, at a meeting with Doug. One afternoon, he was back at the hotel, doing his medical stuff, so I took a little stroll to see what was going on.

I ended up in the Red Light District. It's world-famous for half-naked prostitutes in brothel windows, raucous bars, marijuana-smoke-filled "coffee shops," spectacular strip shows, and mind-boggling museums.

I was walking around, taking in all the sights, when I saw a guy in the street dressed up as a strawberry. The only thing I could think of was, *Maybe he's advertising Smuckers Strawberry Jam.*

So I went up to him and asked, "Why are you dressed up as a strawberry?"

He said, "Oh, this is my bachelor party. Would you like to join us?"

I still have no idea what that had to do with a strawberry, but I was all by myself, with nothing better to do. So, as usual, I thought, *Okay, sure, why not?*

My new friend had about six or seven other guys with him. We all went for dinner and a beer, and then to a live sex show in some theater. That was it. Then they had to go home, even though it was still pretty early.

They lived in the suburbs of Amsterdam, so it was a bit of a trip, I guess. I walked them down to the train station and said good-bye. Yes, I would say the bachelor party in Amsterdam was wilder than the one in Atlanta. It was really pretty neat.

There probably aren't too many women who have been to two bachelor parties in their lives…unless they were working there. I doubt I'll be going to any more, but I'm the type of person who rarely says no. I'm very adventurous. Life is more fun that way.

Chapter 52

Thanks to my part-time job as an outside travel agent, in 1997 I took a nice, long trip to Africa, which was amazing. A friend of mine had seen an ad for an 18-day tour to South Africa and Zimbabwe and told me about it. If you were a travel agent, you got a 10% discount.

So I signed up for the tour, got that discount and had a grand adventure. I was able to take that trip because my son Steve offered to stay home with Doug, to make sure he was okay while I was gone.

Later that year, Doug had to go into Overlook Hospital for surgery on a decubitus ulcer. He had to stay in there for three months. As a result, we had to cancel trips to Spain and Switzerland.

While Doug was recovering, he could only start sitting up very gradually. Because of some setbacks, he could stay in his wheelchair no longer than 30 minutes at a time.

On one of the trips, we had been planning to go to a famous pilgrimage site in Spain, Santiago de Compostela. It's about an hour or two north of Madrid by plane and is supposedly where Saint James the Apostle preached and was buried.

People have been going there for over 1,000 years on a pilgrimage known as the Way of St. James. There are lots of stories of miracles and amazing events connected with this place.

At the last minute before our trip though, Doug started having the beginnings of a breakdown in his skin. We knew, if he sat on an airplane for eight hours, it would get serious.

As I said earlier, when you're paraplegic, you're supposed to push yourself up every 20 minutes to get the weight off your buttocks for a while, so the blood can rush in there and the skin can recover.

You can't very well do that on a plane. We went to a doctor to check it out, but he didn't really know much about our situation. We had to trust our own instincts. I was pretty sure, if Doug flew to Madrid and then to Santiago de Compostela, it wouldn't be good.

Later, one of Doug's colleagues, who did do that trip, told us the town was very inaccessible and difficult to get around in...lots of narrow, winding streets and decrepit, old buildings. It was a good thing we didn't try to do it. In Europe, it was still very difficult for the disabled.

Of course, I was very depressed when Doug and I had to cancel those trips. I always looked forward to traveling. I got over it though. There were plenty more trips to come.

That year Steve transferred from the University of Massachusetts to State University of New York (SUNY) at Stony Brook, to do PhD studies in mathematical models of ecology. He was following in his father's footsteps somewhat. Doug often called himself a mathematical psychologist. Steve was on the track to become a mathematical ecologist. Math can figure into many different disciplines.

1998 rolled around and it turned out to be not our best year. It started with me taking Steve skiing out west to Aspen. I took Steve skiing many times, but this time, we arrived in Aspen on January 6, 1998.

That was just a week after Michael Kennedy, the son of Robert F. Kennedy, Jr., of the famous Kennedy clan, was killed, while skiing on those same slopes.

It had happened on the main mountain at Aspen, where Steve liked to ski. He was an expert skier. I'm just advanced intermediate. I don't push myself too much, but when you're young, you do.

I knew Steve would probably be going down the exact same run where Michael Kennedy had died. I was a wreck thinking about that. It just reawakened all the old pain about Doug's accident.

Sonny Bono was another famous person who died as a result of a ski accident. That was on a run called "Orion" at the Heavenly ski resort in Lake Tahoe. Like Doug, he skied into a tree.

It was a totally nerve-wracking trip going out to Colorado. Aside from worrying about Steve, I had to worry about Doug as well.

I had hired a woman through an agency to come stay with him for the week I would be gone. Steve and I were flying to Denver and then to Aspen. As we were leaving for the airport, the agency called Doug and said she couldn't come.

They said they'd send somebody else over in two hours, but Steve and I had to leave right away, if we were going to catch our plane. I was a wreck the whole way out to Denver. Until I could call and confirm that someone had actually showed up, Steve and I thought we might have to turn around and fly right back again.

A new woman did arrive and she stayed for the week. As always, though, life was stressful. I hated leaving Doug all by himself and just hoping that someone would show up.

He was still recuperating from decubitus ulcers. By May, he was finally able to drive to Rutgers for important meetings and to remain in his wheelchair for extended periods of time.

It was always back and forth with his condition. In June, we flew to the University of Illinois at Champaign/Urbana for the joint meeting of the Classification Society of North America and the Psychometric Society. Unfortunately, it led to a recurrence of Doug's skin problems, so we had to cancel a trip to Rome later on as a result.

In July, 1998, we purchased a wheelchair-accessible Dodge mini-van to help with transporting Doug. Doug's partial loss of the use of his left arm had made it difficult for him to transfer in and out of his Buick LeSabre. He had to use that left arm to pull the wheelchair in and out of the car, so he was putting stress on that arm all the time.

Doug had a physiatrist he went to, who oversaw his whole condition and all the various procedures he went through. The job of a physiatrist is to maximize what a disabled person can do and assist then in adapting to what they can't do. He recommended we get the van.

Doug's physiatrist told him, "You know, if you keep using that left arm so much, you might eventually cause yourself to lose total use of it. I think you should get a wheelchair-accessible van, to avoid all that stress on your arm."

He said even if Doug tried to use his right arm instead of his left, he might just lose the use of that arm too. It was too much wear and tear on one limb. So we bought the mini-van.

With his new mini-van, Doug was supposed to be able to drive right from his wheelchair, which fit behind the steering wheel of the van. We were hoping Doug would soon be independently mobile again.

Unfortunately, even after we went through all this, it didn't work out. Doug tried driving once or twice, but his posture and balance were so bad, he couldn't do it. He kept falling into the wheel. He couldn't control himself or the van and it was just too dangerous to let him keep trying. So from then on, either I drove Doug, or someone else did.

That year we also spent a lot of time going up to the Helen Hayes Hospital in Haverstraw, New York, where they do a lot of spinal cord injury rehabilitation. Doug was part of an experimental program there. It took us up to two hours to drive there for these sessions.

Doug was being studied by an unusual group of rehab technologists, who were looking for engineering solutions to skin breakdown. They were hoping to correct Doug's posture by creating a new wheelchair, to relieve some of the pressure on his skin.

Doug was fitted for this new type of wheelchair, but it turned out to be terrible. It never worked. It was frustrating that we had to drive that hundred miles up there and back so many times, just to end up with something that didn't work. I guess that's why it was experimental.

Chapter 53

Doug's new mini-van only had about 6000 miles on it when we bought it. It had belonged to an MD, but then he had died. It had been modified by a company, which customized Dodge Caravans, to make them wheelchair accessible. It costs a lot of money to do.

We had to get a mini-van, because a regular van wouldn't fit in our garage. Doug couldn't be going outside in his wheelchair in the winter to get into his car. He might roll down that hill.

The new mini-van was equipped with all the latest technology to make it totally wheelchair accessible. You could remove two of the regular seats, the driver's seat and the right passenger seat, to be replaced by the wheelchair. In either spot, the wheelchair would be attached to the floor, so it wouldn't move.

That was done with an EZ Lock wheelchair docking system. It's a system of brackets that secures a wheelchair to a vehicle floor. This is in line with ADA regulations, to keep wheelchair passengers safe in a moving vehicle. The system was supposed to be easy enough for the wheelchair user to do it himself, but it wasn't that easy.

Whether he was driving or not, Doug would always have to enter and exit the van through the big sliding door on the right side. It had a metal ramp, which came down automatically when you opened the door and back up again when you closed it. There was a little button that opened and closed the sliding door and the ramp.

For Doug to drive, the driver's seat of the van had to be removed, so he could sit at the steering wheel in his wheelchair. To get there, he would wheel up the ramp, across the inside of the van, and then turn his chair to position it at the steering wheel. The van had hand controls for Doug to drive it, but after all this, it turned out he really couldn't do so after all.

The problem was that, since Doug had such poor balance due to his paralysis, he would end up falling into the steering wheel. He couldn't sit straight up, because his injury was right at the nipple line. It was too dangerous for him to drive. That's when I started driving him to work, which was only one day a week. So it wasn't that bad.

Since Doug was just a passenger now, all our procedures had to change. He would roll straight up that ramp and stop in the back of the van, facing sideways, away from the door he just came in. Once he got up in there, he couldn't turn his wheelchair in any direction. There was

221

bench-style seat in the rear for other passengers, behind where Doug entered and exited.

We would lock the chair down to the floor with the EZ Lock hardware. When Doug wanted to exit, he would have to roll down the ramp backwards again. The ramp was very narrow and we always had to watch carefully, to make sure Doug didn't go off the side of it.

After we got the van, I also couldn't leave my car in the garage whenever Doug was coming home. He needed extra space beside the van for the ramp to come down, so he could exit and turn his wheelchair.

After Doug got out of the van in our garage, he would wheel himself up to the front of the van. Then he had to turn left a little, to get to the foot of the entry ramp into our house.

To leave space for him to cross in front of the van, we now had to park it a little farther back and to the right. We couldn't close the garage door. The rear of the van was sticking out. The door was also left open for carbon monoxide reasons, but it didn't stay open for long.

After Doug got into the house, whoever was driving would move the van over to the left and further in. That way, I could get my car into the garage and close the garage door.

I always had to put my car in the garage later than the van. If Doug had to go to work in the morning before I was planning on leaving, then I had to park my car outside the night before, or else get up early and move it.

The ramp we had built to go into the house was actually very handy for carrying things in, as well as for Doug. When we were cleaning out the house, bringing in groceries, or whatever, it was much easier using a ramp than going up and down a big step.

It also made things easier when Doug had to be transported by ambulance. For years, whenever he had to go into the hospital or come back, the paramedics would ask how many steps there were for them to navigate. They were always happy to hear we had absolutely no steps for them.

The classes that Doug was teaching at Rutgers were three hours long. He had to be there an hour before to prepare and usually stayed an hour afterwards to talk to students, so when I was driving him, I had five hours to kill.

Talking to my son Greg on the phone one day, he suggested I should go into New York and have some fun with that time, instead of just waiting around. So sometimes I'd go into the city and listen to jazz.

Doug's teaching assistant from Turkey saw what I was doing and asked why we didn't just hire someone to drive him. The reason was I knew how to deal with Doug. No one else could really handle everything he needed. It was easier and less stress for me to do it myself.

Anyway, one time while Steve was working on his doctorate, we made plans to meet for dinner on Park Avenue. I had already dropped Doug off at Rutgers, so I was in the van.

The restaurant was on Park Avenue and 20th Street. I parked on the north side of 20th Street, facing east. The passenger side of the car was toward the passing traffic. I was in the van, digging in my purse for quarters to put in the meter. I must have accidentally hit the button for the sliding door and the ramp, because, all of a sudden, the sliding door of the van opened up and the ramp came down. It hit the tail-end of a car that was going by.

I was so upset. I couldn't believe it. I went to talk to the man who was driving the car that got hit. I said, "I'm so sorry, this is the van for my husband who's disabled. I just dropped him off. I'd really rather not go through my insurance company, so can you just get an estimate and send it to me? I promise I'll take care of it."

I gave him my personal card, which I always carried and he said that it was all right. The damage to his car, which was a Blazer, was minor, so he agreed to avoid the insurance company.

He was so nice. Later, he got me an estimate, which seemed sort of high to me. So he went and got another estimate, which was $300 less. I sent him a check, of course.

Anyway, after all this excitement, I walked over to the restaurant. I was still shook up, so I went to the bar and ordered a glass of cabernet. As I was sitting there, looking around, I saw a man in a wheelchair and I thought, *Gee, that looks like John Hockenberry.* His photo was on the front page of his book, which I had read.

Then Steve showed up. They gave us a table upstairs, where we had a very nice three-course meal. When we came back downstairs, I asked the waiter if that man was, in fact, John Hockenberry.

He said, "Yes, it sure is."

In case you're not familiar with him, John was a reporter for Dateline NBC. He won four Emmy Awards and three Peabody Awards. He's also a prominent figure in the disability rights movement.

He was paralyzed in a car crash at the age of 19, which left him paraplegic from the chest down, like Doug. He had been hitch-hiking with a friend, when two girls picked them up. The girls hadn't slept all night and got into an accident. His life was changed ever after.

He's a fascinating guy. I loved his book, *Moving Violations*, which is a collection of short stories about his life. So I went over to meet him.

He was sitting with three other people. I introduced myself, "Hello, I'm Sylvia Carroll. My husband, Doug Carroll, is paraplegic. Are you John Hockenberry?"

He was very gracious. He said, "Yes, I am and this is my wife and these are my friends. We're celebrating the 19th anniversary of my accident. 19 years being paralyzed."

I knew John had started school majoring in math, so I said, "This is my son Steve, he's working on a doctorate in mathematical ecology and evolution at Stony Brook."

Then we chatted a bit. It was really neat that I got to meet him, especially after the crazy accident I had just had with that van. It was nice to let him know how much I appreciated his work.

Chapter 54

In our modern world, where we're so connected to everything 24 hours a day with cell phones, tablets, computers and so on, it's hard to remember that once answering machines were a big, new thing. It was in the late 70s and early 80s that they started becoming popular in people's homes.

After Doug's accident, when we were in our new house in Warren, once in a while someone would tell me, "Oh, I'm going to call you tomorrow."

It might be someone I was going out with, or a nurse, or a tradesperson, but, since I was out doing things most of the time, I would say, "Okay, what time are you going to call?"

Then I would expect people to call when they said they would. It was very frustrating to rush home to be there for a call…and then it wouldn't come. So one summer, when both my sons happened to be in Europe, I thought to myself, *I'm going to get an answering machine. I'm tired of racing home for a call and then the person doesn't phone when they're supposed to.*

Once I got the answering machine, I just loved it. It was so convenient. Still, I was always afraid one of my friends would say something inappropriate that would get recorded and heard by someone else in the family. Fortunately, they never did. My friends were discreet, which was good. I didn't want my sons to hear anything like that.

My whole family was dealing with a difficult situation and under a lot of stress every day, so we had to try to be sensitive to each other's feelings. The first three years after Doug's accident were the most difficult for all of us. At times Doug would get very upset and he'd yell in anger. It was easy for me to feel whatever he was yelling about was all my fault.

Doug was very frustrated with his situation. For some reason, I would take responsibility for his feelings and take it out on myself. I talked to a couple of psychologists about it and finally learned not to do that.

I realized I didn't need to feel responsible for all this difficulty we were in. In fact, if you thought about it, following my advice that fateful afternoon at Mont-Tremblant would have avoided it all. Maybe Doug felt responsible and that got him down.

It was funny. All of Doug's life, his father wouldn't let Doug do anything dangerous, like play football in high school. He was always afraid Doug would have an accident. Maybe that was some kind of premonition.

Doug was accident-prone. He was tall, 6'4", and a little uncoordinated. He wasn't an athlete by any means. He wasn't overweight, but he had a large frame. He got that from his mother. She was big-boned. His father was smaller-boned.

Anyway, whatever the cause, I discovered that when Doug got in a bad mood, I should just walk out of his room, close the door and let him work it out for himself. That was the only way to handle it.

Sometimes we might have fights or the problem might be as simple as that he'd dropped something on the floor and was upset that he couldn't reach it. He had reachers to do that, but sometimes they didn't extend far enough.

People in wheelchairs use these reachers a lot. They're about two feet long with pincher claws on one end and a handle on the other with a squeeze control to close the pinchers. They help disabled people extend their ability to pick things up without moving too much.

Doug was normally settled into the king size bed in the master bedroom of our home. At first, I slept in there too, but eventually I moved to my own bedroom on the other side of the house, where the boys had their bedrooms.

The problem was Doug would work all night in bed, sometimes blasting the TV the whole time. I don't know how he could work. I sure couldn't get any sleep there.

Looking back, I would say Doug had problems with depression too. Even though he took a lot of pills, he never took anything for depression that I know of. He did take Valium to prevent spasms in his legs, which helped him sleep at night, when he did sleep.

You would never know it from the happy holiday letters Doug wrote, but every Christmas he would turn into kind of a Scrooge. He didn't like the holidays. Actually, he was always sort of like that. I guess he got worse as time went on.

Our yearly holiday letters generally just went into the upbeat highlights of our household, but behind the scenes, there were a lot of medical issues we had to deal with all the time.

There were always lots of nurses coming and going in our home. One time in our early years in Warren, one of the nurses from Overlook Hospital said to me, "Oh, you must be so stressed out with all this."

226

I just said to her, "Oh, no, I'm fine. I belong to a massage group and I have a lot of friends, so it's all okay."

Doug's great escape was his work. In his office at Rutgers, for many years Doug had a very good secretary from the beginning. She was with him for a long time. He was very nice to her. He would take her out to lunch. Sometimes he would even take her, her husband, and me out to dinner, which is unusual for a boss to do.

Whenever we traveled, he always brought her back a really nice present. He would also talk to her at home on the phone in long conversations. Sometimes it sounded like she was his girlfriend, the way they went on. Anyone coming in the room would have thought it was an intimate conversation, but I wasn't jealous. He was just being nice.

Then one time he was in a rehab facility recovering after a surgery for the decubitus ulcer on his buttocks. He had to be in rehab for three months, while it healed, and stay on a special Clinitron bed.

Every time he went into the hospital or rehab, they would order a Clinitron bed for him. They use these beds in hospitals for people who are paralyzed. It was a very expensive piece of medical equipment, which cost about $40,000. It ran on electricity and had glass beads in it, which rotated all the time. The motion and controlled temperature were supposed to help prevent decubitus ulcers.

It would take a while for the company to come set up the Clinitron bed. Doug always had to have a special room to stay in, because the bed's motor would make noise. Other patients would get upset, so they had to isolate him.

So, anyway there was Doug, stuck in his Clinitron bed, when one Saturday morning his secretary and her husband came in to see him. Lo and behold, she gave her notice that she was resigning.

Her daughter had had a baby and she had decided she didn't want to work any more. She wanted to help take care of the baby. Now that's what I call a very conventional woman, very traditional.

I think her husband worshipped her, by the way. They had all these little pet names for each other. I, however, thought it was really mean, to leave Doug in the lurch when he couldn't even go into the office to see what was happening. I was really angry when I heard what she had done.

Now Doug had to hire a new secretary, but he couldn't even interview anyone while he was in rehab. Finally, he did find a lady, who turned out to be pretty nice. She was a lot younger than his first secretary and maybe more appreciative. She gave Doug a pen set one year as a Christmas present.

Good help is hard to find…and good to find.

Chapter 55

My son Steve once wrote an essay for his school health class. It was five pages long and he got an A+ on it. It was about his dad's accident and about his family's life. His teacher didn't know his father was paraplegic until she read his paper.

My kids never talked to anyone about it. Even when Greg's counselor in middle school came to our house, he didn't find out until he got there. The boys couldn't go around to all their teachers and say, "Oh, my father had an accident and he's in a wheelchair." That just doesn't work. If I met people, I would tell them pretty soon that my husband was paraplegic, but the boys didn't do that.

So in his essay, Steve was describing how, when I went away on vacation I would be a different kind of person. He said I was happiest when I traveled. I wasn't happy most of the time, but when I traveled, I was. It was true.

Some people just come alive when they travel and I've always been that kind of person. Travel took me away from the stressful situation at home. Steve enjoyed traveling too. I took him with me a number of times.

So the comment the teacher wrote on his paper was, "How awful." She was referring to how awful our situation was for Steve to grow up in. With Doug being paralyzed, it was indeed difficult. Most of the time I felt an overwhelming responsibility in my life…but our life wasn't "awful." We found ways to make it happy and fulfilling.

I'm not the typical person. If I was, I wouldn't have been able to do what I did and I wouldn't have led the life I did. I have no complaints, especially now that I don't have any stress any more. Sure, you always have a little worry about one thing or another, but my life now is so much easier than it used to be.

From the outside, everything looked hunky-dory at our house. You had to be in it to really understand the difficulty. Aside from all the terrible medical problems, we had a good life. Many people who have emotional problems or mental problems are probably much more miserable than we were.

Doug was amazing. He would never give up. He just got lost in his work and he was happy there. In his brain, he wasn't disabled. He would say, "All I need is a new body."

Now that I'm living in a relaxed situation with no stress, I can see how my whole earlier life, including the way I grew up and many of the things that happened along the way...all made it possible for me to deal with the situation fate dealt me.

Sure, I drank a lot of liquor, especially at first. When I was up in Montreal, right after the accident, I started drinking. I couldn't believe this had happened. We had had such a good social life and family life.

Before Doug's accident, we both had careers and we had kids. With all that responsibility it's not easy, but we had a great life, which included socializing, traveling and so on.

After Doug's accident, we weren't invited to as many things. One of our friends had a boat and we couldn't do that, because Doug couldn't get in the boat. Some people didn't invite us into their homes anymore, because they weren't wheelchair accessible.

The accident affected our social life somewhat, but not a lot. It did affect all kinds of other things you would normally never even think about.

When I got home from taking Doug to work in the mini-van, I'd have two or three glasses of wine, just to relax after all the exertion. I used drinking as an escape...and it did help me get through.

Doug and I both went to parties and enjoyed drinking before the accident, but it escalated afterwards. I didn't know how else to deal with it. What was I going to do?

I had two little boys to raise. I wasn't working and I couldn't have, if I wanted to anyway, with all the new responsibilities I had. My job was now taking care of Doug and the kids.

I see that growing up as an only child of two parents, who were both very independent, helped me deal with the difficulty. Also, being extroverted, finding people, making friends, being social...it all helped.

I just met a guy yesterday at the beach, who said, "Oh, you're so easy to talk with. You're so nice."

I've heard that all my life. I always thought it was because I grew up in Miami, where everyone was friendly back then. Up north, people were always hustling and running off to work. They were more anxious, because of the weather and their careers.

My father was very happy go lucky. My mother was more responsible. I took after both of them. Mother missed her friends and parents from up north. She wasn't really happy in Miami, but he was.

So I see this pattern in my life. A friend from Bell Labs back then told me that, of all the women he knew, I was the best equipped to handle my situation. I thought, *No way. I like all kinds of things, but now I'm stuck at home. This should happen to a homebody. She would be home anyway.*

My life was more than just being stuck at home though. I helped Doug in his work a lot. One time he wrote a book with one of his colleagues, spending hours and hours working on it. When the book was finally finished, he was exhausted.

One of his colleagues at Rutgers was worried and told me, "Doug's not right. You ought to take him to the ER."

My son Steve had just walked in the door, coming home from a trip to Europe. I explained the situation to him and said, "Steve, I don't know what to do with Dad."

Steve very wisely said, "Mom, just let him sleep.'

That's what I did and eventually Doug was fine. He had just been tired. He would do that...work himself to exhaustion and then recover.

Because I had been in research myself, I understood his kind of work in academia. I guess I was a good person to deal with this after all, but I didn't feel that way at the time. It affected my whole personal life. I felt tied down, the very thing I had worried about during our wedding ceremony.

I did enjoy my family though. I always had everybody come for Thanksgiving dinner at our home. It would have been too complicated to take Doug out of the house and find a restaurant for all of us.

Doug would get up and join us for Thanksgiving dinner, one of the few times that would happen. Other times, other days, when family was visiting, I would make sure people went in and spent time with Doug in his bedroom.

After Greg got married, he started taking his family to Costa Rica for Christmas. That's why Thanksgiving became our family reunion time.

When we became grandparents, I'd take my grandson in and Doug would hold him. Another time our daughter-in-law's daughter was there and she played her flute for Doug. She had a music stand and sheet music. It was very impressive.

Every Thanksgiving, when we got together, we would also do a family photo for the holiday greeting card. One year, Doug had had surgery on a decubitus ulcer, so he wasn't allowed out of bed. That year, I had him

Photoshopped in with us. Walgreen's did it for me.

Doug couldn't be in the photo we took, but I couldn't send out 80 cards to his colleagues and our friends without him in it. They would all ask, "Well, where's Doug?"

He hadn't died, so I just got it done professionally. That's a great example of how our holiday letters didn't and couldn't show the whole picture of our real lives.

I also got a lot of inspiration over the years from certain individuals I admired, like Marianne Williamson. She's a spiritual teacher who wrote many books based on *A Course in Miracles*. I used to go to her lectures, when I lived in New Jersey.

One of the guys I used to date, David, introduced me to Marianne and used to take me to her lectures. When I lived in Irvine in 1973, she was living in Los Angeles and I went to some of her talks there.

She's very inspiring. She talks about how it's not what happens to you, but it's how you look at things that really matters. How you deal with what happens to you makes all the difference in life.

I went to one workshop she did with another man, Robert Thurman. He's the president of the Tibet House and a professor of Buddhism at Columbia University. He organized a trip, where he took 20 people to Bhutan for ten days, and gave lectures on Buddhism and did meditations.

I was talking to my son about it at the time and he said, "Mom that doesn't sound like your kind of trip. You like to go to a lot of different places, not just one and then come home."

He was right. I thought about going, but I'm glad I didn't. I wouldn't want to spend ten days in Bhutan. I spent four days there later on another tour. I wouldn't want to go that far without also seeing Tibet, Nepal, Bangkok, Dubai and all the other places I visited on this other trip.

I do admire Robert Thurman though. The workshop he and Marianne did was about dying. Most of the people there were health workers. I got to talk to him at breakfast one morning and I asked, "Do you really think there's anything after you die?"

He looked at me very deeply and said, "Yes, I do."

That was very meaningful to me, because he is a Buddhist spiritual leader. I believe he knows what he's talking about. I admire people like that. I like hearing their ideas and beliefs.

Chapter 56

In 1999, Doug and I both turned 60, just 18 days apart. I threw Doug a 60th birthday party at our house. Both Greg and Steve were there. Steve's best friend, Jay, even came too. We had 40 people altogether.

Of course, I couldn't make it a surprise party, because Doug had to be dressed and out of bed for it. When I told him what I was doing, he said he didn't want a lot of people. So 40 people was a small crowd for us.

Doug was still teaching at Rutgers. The school has three campuses, Newark, New Brunswick and Camden. Doug's office and his classes were in Newark. I would drive him there once a week, when he was teaching. They wanted his name on the faculty because he was famous, but he didn't have to teach that much.

Doug's contract was just to teach PhD students, but one semester in 1999, they asked him to teach an MBA course to undergraduates. Doug didn't like teaching MBA students, because he felt they didn't have a very good attitude.

MBA students weren't like PhD students, who were more academically oriented and in awe of their professor. The MBA kids just wanted to get their degrees, get out of there, and go make money. Their teacher was just a necessary means to that end.

One time after I dropped Doug off, I was still outside his door when an MBA student walked in to see him. He closed the door, but I could hear him out in the hallway. He was loudly demanding that he receive an A. He actually said, "I demand that I get an A!"

That's not the end of the story. The day of the final exam, Doug noticed this same student walking out of the test room with a girl during a break. After the break, they both came back in and continued taking the test.

When Doug graded their finals, he saw that they both had made exactly the same mistakes. In all his years of teaching, he had never seen that happen before. His colleagues told him he should turn them in, so he did.

As a result, they were told by the administration that they could either be suspended, or else just not receive credit for the course and retake it the following year. They chose the latter.

After the way I had heard that guy talking to Doug, I was afraid they might come to the house and shoot us, but nothing more came of it.

The year 2000 brought a whole new millennium, but our lives didn't change that much. We attended a Classification Society meeting in Montreal and got to see our old friends Al Bregman and wife, who had helped us so much after Doug's accident. That was nice.

Unfortunately though, we had to cancel a trip to Europe for meetings in Belgium and Denmark, because of a skin breakdown Doug had.

2000 was the year I did go to Russia on my own for a one-week tour. That's where I bought the chess set for my son Steve, which got stolen.

Hank and Debbie Gran visited us and we saw *Music Man*. He and Doug were best friends from Jacksonville. The Grans stayed at the Manhattan Club. They invited me over there and we were sitting around, having wine and cheese and crackers.

Then Debbie, Hank's wife, asked me, right in front of Hank, "Sylvia, why did you marry Doug instead of Hank?"

I was flabbergasted. Hank and I had had a few dates in college, but it was never anything serious. She was Hank's second wife. It seemed like a strange thing to ask and I didn't know what to say. All I could think of was, "Well, I met Doug first." Funny.

Whenever Hank would come to visit, Doug would generally ask for some private time with him. After they were alone, Doug would ask Hank if he was still religious. Hank would say yes and Doug would ask, "Why do you still believe all that?"

Hank was also a scientific guy. I guess Doug was trying to figure out why Hank would stay the way he always was, while Doug would change. They had gone to the same strict Southern Baptist church together. Doug had even been the youth pastor at the church one summer as a teenager.

Doug told me he went to church because he loved his mother and she wanted him to. His father didn't usually bother with church, except maybe once in a while a Unitarian one.

His father was disillusioned with religion. He had been brought up Catholic, but when he married Doug's mother, his own father disowned him. Catholics back then were very strict about marrying non-Catholics. All these people, arguing over God, it's crazy. I don't get it and Doug didn't either.

2001 was the year that really brought a lot of change, as everyone remembers. It touched us in many ways.

Steve had been doing his PhD dissertation in mathematical ecology,

234

while also working for an ecological consulting firm. All of a sudden, in January, 2001, with no warning, he very unexpectedly left his studies, his job and his apartment to just take off.

He had decided to drop out and reassess his life. He ended up in San Jose, Costa Rica, where he started backpacking through Central America for five months. During his travels, he met a beautiful Danish girl, Camilla. She was studying Spanish and working in a medical clinic in Antigua, Guatemala.

In June, Steve came back to the States to tell Doug and me about his new plan for his life. The first thing he said was, "I'm getting married."

Doug said, "Congratulations."

Meanwhile, I started shaking inside. When he was a student at Berkeley, Steve had told me he was never getting married. Then Steve said, "We're moving to San Francisco and I'm finishing my doctorate."

Camilla had already gone back to Sweden from Guatemala, before Steve came back to the States. In July, Steve flew to Copenhagen, to spend two months with her in Malmo, Sweden, which was about 20 minutes from Copenhagen.

Steve met her parents while he was over there and they liked him. Everyone always likes Steve. She was packing up her things and finding a new home for her cat. Then in early September, they flew out of Copenhagen on the same day, on different airlines, arriving about half an hour apart.

I went to pick them up at Newark Airport. As we were walking out of the airport terminal to my car, we had a great view of the World Trade Center.

I said, "Oh Camilla, look at that. That's my favorite building in New York. You should get Steve to take you there sometime."

When we got home, Doug joined us and we had my famous lasagna, salad, and garlic bread for a nice dinner in the dining room. The next day I took them both out for lunch in Warren.

The following day, Camilla got all dressed up in a beautiful black lace outfit. When I asked where they were going, she said, "Oh, Steve is taking me to Windows on the World in the World Trade Center for dinner." This was September 7, just four days before those buildings disappeared in rubble.

On September 11, I had plans to go with a friend, Bill, to Block Island, which is about an hour and a half ferryboat ride north of Montauk, on the other side of New York from us.

Bill came at 11 am to pick me up. He met my entire family, Doug, my two sons and Camilla, and then we left. We were going to go first to Montauk, on the tip of Long Island, where I had reserved a room. We wanted to spend the night there and then take the ferry the next morning to Block Island. He had reserved a place for us to stay overnight and then we'd come back home the following day.

On the trip to Long Island, we had to cross the Goethals bridge. We got there about noon, but the bridge was closed. All the bridges in the area were blocked because of the terrorist attack that morning. So we had lunch at a restaurant and ended up waiting there all day.

They wouldn't open the bridge that day. We even met the mayor, but he couldn't do anything about it. So we had dinner at the same restaurant, gave up, and came back home

When we got back to my house, I told my friend he could sleep over and we would go to the Jersey Shore at Sandy Hook the next day. I went in to see Doug and said, "Hey, where are Steve and Camilla?"

Doug said, "They left for California in Steve's car. I tried to talk them out of it, but they insisted on going today."

Well, they were headed in the opposite direction of the attack and there was nobody on the roads that day. They spent the night in Atlantic City and then went on. They left so suddenly because she was afraid. It was her first time in the States and a few days after she arrived, there was a terrorist attack.

Everybody remembers where they were on September 11, just like they do for the day Kennedy was assassinated. I was living in Germany that fateful day in 1963.

It was a Friday night and I had a date with an American, who was in the military. He was the one who told me the president had been shot. JFK hadn't died yet. I didn't find out he died till the next morning. Then my friend took me over to the base, where he worked. All the German waitresses were crying. They loved Kennedy.

Steve and Camilla got to San Francisco safely and were married on October 13, 2001.

Chapter 57

Doug took another sabbatical to California in 2001, to work on a couple of books and be a visiting professor at UC Irvine. It wasn't easy to move 3000 miles out there for six months, but we did it.

We lived in a small apartment there with two bedrooms. I was in one and he was in the other. Again, because of Doug's all-night work habits, we couldn't sleep in the same room. He was a night owl. His bedroom was his workplace, and I respected that.

Before we moved out to Irvine though, I laid down the law. We were going to be living in a small, two-bedroom place with just one bathroom. I wanted Doug to know, if he mistreated me, I would leave.

So I hired Joe again to come over and talk to Doug, to make sure he would promise not to yell at me or start any fights. I just couldn't put up with it in a small apartment like that. There was no place to go.

We made that agreement and everything worked out fine for those six months. I was glad I had it verbalized before we left. I needed Doug to know how I felt about living in small quarters with him.

That year we also attended a Classification Society of North America meeting in St. Louis, Missouri. When we were there, Doug was taking a taxi each day to the meeting. One day, as he was coming back, the cab driver told me, "He's bleeding."

Doug had had a skin breakdown and was bleeding right through his pants. Fortunately, it wasn't too serious and we got through that year without having another surgery.

One funny thing, while we were at a meeting at SUNY Stony Brook that year, we met Steve's advisor for the first time. His name was Lev. He immediately said to Doug, "I can certainly tell you're Steve's father."

People were always commenting on the resemblance between those two. We also met many of Steve's classmates and professors while we were there. They were glad to hear he was doing well.

Unfortunately though, after Steve and Camilla had lived together for six months in San Francisco, she left to go back to Copenhagen. She had dropped out of school before going to Central America and she wanted to get her high school degree.

Meanwhile, Steve decided to come back to New York to finish his doctorate. Camilla was going for a high school diploma, while Steve was going for a PhD. Maybe not the best match....

Once Camilla was back in Copenhagen for a few weeks, she emailed Steve to ask for a divorce. Three days later, Steve called me to tell me their marriage was over.

Getting a divorce turned out to be complicated, but it was an amiable. Since she was a Danish citizen, they had to do it through the Danish consulate.

Meanwhile, Doug's mother was ensconced in a retirement home. She had lost her husband a few years earlier. Now she was losing her memory. She would tell us, "I can't remember what I did today, but I had a good time doing it." She was sweet.

Meanwhile, I don't want you to think that Steve was the only one having lots of life adventures. Greg graduated from chiropractic school on December 17, 2002, but it was a bumpy road getting there.

Greg was two semesters away from graduating from Rutgers with a degree in Psychology, when he decided he wanted to go to Australia and New Zealand instead. Maybe my two sons got the travel bug from me, I don't know, but they sure had it.

Doug didn't approve of Greg's plans, of course, but he couldn't do much about it. Greg was of age and paying for his own education. When Doug realized Greg was serious, he said, "Well, if you're going to go, you might as well go to college while you're there."

That was Doug's idea, not Greg's, but Greg agreed and took off to spend a year in Australia. Then, one fine day, he called me about 9:00 in the morning and asked what I was doing.

I said, "I'm just getting up."

He said, "Well, you better sit down."

I said, "Oh, no, why? What's happening?"

"I'm back in New Jersey."

When Doug heard this, he went through the roof. He had paid $10,000 to send Greg to Butler University in Sydney to study psychology. But that's what he got for trying to control headstrong Greg.

After Greg finally settled down and got his Doctor of Chiropractic degree, he moved to Boca Raton in the beginning of 2003. He had a classmate, Javier, who was from there. They were going to start a practice together.

The whole thing was a very weird story. I happened to be in Florida for ten days at the time, visiting family and friends. On a beautiful Sunday, I was heading down to Key Largo, to see a friend. I had just

238

gotten onto the Florida Turnpike, when Greg called. He wanted me to turn around and come up to see him in Boca Raton. It was in the opposite direction.

I told him, "I'm on my way to Key Largo, Greg."

"Oh, but tonight is the only night I can see you."

I had been planning to see Greg Tuesday night. Now he was changing it. So I called my friend in Key Largo to adjust our plans. Fortunately, he was okay with it.

It was about 1:00 in the afternoon, so I told Greg, "Well, if I have to come up there tonight, at least I'm going to go to Haulover Beach this afternoon." I wanted to enjoy the clothing-optional beach in Miami, which I loved.

He said, "Fine, just come on up here for dinner."

So I left Haulover a few hours later, wearing casual shorts, with sand in my toes and an all-over tan. I had just started driving up I-95, when the heavens opened up and a torrent of rain came down. People couldn't see to drive. They were pulling over and stopping.

They do that a lot in Miami. You'd think they were in a blizzard. I'm used to driving in blizzards though, so I just kept on going, very slowly. It was scary, I admit. It's amazing how the tropical rain can be so blinding.

I finally arrived at the home of Javier's father, where Greg and Javier were staying. I told my son I wanted to take a shower and change my clothes for dinner. He showed me where the bathroom was, then I got cleaned up, and put on a nice outfit.

When I opened the door to come out, there was Javier's father. I didn't know who he was and I guess he didn't know me, so we just stood there for a moment, sizing each other up. Then Javier arrived and introduced us. His father seemed very strange to me.

I don't think he was emotionally all there. His wife had died a few years earlier, so maybe that affected him. He had a girlfriend now, who lived in Austin, Texas. He was planning to sell that house and go live with her.

So, I went out to dinner that night with Greg and guess what. Somehow he talked me into the idea that Doug and I should lend him $25,000 to start their new practice. That's what was so urgent. Like a good mother, I agreed to it, with Doug's approval.

That night Greg let me sleep in his bedroom, while he took the couch in the living room. The next morning, I needed coffee, so I went out to the kitchen. I was in my nightgown and my hair was a fright, as usual in the morning.

There in the kitchen was Javier's father. He started talking to me, so it was too late. I couldn't go back and get myself fixed up. I just stood there drinking coffee and trying to converse with him.

In the course of our conversation, I said, "I'm going back to Miami today."

He said, "You're going to drive down there by yourself?"

I answered, "How do you think I got here? I drove up yesterday in that terrible rainstorm."

He seemed to be afraid of everything. That's the kind of guy he was. He did eventually leave and move in with his girlfriend in Austin. It turned out that, in spite of his lovely house in Boca, Javier's father was totally broke.

So Doug and I were the ones who lent these two guys the money to set up their practice. Without us, they wouldn't have had one. In retrospect, it was a foolish thing to do...but it all worked out.

Chapter 58

When Doug and I loaned Greg that $25,000, we did it right. I had a lawyer write up our loan agreement with a payment schedule and interest included. I'm glad I did.

Shortly after we turned the money over to them, Greg found out Javier was doing drugs. As we saw at Colorado University, that was a definite no-no for Greg, so he just up and took off for Costa Rica, leaving the whole practice to Javier.

We had really loaned them the money for Greg's sake, but when he left, it was now Javier's responsibility to pay us back. He was the one who owned the practice.

I think Greg had suspected all along that Javier was doing drugs, but once they started working together, it became clear he couldn't deal with it any longer. That was actually a good thing in the long run.

Greg had passed his boards, so he could practice anywhere in the U.S. He had heard Steve and me talk about how great Costa Rica was from a trip we had taken down there. He had also heard about other chiropractors who were practicing there. You didn't even have to have a license, but you did have to have a work permit.

I think Greg also liked the Latin women. He's a blonde and, for him, opposites attract. I recently came across his high school prom picture. His date back then had long dark hair. Even Javier told me that Costa Rica would be great for Greg, because he liked Hispanic women. Javier knew what Greg liked.

After he got down to Costa Rica, Greg asked me go to the Costa Rican consulate in the financial district of New York, to get papers he needed to work down there. Greg was always asking me to help him. That's why I'm glad he has a wife now. She can do it, instead of me. Before he had a wife, I was always hearing, "You have to do this, you have to do that, and so on."

Greg happened to know an American fellow from Virginia, who had a practice down there in San Jose. Greg partnered up with him, to start a second practice. They opened a chiropractic clinic in Escuzu, the elite area of San Jose, where a lot of Americans live.

While Greg was living and working down there, his apartment got robbed. He had just moved into a new place near his practice, which didn't have bars on the windows yet. That is kind of necessary there.

He had just gotten his security deposit back from his previous apartment, so he had at least $500 in cash on a table. The thieves took that, plus his beautiful leather jacket. When he came home for Christmas, he had no jacket to wear. We had to immediately go to a department store and get him one.

Meanwhile, the whole time he was down there, Greg was trying to get Javier to pay us back the money we had loaned them. We were on good terms with him though.

One time I went to visit Javier, he had a new girlfriend, who later became his wife. She had grown up in Boca and did skincare. He had grown up there also. Everyone knew everyone else and Javier was a success story. The newspaper even did an article about the hometown boy who came back and became a big chiropractor in town.

Javier invited me to dinner that time, but then his girlfriend told me he was very sorry, he couldn't take me out after all. He had to go to a fancy black-tie event with some big lawyers. Chiropractors are always working with lawyers.

She said I could go with them to the event, but I really didn't want to. I was kind of irritated that I didn't even hear this from him. My relationship with Javier was crazy, but then, many things in my life are crazy.

Whenever I came to Miami, Javier would invite me over to his house. It was a million-dollar home on the Intracoastal Waterway in Lighthouse Point, which is a very expensive area.

When I was in Florida, I would call Javier. I had a good rapport with him. Javier was a big spender and he was very nice to me. Once he invited me over for cocktails and then took me out to dinner.

He had a yacht, which he took me on with his wife. We went to Cap's Place. It's a famous seafood restaurant on an island near Lighthouse Point. You can only get there by boat.

In spite of everything, I thought he was a good guy. I was like a mother to Javier. In fact, I would tell people I had a third son now. I was actually very proud of him.

One time he was out on his yacht and a little boy fell off someone else's yacht. He jumped in and saved the little boy's life. The story was on the front page of the local newspaper.

Javier would also have me come visit his practice. He had a massage therapist on staff. When I went there, he would always ask, "Would you like a massage today?"

So I would always say, "Sure, that would be great."

I'd get the massage and then he would introduce me to everyone. He'd say to his people, "Without Sylvia, I would not be here today." That made me feel good.

Finally, one time when I was down in Florida, Javier drove down from Boca to my motel in Miami, to pick me up and take me to dinner. After dinner, he said, "Sylvia, please figure out how much money I owe you, because I want to pay you off now."

And that's exactly what he did. He actually paid us in full earlier than the terms of our agreement. Greg was happy about that and I was too.

At that time, his wife told me that he had been on drugs, but that he had been to rehab and was doing well. She was nice looking and they had two beautiful sons. Javier actually went to rehab twice. He still kept the business going though. He expanded to three clinics and even had an MD working for him at one point.

Then, one Christmas, he and his wife threw a party on December 22nd. After the party, he took a gun he owned and went outside, high on something evidently.

He started walking down the street and went into an apartment complex. He knocked on somebody's door. Nobody would open it, so he went across the street. I don't know what was in his mind, but he started shooting at the Lighthouse, Florida, police station. Not smart.

A cop came out of there and returned fire. He shot Javier four times in the torso. Javier ended up needing four surgeries to recover. After that, he went to jail. He's still alive, but his wife divorced him and took their two little boys. It was terrible.

Meanwhile, Greg ended up staying down in Costa Rica for two years. He met a girl down there. One day he called me and said, 'Mom, I have a girlfriend…and she has a daughter."

I had always seen Greg as kind of self-centered. I told him I was surprised he was willing to take on the responsibility of a little girl who wasn't even his, but he just said, "You can't plan these things, Mom."

It's true. Love changes everything. It can put you in all kinds of situations you didn't expect. My life surely proves that.

I went to visit Greg in Costa Rica, the second year he was there, to meet his new girlfriend and her baby girl. We all three went to Jaco for the week-end. It was a nice way to get to know her.

243

On the way home, I met her parents. Her father was real friendly, showing me photos, while I showed them pictures of my family too. They did not speak English, so I used my little Spanish and Greg was impressed.

Then sometime after I returned to the States, around 11:30 one Saturday morning, I was getting ready to go to a party in Philadelphia, when the phone rang. It was Greg. He said, "Mom, what are you doing?"

I said, "I'm getting ready to go out of town."

"Oh," he said, "Okay, I guess you don't have time to talk then. We'll just talk tomorrow." And that was it.

The next morning I called home, to check my messages and see how Doug was doing. My answering machine was blowing up. Maria, Greg's girlfriend, had left a frantic message, crying, "Do you know where Greg is? I can't find him."

I called Doug and he said Maria had just called him as well. We didn't know anything. She just kept calling and calling, in tears, "Where is he, what's going on?" It was a mess.

When I got home from Philadelphia about 7:00 that evening...surprise! Greg was in the kitchen of my house, with all his luggage. He never told me he was coming. He just showed up. I was in a total state of shock.

Greg hadn't told anybody what he was doing. He just left his business, his girlfriend, everything. Later he told me his partner had already left also and gone back to the States. If Greg had stayed there by himself, he would have gone under, so he just decided to cut his losses.

He felt that, if he had told Maria he was leaving, she would have tried to stop him. He didn't want anyone interfering with what he felt he had to do. He wasn't going to talk about it or have anybody try to talk him out of it. He's hard-headed. When he makes up his mind, that's it.

Still, it was a big mess. Greg had left his car at the airport in San Jose with the keys inside. Later, he told Maria where to find it. She retrieved it and he signed the title over to her. She eventually sold it. Eventually, Greg did go back to Costa Rica for her and they got married at her home.

Meanwhile, Greg had three offers for positions in the States. One was in Arlington, Virginia; one was in Arkansas; and one was in Columbus, Ohio.

The offer in Columbus was from two guys he had gone to chiropractic school with, so he went there. He felt it would be a good place to raise a family. He stayed there for eleven years and did very well.

Chapter 59

When I think about my life with Doug after the accident, it was truly amazing all we accomplished together, considering all we had to deal with.

Our trip to Costa Rica was a good example. Doug had had to cancel a couple of trips in 2002, because of skin breakdowns. So when he got better, I said to him, "If you could go anywhere in the world, where would you like to go?"

He said Costa Rica. Since Greg was living down there, it was a natural. Doug and I decided to go down there in early September. We flew back Sept. 11, the one-year anniversary of the World Trade Center attack.

I had made the reservation without thinking about the date. When I realized it, I was concerned that something might happen. Doug said, no problem that was the safest day to fly back, because the security would be so tight.

I arranged to get a wheelchair-accessible van with a driver for us, while we were down there. He was a Japanese fellow from Chicago, who had recently married a wonderful woman from Nicaragua. They were going to shepherd us around for a week.

When we got on the plane to go, we had coach seats, but Doug couldn't get his wheelchair into coach. That was often a problem, just getting on and off planes and getting him down the aisle. They had to seat Doug in first class, where the aisle was wider.

I said, "Don't worry about me. I'm fine in coach."

My first priority was always Doug. Believe it or not, his pillow was another issue. When he was in the wheelchair or sitting up, he always kept one behind his head. Since he had broken his neck in the accident, his neck always gave him problems. The pillow helped with that.

He actually had three or four pillows back there when he was on an airplane, but eventually one would always fall down. Then he would start yelling for help, almost screaming, in fact. I or someone else would have to go over and readjust it.

By the time we got to Costa Rica, Doug was in so much pain, it was unbearable. Our Japanese driver and his wife picked us up and they could tell he was in bad shape.

They took us to the Holiday Inn and that was it for the day. Doug and

I had one room. I gave him the bed, of course, and ordered a rollaway bed for me.

That night Doug wouldn't stop talking. I couldn't sleep. We had a big fight over it. I threatened to get a room for myself, but he wouldn't let me leave. What a night.

The next day he was better and wanted to take a tour. When the driver came over, he was surprised. He said, "After I saw the condition your husband was in yesterday, I never thought you two would want to do anything today."

Doug was tough. Even though something was always going wrong, we just did our best to fix it and keep moving forward. Some of the things we did on that trip were to take an aerial tramline through the rain forest and a boat trip on the Tortuguero River in the National Park.

The resort where we stayed at the National Park was not wheelchair-accessible. Doug was able to get into the restaurant to have lunch, but when we took him to our room, they had to put an extra mattress on the bed. That was necessary, to make it the proper height for him to be able to transfer from his wheelchair onto the bed.

This was all part of being paraplegic. We were always having to change things around. The rest of the resort grounds were really not accessible, so Doug got some much-needed sleep. He was also reading a book on coral calcium that Greg had given him.

Greg came with us when we went to the aerial tram. While we were all together, Doug and Greg got into an argument. Doug told Greg that I had just bought myself a Jaguar. Greg was shocked, because he thought that must be a lot of money.

Actually, it was just the X-Type that came out in 2001. It was a lower-priced Jaguar, around $30,000, no more expensive than any other new nice car. Steve had thought it would be good for me and I liked it.

I hadn't told Greg, but Doug just had to tell him and get him riled up. So then Doug followed that up by declaring that all cars look the same anyway. Greg, of course, disagreed, so then they got into a big debate over that.

Their next argument was over sharks. Doug said they don't bite and Greg said, of course, they do. They went on about that as well.

This whole time, I was just sitting there wondering, *Is this a real conversation?* I guess it was just a father and son marking their territory.

To show you the dynamic between those two, once Greg drove all the way to Pennsylvania to buy a lottery ticket. He was excited about it and all the money he might win. When he came home, he went into his father's room and told him what he had done. He forgot he was talking to a world-famous statistician.

Doug said, "Do you know what your chances are?"

Greg said, "At least I have a chance."

Greg always liked having money and nice things. When he was growing up, there was a boy who lived down the street. His parents weren't that educated. The boy's father owned a body shop. I guess they had money, because they were always giving their kids expensive presents.

Greg would see this and ask for the same things his friend was getting, but we would just say, "We don't care what he got. We're not giving that to you." So Greg grew up determined to make his own money, so he could have what he wanted.

On that same trip to Costa Rica, the three of us went to some kind of zoo. They had sidewalks, so you could go around and see everything. Greg was pushing Doug's wheelchair. Greg's a big guy, over 6'2" and he works out, but it was still difficult. He did a great job showing Doug around. In spite of their differences, they really loved each other.

That night, I walked down to the beach to watch the green turtles hatch. That was amazing, to see all those little creatures scurrying for the ocean.

The guide had an infrared light, so we could watch them without bothering them. It wasn't wheelchair-accessible, of course. You can't put a wheelchair on the sand at all.

The next day, early in the morning, I took a boat for a little ride. After that, Doug and I did a lot of sightseeing on the rest of our trip. Costa Rica is a truly beautiful place.

I am a pioneer. I do all these things that many people are afraid of. I often do them before most people do. Greg is similar. He says he does everything one time. He even went hang-gliding, when he was in New Zealand. Now that's one thing I would never do. It's suicidal to me.

There was a nude beach in La Jolla, when we lived out there. They had hang-gliding up above that beach, where people took off from high cliffs overlooking the ocean.

The only problem was, if the wind hit just right, they would be blown right back onto the rock face and die. It happened all the time, but people still kept doing it.

Chapter 60

In 2004, Doug and I both turned 65, another milestone in our lives. I chose to celebrate my birthday by going on a 10-day tour to Guatemala and Honduras that would coincide with my big day. It was a wonderful birthday present to myself.

The guide for our trip was a woman from Algiers, who was married to a Guatemalan man. Her name was Virginia. At the beginning of our tour, she had some questions she asked us, to gather information about the group.

One of the questions was if we were celebrating something special during the trip. So I wrote down that it was going to be my 65th birthday. I didn't care if everyone knew my age.

Of everyone on that tour, I gained the reputation of being the one who had to go out every night. When I arrived at our initial gathering point, the Hyatt Tikal Hotel, in Guatemala City about 11:00 on a Friday night, I asked Virginia where was a good place to go the following night.

She said, "Oh, no, you can't go out here. It's not safe." That didn't sit well with me.

The next day, Virginia had us out touring and sight-seeing till about 2:00 in the afternoon. Then we went back to the hotel. There were two single men on this trip. One was older than me and one was younger. So I asked each of them if they'd like to go out. They both said no.

That didn't stop me. I had my travel guidebook, so I looked up what it recommended for nightlife. I saw an area called Zona Viva. It was supposed to be an affluent district with a lot of bars, restaurants, hotels, discothèques, and shopping.

So, I went down to the doormen and asked if I could get a taxi over there. Another doorman, who was just getting off duty, overhead me and said, "Oh, I'll give you a ride down there. In fact, if you don't mind, I'd like to go with you."

That made me a little nervous, so I responded, "Well, let me check with my tour operator first." Then I went to find Virginia.

She just laughed and said, "Oh, no problem, he's fine."

Unfortunately though, by the time I got back to the desk, he had disappeared. So I just got a taxi to go there. Because I was still nervous about the whole thing, I asked the taxi driver to come back and get me in an hour and a half.

Once he dropped me off, I walked around a little and then went into a bar/restaurant where they had live music. A nice Guatemalan man there asked me if I'd like to go back to his apartment. Right off the bat, he just propositioned me!

I laughed and said, "Oh, no I can't do that."

So he said, "Well, how about having lunch next Tuesday?" He was persistent.

I just answered, "Sorry, I won't be here, but thanks anyway."

Then I met another guy, from Santiago, Chile, which I had visited before. I liked him and we danced together until the taxi driver showed up on time to get me. Then I went back to the hotel, my virtue still intact.

The next morning I went in to breakfast and everyone was asking, "Oh, how was it?"

Somehow they had all found out that I was out gallivanting by myself. I'll tell you, a lot of people on that tour started living vicariously through me.

As brave as I was though, there were still some places where you really couldn't go out at all. I wasn't crazy. I would always ask first.

When we got to Copan in Honduras, it was the day before my birthday. I went up to the reception area of the hotel and asked, "How do I get into the center of town?"

They said, "Oh, we have a van that can take you."

Virginia was walking by just then and she came over. "Sylvia, aren't you tired?"

"No," I said," I'm not tired. I want to go out." I only had one more night to be 64!

So that night I took the hotel van into town and met some really nice people. I told one man there that the next day was my birthday and he bought me a drink. Then I met a couple from England and also told them I was celebrating my birthday the next day. They said, "Oh, please, come back, we want to celebrate with you!"

I got back to the hotel safely, all primed for my big day, January 21. The next morning, everybody was asking me, as usual, about my previous night's adventures. Our schedule for the day was to go into town and take a tour of the ruins there, then have a nice lunch among them.

As we were having lunch, I was sitting with five other people and suddenly everybody started singing "Happy Birthday."

I blushed a nice, deep pink. Then they all stopped. I was usually so adventurous, that they never expected my reaction. Everybody was laughing. They couldn't believe that gutsy, bold, little Sylvia would be embarrassed by people singing *Happy Birthday*.

Then Virginia came over and gave me some earrings and a little doll. It was really sweet. I never expected them to throw me a birthday party right in the ruins there. It was definitely a surprise.

After lunch, we were supposed to go to a museum. I had already seen it before though. I really didn't want to go to the museum again. Then the younger single man on our tour, who was from Vancouver, came up to me and said, "Sylvia, how would you like to go out for a beer now?"

I said, "Great!" It seemed like a nice way to finish the day.

We all climbed back on the bus to go to the hotel. Once we were on, Virginia had an announcement. She said, "Now when we get off the bus back at the hotel, I want everyone to follow me. I need to talk to you about something."

I thought to myself, *What is this? That's strange. She's always talking to us on the microphone anyway...why not just do that?*

Anyway, when we got back, she led us through the hotel lobby, past the bar, to an outside patio area. Another surprise!

They had a whole private piñata party set up there for me, to complete the day's celebration. I ended up breaking the stick instead of the piñata. But it was a fantastic birthday and a great way for me to turn 65.

Later on, I picked up all my birthday messages from the hotel. I didn't get to talk to any of the callers, because I wasn't there when they called, but I was touched that they had reached out to me, all the way down in Guatemala.

Doug had called and left a Happy Birthday message. Greg, who was still living in Costa Rica at the time, also called. Plus, another good friend from the U.S. left a message. It was lovely.

My friends tell me I have the richest, most interesting life of anyone they know. They support me and give me a lot of credit for all I've done...and continue to do.

Those are the kinds of friends you need in life.

Chapter 61

As time went on, Doug's various disabilities were escalating...and so were the procedures he had to go through in order to keep working.

In 2004, his decubitus ulcer had become so serious, we had to cancel a trip to Chicago in July. In order to deal with the situation, he eventually had to go through a type of plastic surgery called a "flap surgery."

This is generally one of the last and most serious options in trying to heal a decubitus ulcer. It involved his plastic surgeon first removing the necrotic, or dead, tissue from the wound. Then he had to separate and pull skin from the surrounding area over the wound to cover it and hopefully heal it.

After that surgery, Doug had to once again spend a lot of time in bed recuperating. He was going to do it at home, since we now had our own Clinitron bed set up in his bedroom.

We had gotten the bed some time before. It was recommended to us, to help prevent the decubitus ulcers. Even though Doug used it, the ulcers still kept getting worse. That was why he needed the flap surgery again.

Doug continued teaching that semester, from September through December, while he recuperated. He couldn't sit up in his wheelchair, so he taught his students right there in our home, from his Clinitron bed in his bedroom.

Doug had this three-hour class once every week. His teaching assistant at the time was an Indian man, who had a three-year old son. His wife had just had another baby and she didn't feel she could take care of both kids at the same time, so she told him he had to bring their toddler with him to our house.

Every week, the teaching assistant would arrive with his little boy, then go into the bedroom to set up an overhead projector and screen. That was what Doug used to display his notes and teach the class.

Meanwhile, I was the designated baby sitter for his little boy. He was really hyper. Between the extra time before class and after class, the TA and the students were actually at our house for about five hours, which I had to fill, to keep this little boy occupied.

There were no sidewalks in our neighborhood. If the weather wasn't too bad, I would take him for walks. I had an ulterior motive for that. I wanted to try to make sure he didn't break anything in our house.

During these five hours, I also had to go out and buy pizza for the class for everyone to eat on their break. I had to time this so that the pizza would still be warm when they were ready.

I tell you, by the end of the day, when they all left, I was a wreck. I always needed a couple of glasses of wine to calm down and relax. What an ordeal.

But that was our life.

Around this time in 2004, there was one bright spot. I got to meet Christopher Reeve. I had read his book about how he dealt with his accident, which rendered him quadriplegic, and really enjoyed it.

I met him up in Williamstown, Massachusetts. I was there with a lawyer friend for the weekend. I had asked about a really good place for dinner and was told to try Main Street Restaurant.

This was a Saturday night and we didn't make a reservation, so when we got there, we couldn't get a table. We just ate at the bar instead.

About three barstools away from us, there was a young woman sitting alone. This little boy kept running up to her and then scampering back around the corner into another room.

Then something came on TV about the movie *Rear Window*. So this girl started talking to me about it. She told me she was one of the nurses for Christopher Reeve and that he was right around the corner having dinner with his wife Dana. Christopher was starring in a new movie, a re-make of *Rear Window*, in which he played a quadriplegic.

So I said, "Oh, I'd like to meet him. Do you think I can go in there?"

She said, "Well, after he finishes his dinner, it would be okay."

So we finished ours and then I just walked in there. He was sitting at a table in the back with his wife. I went up and said, "Hello, Mr. Reeve, I'm Sylvia Carroll and my husband, Doug Carroll is paraplegic. He teaches at Rutgers University, but he's recovering from a decubitus ulcer surgery right now."

Christopher was very gracious. He said, "Nice to meet you, Sylvia, please tell Doug I wish him a speedy recovery, so he can get back to teaching."

He was a true gentleman who inspired a lot of people. He will be missed.

Meanwhile, at our house, the complications kept coming. It was also in 2004, that we had to get Doug some mechanical assistance to get in and out of bed.

Doug was a big guy. Nobody could ever lift him on their own.

Paraplegics like him generally use a sliding board, if they have the use of their arms and are strong enough.

Doug had done that in the early years after his accident, but now he needed help. As he got older and weaker, he wasn't physically able to use the sliding board any more to transfer himself from the bed.

One of the other reasons we had to do something was because of Doug's skin problems. They were so serious now, the sliding board would make things worse.

Even with his pants and underwear on, moving across that board created a lot of friction. The rubbing against his skin would cause a skin break-down. We needed something to avoid that.

A Hoyer Lift was the solution we turned to. It made it much easier to transfer Doug from his bed to his wheelchair. It was a hydraulic lift with a fabric sling that went under his hips. We had to roll him back and forth enough to get that sling under his buttocks. Once we did, it created a kind of basket for him to sit in.

When Doug was positioned in the sling, you had to use a pump on the Lift to actually raise him up off the bed. Ours had a manual pump. They also made an electric-powered one, but we just used the manual one.

When you engaged that pump, it raised him off the bed. Then you could swing him over to where his wheelchair was, next to the bed, and lower him into it.

We had never used a Hoyer Lift before that, but Doug needed it during the last seven years before he died. We started with it after our first live-in health aide, Arunas, came on board with us.

Arunas was a skier and very strong,. He was only 37, very healthy, and worked out a lot. He was in good shape, but the Lift was still necessary, even for him.

Over the years, we had had many different health aides. At first, I would just hire someone for so many hours a day. I always needed some assistance, especially the last 15 years or so. By the last seven years though, we needed live-in help, 24/7. I wouldn't have been able to go anywhere without someone I could trust.

Arunas was with us for a year and a half. Then we had another live-in, Inga, who was only with us for about six months. Those were a terrible six months. We found out she was on drugs. Then our final live-in, Tammy, was with us for five years. She was great and we are still friends today.

I wouldn't have made it without them.

Chapter 62

We had a financial advisor, Bruce Tucker, who also sold life insurance. About ten years after the accident, when Doug was 50, Bruce had recommended we try to get long-term care insurance, so we applied. Bruce even came over to our house and helped us fill out the forms.

I wanted to get it mainly for Doug's situation. They don't usually give it to people with a spinal cord injury, so we both applied, hoping that would help us get it for him.

Bruce helped. He fought like mad to get us covered. He wrote about how we traveled all over the world and how, even though Doug was paraplegic, nothing stopped him. Lo and behold, we both got the coverage.

What they gave Doug at first was just for a nursing home facility, extending an indefinite period of time...forever, basically. What they gave me covered both nursing home and home healthcare, but it was just for four years. Usually, when a person goes into a nursing home, they don't live more than four years. That was the rationale behind that.

Our thinking was that, if something happened to me, Doug would still be taken care of. It turned out Doug's premium was about $600 a month and mine was $800.

After about ten years, they offered Doug home healthcare in place of the nursing home coverage. We took it. That's what we used to pay for our health aides for about 15 years on and off. It really helped.

We paid them by the hour. I would have to fax in their hours and sign a form to the insurance company. It was a lot of paperwork, but it was worth it. The last six and a half years of Doug's life, we had a live-in, seven days a week. That was around the time his situation really began to decline.

It all started with the bowels. Taking care of Doug's bowel problems and accidents was getting more and more difficult. He had no control over his bowels, so there would be accidents from time to time.

For example, one Saturday, I was supposed to meet a friend at a nudist resort for a nice little getaway. As I was getting ready to leave, Doug called me into his room. He had made a terrible mess all over the bed.

I didn't have any choice. I had to clean it up. It took me a couple of hours. I had to change the sheets, while Doug was still in the bed, which involved rolling him back and forth to get the linen off and on the bed. It was hard.

Another time we were at the Metropolitan Opera with Doug's best friend from Princeton, Bert, and his wife. Doug had another bowel accident right there in his wheel chair, in the middle of the audience at the opera. Doug was aware of it and we could all smell it. It was very embarrassing.

Finally, we felt it would be better for Doug to get a colostomy, rather than continuing to do the manual bowel routine he had done all those years. It was just getting to be too much time and trouble.

With a colostomy, the feces would simply empty into a plastic bag, similar to what we were doing with his urine bag. I found a surgeon to do the procedure at Overlook Hospital nearby.

Even though we had decided to do a colostomy, Doug ended up getting an ileostomy instead. The difference between the two is where the feces exit the intestines. With an ileostomy, they exit from the ileum. The ileum is the very last part of the small intestine. With a colostomy, they exit from the colon. The colon is the large intestine, after the food has traveled farther down the body.

I wasn't at the hospital the day of Doug's surgery. I had already made plans to leave for France with three of my friends that day, long before we set the date for the surgery. So I asked my son Steve to be there instead.

The doctor who was going to perform the surgery was not familiar with spinal cord injuries, which turned out to be a big problem. He had looked at an x-ray of Doug's colon and, for some reason, thought it would be better to attach the bag to the ileum, rather than the colon.

Steve was only there as emotional support for Doug. He didn't have any medical knowledge, so when the doctor told Steve his change of plan, Steve agreed. None of us knew what an ileostomy was or that it would create so many problems for Doug.

I had never even heard of an ileostomy before this surgery. If I had been there that day, I wouldn't have known to challenge his decision. I felt bad about it afterwards, but there was nothing I could have done. He was the doctor. He was supposed to know what he was doing.

As a result of his error in judgment, however, Doug almost died.

When I arrived in France, I called Steve to see how the surgery had gone. He told me what they had done and that Doug seemed okay.

Then after the operation, Doug couldn't keep any food down or even stay hydrated. He eventually came home, but had to keep going back into the hospital, because he was so sick. He started losing a lot of weight.

Doug went in the hospital five different times before we figured out what the problem was. I would call the surgeon and he would just say, "I didn't do anything wrong. I did the surgery right. He has a medical problem."

Meanwhile, Doug just kept getting worse, so bad he ended up in the ICU, on a respirator. He was close to dying.

That's when I called Greg, who was living in Columbus, Ohio, and told him, "Dad's on a respirator." Greg, as a chiropractor, did have medical knowledge. He couldn't take it any more, so he immediately flew in.

We met with the surgeon in the ICU, right in front of Doug. Greg demanded that he reverse the ileostomy and do a colostomy instead. Greg is very aggressive and he has a temper. He actually yelled at the doctor, "If you don't reverse this, you will be killing my father. I insist you reverse it!"

Because of that, the doctor finally reversed the ileostomy. He couldn't do the colostomy yet, of course. Doug was so weak after all this that he had to stay in the hospital another five months, just to recover before going through anything else.

After the surgeon reversed the ileostomy, Doug had to go back to his bowel routine to let everything heal, before we could do a colostomy. In the meantime, we found Dr. Gilder at the Kessler Institute in New Jersey, where they specialize in spinal cord injury rehab.

Dr. Gilder was a urologist, who worked with quadriplegics and paraplegics. He told us he never would have done an ileostomy. An ileostomy is generally only done if someone has cancer of the colon and part of their colon has been removed. It's supposed to just be a temporary procedure, while the colon is healing. They reverse it later. A colostomy is what you do for a permanent solution.

We had gotten the wrong doctor and he had made a bad decision. He evidently didn't know much about spinal cord injuries. He shouldn't have done an ileostomy. It was so high up in the digestive tract that Doug couldn't keep his food down or get enough nutrition from it.

After they reversed the ileostomy, Doug was in the hospital five months, just to recover his strength. He was so weak the whole fiasco almost killed him.

The amazing thing is Doug was still working through all this, even when he was in the ICU on a respirator. He only had five PhD students and one class a week. If he couldn't lecture, he'd get his TA to do it for him. He had really good TA's. Still, he had to prepare and grade the final exam for his class.

After his students took the exam, I carried the test papers over to Doug in the ICU. He graded them there, on the respirator, and then handed them back to me. I went home and called the grades into the department secretary. That was our semester.

No one at Rutgers knew any of this was going on. Doug never told them he was in the hospital, unless he had to. Every time he went into the hospital, he tried to hide it. He didn't want his colleagues to know, if he could avoid it. As brilliant and famous as he was, he was always worried about losing his job.

So finally, after five months of recovery, Dr. Gilder ended up doing the colostomy on Doug...and that worked. Doug had that colostomy for a long time after that, with no problems about his bowels.

We were very upset with this doctor who had done the ileostomy though. We were going to sue him, but when we looked into it, we found we couldn't. He did the actual surgery correctly, as he had kept insisting throughout the ordeal.

It was just the wrong surgery. The problem was that he made the wrong judgment, what they call a "judgmental decision." Technically, he wasn't legally at fault.

Go figure.

Chapter 63

The doctor who gave Doug the ileostomy really screwed up and he really screwed Doug up. While Doug was in the hospital, recovering from reversing the ileostomy, he was diagnosed with stage four renal (kidney) failure.

When people are in stage four renal failure, that's the end. It only goes stages one through four. Doug was there, as bad as it got. He had to start dialysis.

No matter how old you are, if you reach stage four renal failure, dialysis is free. The government pays for it. We didn't have to pay for the machine or for the materials associated with it.

But dialysis shortened Doug's life. When you're on it, your skin becomes very fragile, so you are even more susceptible to skin breakdowns. That's what finally killed him.

Before the ileostomy, they had given Doug a test, to determine if he had any kidney malfunction. I asked his kidney doctor then what the test showed. He said there was no kidney failure.

After the ileostomy, though, Doug was suddenly at stage four. Something happened. When I went to the kidney doctor, he denied ever telling me that Doug's test was all clear. He was obviously trying to protect the surgeon. These doctors cover for each other.

Most people on dialysis go to a center for it, about three times a week. With Doug's situation, he couldn't possibly do that. With his skin problems, he had to have home dialysis.

To avoid getting a decubitus ulcer, we couldn't put him into a wheelchair, take him to a dialysis center, and have him lie there for three hours on some uncomfortable mattress thing. Doug had to be on his Clinitron bed for dialysis.

It was about six and a half years that Doug endured this painful procedure. They had to put needles in his arm. Sometimes he would complain to his neurologist about the pain and he would give him medication to make it hurt less, but the stress really got him down.

A couple of times he got so depressed, he said, "I might as well just give up."

I don't know if it was because of his work or his medical problems, but he was down. I would give him a pep talk and tell him, "Things will be okay. We need you! Keep plugging away. Things will get better..." And so on.

Doug's depression was probably mostly because of the medical issues, but he was also worried about losing his job. My kids thought that was ridiculous. No one else could ever imagine him getting fired, but he could.

His work was a big part of what he was living for. His list of priorities went: family, friends, work. He would have been devastated if he didn't have his job, but there were lots of politics at Rutgers. Doug was involved in some of it and he would get frustrated about it.

While Doug was in the hospital recovering from the ileostomy reversal, we hired Arunas to be our first live-in health aide. He was living in our house, but he didn't have much to do at first. His main duty every day was to take Doug *The New York Times*, which Doug loved, and visit with him.

When he came home, Doug had to continue dialysis, so Arunas had to take instruction on it from DaVita, the company that made the machine. The DaVita dialysis nurse came to our home for that.

Doug was on dialysis for the last six years of his life. The machine was set up next to his bed. We had to have special plumbing done to get it in there. We ran pipes from the basement on one side of the house all the way over to the other side, where Doug's bedroom was. That cost about $3,000.

The installation process was very stressful. It was complicated, noisy, and expensive. It took two days to get it done and I had to be there to supervise. The workmen came and didn't know how to do it, so they had to come back again. It seemed my life was just one problem after another.

Once the plumbing was all put in, two pipes came through the wall next to Doug's bed. Water had to run into the machine and water had to go out again. Each pipe had a faucet with tubing on it, so we could turn the water on and off for the dialysis.

I came to realize at this point that Doug was on life support in our home, which depended on electricity. Doug's life support system included both the Clinitron bed, which we had gotten before we got the dialysis machine, and, of course, the dialysis machine itself.

One time, we came back from New York and it was snowing. We couldn't get the car up our long, sloping driveway, so we had to get Doug out of the car and into his wheelchair. My next-door neighbor helped me push Doug all the way up to the house. Otherwise, we would have been stranded out there.

After that, we bought a generator for the house. Doug's Clinitron bed had these glass beads in it, which had to be rotating all the time. If the power went out, the glass beads would just create a solid layer, instead of moving around. The bed would get as hard as a rock and Doug would get a skin breakdown in no time. Even more urgent, without power for the dialysis, he would get very sick.

The winters were getting worse. We never knew when we might lose electricity. Doug couldn't survive without it. As it turned out, we did lose electricity at times, so it was really good we had that generator.

Originally Doug just wanted me to get a generator for his room, to supply the medical equipment. His room was on the opposite side of the house from the rest of us, but still I had to live there too, as well as cook and so on, so we needed electricity as well.

How would we survive to take care of him, if we had no heat, light, or power? That was another example of how I had to be the practical one.

People have no idea what it's like to care for a patient full-time. Our whole lifestyle was terribly complicated. Even just lying in the bed, Doug would have to wear special booties on his feet, so his heels wouldn't start getting decubitus ulcers. That could happen, just from the pressure of his feet on the bed.

At times, he did get skin breakdowns on his feet. In fact, once it got so bad, he had to have a toe removed. Somehow, it got infected and it had to be amputated.

Another time, Doug caught another infection. There was something going around the hospital, called MRSA. It's an infection caused by a type of staph bacteria. It's become resistant to many of the antibiotics used to treat most infections, so it's very difficult to cure. We had to wear gowns and gloves to go in and visit him.

When you have a spinal cord injury, you're supposed to move around and change position as much as you can. You can't just lie on your back all the time. You should lie on one side, then the other, and so on.

Years ago, they used to have a bed that would rotate the patient, but we didn't have that. Instead, the health aide would give Doug lots of pillows, to help him lie on his side. They tried to keep him off his buttocks, because that's where the pressure builds up the most.

The Clinitron bed did help protect his skin somewhat, by providing lower pressure and adjustable temperature. The glass beads rotating inside created some movement and air-flow under Doug, which helped.

That ileostomy surgery was a real turning point in Doug's life. He might have lived a little longer and more comfortably, if it hadn't been for that big screw-up.

But we can't go back...we have to just move forward in life.

Chapter 64

Our first live-in health aide, Arunas, was a great guy. He had actually been an MD in Lithuania, before he came to the U.S. He was an expert at taking blood and was very helpful in many ways. After a year and a half though, he left us to move up to Worcester, Massachusetts, for a position at a hospital there.

Before he left, he found us another live-in, who was also an MD from Lithuania. Her name was Inga. Unfortunately, Arunas didn't know that Inga was a drug addict.

She was married to a nice enough man, who was also a live-in. He took care of a patient who lived down at the shore. He was very handsome and very nice. Sometimes he would visit Inga and bring her food. They had three children back in Lithuania, so they were still cooperating to support them.

In addition to her husband, Inga had a boyfriend. He was a maintenance man, who lived about an hour and a half south of us, in a retirement community. He would come spend every weekend with Inga at our house.

They stayed in her bedroom on my side of the house, so Doug had no idea what I was going through with them. It was like living in hell.

They both smoked cigarettes. When I hired her, I told her, "You can't smoke in the house, only on the patio." I never caught her with a cigarette burning in the house, but smoking turned out to be the least of the troubles Inga inflicted on us.

It's very difficult to find someone who's medically trained, to take care of a paraplegic like Doug. You can't just hire someone off the street with no medical background. All the live-ins we hired were former physicians from other countries.

So even though Inga and her boyfriend were living on my side of the house and driving me crazy, I never went into detail about it with Doug. I felt it was just something I had to put up with, in order to have a live-in stay with us.

There were lots of things Doug would get upset about, so if there was a problem at home, we usually just didn't tell him. We didn't want to worry him or hear him complain about it. He had enough to deal with already, between work and medical problems. If there was something Doug didn't absolutely need to know, we didn't discuss it with him.

Well, we had an E-ZPass to automatically pay tolls for expressways, tunnels, and bridges. As I was examining our E-ZPass bill the winter that Inga started with us, I noticed over $100 in charges for the Garden State Parkway.

I never used the Garden State Parkway in the winter. I knew it wasn't me, so I checked the bill and saw it was for Doug's mini-van. When I checked the mileage on the mini-van, I saw it was 2000 miles more than it should have been.

I can only guess now that on Saturday mornings Inga and her boyfriend were going off and buying drugs. Inga's husband had told me she was an addict, but I had been hoping it wouldn't affect our situation.

One day in June, her husband had called me and asked me to meet him at the shore, near where I went to the beach at Sandy Hook. When I did, he asked me if I had paid Inga that week.

I said, "Yes, she got $135 a day."

He said, "Well, she must be back on drugs then, because she hasn't given me any money at all for the kids." That's when I found out she was an addict. I didn't know what to do.

Then in early August, I came home from the beach around 10:00 at night. Inga was in the family room and said something to me about Doug. I could barely understand her, because she was about to fall over. Silly me, I just thought she was tired.

So I said, "Inga, why don't you just go to bed?"

By that time, her husband's patient had died and he had moved into our house. He was living in her bedroom with her. Doug knew nothing about all this. I felt there was no reason to tell him. He would just get upset and then I'd have more problems to deal with.

I have to mention one other thing. Over the years, I had always left my purse on a kitchen chair. That was my spot for it. Then, when Inga first came, I started thinking I was losing my mind.

I usually kept about $80 cash in my wallet. I would check after a couple of days and suddenly there would be only $40. I usually just put everything on my credit card, so I couldn't figure out where all this cash was going to. I didn't remember buying anything with cash.

So anyway, that night Inga went to bed and I did too, thinking nothing of any of this. The next morning, when I got up, Inga was wearing sunglasses. She said, "Oh, I had a little accident with your car last night."

The car she was referring to was a Mitsubishi that had belonged to

Steve. Since he was living in Philadelphia at the time, he didn't need it. He had turned it over to me and it was now on our insurance.

The car wasn't worth much, maybe $2000, so I had removed the collision coverage. I allowed Inga to use the car when we needed her to go buy groceries or something. I really didn't want her using the van.

That morning we had to take Doug to Overlook Hospital for wound care, so Inga asked me if I would mind taking him. I said, "Inga, I will drive, but I need you to come with me, to help with the wheelchair."

She came along. As I was driving the van with Doug in the back, I noticed Inga was shaking. She must have been coming down from some drugs. Anyway, we took Doug in with no incident and then came back home.

That's when Inga told me I had to go talk to the police, to get the Mitsubishi back. Evidently, there was a certain place in Warren where the police sent you if your car had been towed after it was in a wreck.

I didn't go to the police station. It was another place. The man I talked to there was really nasty to me. I told him, "You know, I'm not the one who totaled the car. I'm the one who owns it."

I had to pay $450 to get it out. Next, another person, who worked there, led me to a town about four miles away, to get the Mitsubishi. I followed in my car. When we arrived and I saw the car, I was flabbergasted.

All four tires were flat. Some strange bags were all over the inside of the car. I didn't know what they were, so I asked, "What are those?"

They told me, "Oh, those are the airbags."

Right, the airbags had deployed. As I pieced the story together, I discovered Inga had gone out the night before, after I thought she was going to bed. She ended up totaling the car. Then she was arrested and her husband had to go bail her out. I slept through the whole debacle.

Later, her husband told me that about 15 minutes after she had come into their bedroom, she said, "I'm going to go buy a pack of cigarettes."

He asked her, "Where did you get the money?"

She said, "Sylvia gave it to me." That, of course, was a lie.

She had stolen money out of my wallet again. She ended up driving two miles and hitting a person's mailbox along the side of the road. The police gave her three tickets, for a DUI and two other offenses.

When I finally found out about all this, I couldn't deal with it any longer. She was giving Doug dialysis! Anything could happen. But Doug wouldn't let me fire her until we found another live-in who could do dialysis. That took a while.

Chapter 65

Our next candidate for a new live-in was Tammy. I found her through an agency in Princeton and got a good reference for her. Doug was back in the hospital, so we had Tammy come there for an interview.

We didn't want Inga to know we were looking for someone else. There was no telling what she might do. Doug wouldn't let me fire Inga until we had a suitable replacement for her. If he didn't have someone to help him, he couldn't work. And he never wanted to not be able to work.

You'd think Inga would have figured out we were going to fire her when she totaled our car, but she was oblivious. After we decided to hire Tammy, I finally gave Inga the word.

The day she was moving out, I was afraid to be in the house alone with her. I thought, *Hey, she could kill me. She could just grab a knife and go crazy because I fired her.* I had always worried about that kind of thing.

So I called our financial advisor, who lived in the same town. I asked him to, please, come over and pretend he was going over some business stuff with me in the dining room until Inga was gone. He very graciously played his part, while Inga packed up and left.

After she was gone, I went in and looked at her bed. I was shocked. Both the sheets and even the mattress had holes in them from cigarette burns. It was truly amazing she didn't burn the house down around us.

As far as I had known, while she was working for us, she and her boyfriend were always going out on the patio to smoke. Obviously they were also smoking in bed. I don't know if they passed out with cigarettes burning or not, but they sure were careless. That was Inga.

Doug had sort of liked her. He thought she was pretty good, but considering how easily she could have killed him, the rest of us were having a fit about her being there.

So after we hired Tammy, the next step was getting her trained to do dialysis. Arunas, our first live-in, was very smart and had learned it quickly. Inga had also picked it up easily, but after she totaled our car, she had to go.

Tammy, on the other hand, had a hard time of it. She was from the country of Georgia and may have had a language problem. She spoke English, but not perfectly.

The dialysis people were coming over to the house to train her, but after two weeks they pulled me aside and said, "It's just not going to work out with her. She can't learn it."

Tammy wouldn't give up though. She wanted the job so badly, she begged me to give her another chance. She was getting paid $150 a day, seven days a week. If she couldn't do the dialysis, she couldn't have the job. So I asked the trainer to continue with her.

I didn't want to learn it and Doug didn't want me to. If I somehow accidentally killed him, I would never forgive myself. Plus, I had too many other things to deal with anyway. We both agreed it shouldn't be my responsibility.

Dialysis was a four-hour process, done five days a week. We had to do it in the morning, before Doug went off to teach. He always tried to sleep through it and wake up around noon to start his day.

Anyway, after three or four weeks, Tammy finally learned it. I was glad I was patient. Tammy stayed with us for five years, right up until Doug died. In fact, we're still in touch and I took her out for lunch recently when I was up north. It turned out it was her birthday.

Dialysis became a big part of our lives. One time the machine sprang a leak and rotted out a part of the floor. It left a hole next to Doug's bed, so we had to get the floor re-done.

That was another near nervous breakdown for me. It was really tricky, because everything had to be done in one day and I had to organize it.

I had to schedule the dialysis people to come disconnect the equipment and put it in the study next-door to Doug's room the day before the floor was to be done. Then the next morning, Tammy had to wake Doug up at 6:00 am, get him into his wheelchair, and take him into his office at Rutgers.

In the meantime, once Doug was out of bed, I had to have the Clinitron bed people there to disassemble the bed. That is not an easy thing to do. It takes a couple of hours, because of all those beads inside the mattress. It's very heavy. You can't just move it. They had to take it apart, to get it out of the room.

The bed people were supposed to come at 7:30, so Doug had to be out of the room by 7:00. In turn, they had to get the bed out before the floor people arrived at 9:00.

We had to remove everything from the room. There was one storage cabinet built into the wall, which couldn't be moved, so they had to work around that.

Then the flooring people had to come and replace the wooden floor with linoleum, which looked like wood. We had to be practical, in case there was another leak.

The floor people had to finish as soon as possible, so we could set everything back up again. We had to finish the new floor in one day, because Doug needed to sleep in his bed that night. The Clinitron people still had to come back and put the bed together before the day was over.

My stress was that, if one person didn't show up at the right time and do their job on schedule, none of it would work out. It all had to be synchronized and completed on that day.

There was no other place in the house Doug could sleep. He couldn't even get into any of the other bedrooms. The doors were too narrow and, of course, they just had regular beds anyway, not the Clinitron bed.

It was touch and go. Doug came home from work about 4:00 and was in the family room, trying to sleep in his wheelchair. They were still working on putting the bed back together. That was a big mess.

I almost had a nervous breakdown over the whole thing. The next day the dialysis machine had to go back in, but by then the pressure was off.

I never knew anyone who had as many medical issues as Doug did. It wasn't just his own body. It was also dealing with all the different kinds of equipment he needed, like his motorized wheelchair.

Originally Doug had had a regular wheelchair, which he could roll around himself. As he got older, though, he was told he needed a motorized one with special seating, to avoid putting so much pressure on his arms.

The motorized wheelchair had all these buttons, which our grandson Bradley loved. Doug would take him for rides on that thing. Bradley was fascinated with how one button would raise the chair, another would make it go sideways, and so on.

For my part, I wasn't a fan. Doug couldn't really keep track of all those buttons. He wasn't mechanically inclined, so he had trouble remembering which button did what.

Steve told me how he had taken his father to New York, to have dinner and see a play. Doug was in his motorized wheelchair. A couple of times he ran into things, like a plant and a wall, which he scratched, and so on.

I knew what Steve was talking about. One time I had Doug at a neurologist's office in Summit. He ran into the wall there and put a hole in it. I nearly had a conniption. I was afraid we were going to get sued or something.

Any time we went out with Doug in that chair, we had to watch where he was going. Fortunately, no one ever sued us over the damage or asked for remuneration. They just had compassion, I guess.

Still, even with all the problems that wheelchair created, I felt like I would have a breakdown, if anything ever went wrong with it. How would we ever get Doug anywhere?

Another time I had to take him home from work. Actually, it turned out to be the last time ever. You remember, our Dodge mini-van had a ramp that went out the side door for the wheelchair to enter and exit. When you stopped the van, you pushed a button and the ramp went down.

At the same time, the van's whole suspension system also lowered, so that Doug could navigate the ramp more easily. When you brought the ramp back up and the door closed, the car's suspension would return to its normal height. Otherwise, the bottom of the van would hit anything raised on the road.

It reminded me of when I had to drive my father's Cadillac from Miami to New York, with that broken air suspension, which kept lowering the car and dragging on the ground.

Anyway, this last time I was bringing Doug home from work, somehow the button that controlled the van's suspension got stuck in the lowered position and we couldn't get it back up.

It was nighttime. I was driving and Tammy was with me. We did everything we could think of, but we couldn't get the van back up to its normal height. So I had to drive all the way home like that with the bottom of the car hitting the ground for half an hour. It was very bumpy and every bump I hit, Doug would scream, because it hurt like crazy.

His screaming would distract me and make it even harder to drive. Tammy wanted me to pull over, but there was no place to do so, and, even if there were, what would we do then?

So I just drove. The next day, we figured out how to raise the van again. There was another button down near the bottom of the van, towards the back. But that shows you how it was always just one stressful situation after another.

People don't understand the special consideration that's necessary for wheelchair people. One time Doug went to a Japanese restaurant and parked in the handicapped parking. When he came out, a car had parked right next to where the wheelchair ramp was supposed to come down, so Doug couldn't even get into the van.

People who weren't disabled would even park in wheelchair spots. Doug would write them a note and leave it on their car. They really created problems for us.

Chapter 66

One day in 2006, I was at a drugstore around 11:00 in the morning, when Greg called me. He said, "Mom, Maria's having the baby tomorrow. Can you come out to Columbus?"

One thing my life has taught me is that my plans can change at the drop of a dime. Only one thing is certain in life...things are always changing. So I went straight home and got a plane ticket to fly out to Columbus that same evening.

Inga was still our live-in at the time, so she gave me a ride to the airport. It happened there was a terrible thunderstorm that night. The Newark airport even lost its electricity for a while. They had to have the back-up generators kick in.

Most of the flights were cancelled, but I lucked out and boarded mine at midnight. I said to the attendant, "What are the chances we're actually leaving?"

She said, "I would say about fifty-fifty."

Well, we did take off and I arrived in Columbus at 2:12 am their time. I called my daughter-in-law and she said she'd come pick me up...even though she was having a baby the next day. I asked, "Well, where's Greg?"

She said, "He's sleeping."

Maria wasn't in labor yet. She was going to have it induced the next day. She had to be at the hospital at 8:30.

So she picked me up and I got to bed at 3:00 am. I told Maria not to wake me when they left in the morning. Her daughter, Jenny, didn't have school that day, so she could wake me at 10:00. Then I would bring Jenny to the hospital with me.

That's what we did. We were all in the room, when Bradley was born, which is what Maria wanted. She had not planned on taking an epidural, but she was in a lot of pain, so Greg finally told me, "Go get the nurse and have her get an epidural." All went well.

On August 1 of that summer, Maria, Jenny, and Bradley all came to visit us in New Jersey. Doug was in the hospital, but he could see everyone daily. This was the first time he got to see Bradley. Greg and Steve even came for the weekend, so it was a nice family reunion.

After that, they used to do that every year. Maria and the kids would come in the summer for a week, Greg would come for the weekend, and then they would all fly back. Doug was usually working, but it gave me time to take them to the beach, New York, Princeton, or wherever they wanted to go. Everybody came for Thanksgiving too.

So life went on that way for a couple more years, until one day in 2008, I was down in Miami at Haulover Beach. That's the clothing-optional beach there. I was enjoying some time off with some friends, when I got a call from a doctor up in New Jersey, whom I didn't even know.

He was an ER surgeon. What had happened was that Tammy, Doug's last live-in, was concerned about what looked like a hard mass in his groin area. She thought it might be an infection, so she took him to the ER.

We had mentioned this thing previously during Doug's regular visit to his plastic surgeon at the wound care center, but he hadn't felt it was a problem. Now, all of a sudden, the ER doctor had looked at it and said it was a huge infection.

He told me that, if he didn't operate within the hour, Doug would die. I couldn't believe it. I was just beside myself. This was terrible, because there was no way I could be there. I had to give permission for him to operate, which I did.

Since I couldn't get up there in an hour for the operation, I called Steve, who was at our house, and asked him if he could go. I wanted a family member there for sure, so I was glad Steve was at home. He got there in time to see Doug, just as they were wheeling him into surgery.

Afterwards, Steve told me that, just before he went into surgery, his father told him he was proud that he wasn't having a deathbed conversion. He wasn't going to suddenly change all of his convictions, just because it appeared death might be near. That was Doug.

Steve waited and Doug survived, thank God. I guess the doctor didn't realize Steve was there at the hospital, however, because he called me again to tell me Doug was okay. Then I called Steve and relayed the news.

Steve told Tammy the surgery was successful. At that point, Steve decided to go home, because he didn't want to wait for Doug to come out of recovery. That would take hours.

That same year, 2008, we had to put in a new septic tank at our house, which ended up costing us $72,000. The old one had failed. As if that wasn't bad enough, things were complicated by the fact that, since Doug was on dialysis, I had trouble getting a permit from the town.

The city was trying to say we needed an even bigger tank, but it wasn't so. I had to get the dialysis company, DaVita, to send a letter explaining the process and then I had to get the water company to show that we didn't use that much water over a three month period. Dialysis didn't really take that much water.

Just another day in the life of a paraplegic caretaker.

Probably by now, you can see how, when I was out on my own, away from Doug, I tended to flinch every time the phone rang. For example, one time in 2008, I was in New York City, where I had gone to see *Waiting for Godot*. I had seen it before with Doug in the Village, when we were in our 20s and I really liked it.

Now it was playing on Broadway, so I had had a bite to eat in a nice Mexican restaurant and was seated in the mezzanine of the theater. I was in a straight chair, not a regular seat. They had put three fold-up chairs there, to add some extra seats, because it was so full. There were two men next to me, one on either side.

If you don't know this play, it's very slow-moving and heavy. At intermission, I went out and checked my phone. Someone had called me, a woman, and on the voicemail she left, she was crying.

I thought it sounded like my daughter-in-law, Maria. She just said, "Please, call me."

The next voicemail was also a woman crying and she sounded like our live-in Tammy. *Oh my God,* I thought, *Doug must have died.*

Every time anything unexpected happened, that was my first thought. I always expected the worst.

So I called Maria right away and she just said, "Oh, mom, can I call you back in a few minutes?"

I said, "No, Maria, I'm at a play," but she just hung up. So then I thought, *Well, Doug must not have died or she wouldn't be asking if she could call me back.*

I went back into the theater, but now I couldn't concentrate on the play. I actually told the two guys next to me, "Wow, I really thought my husband had just died."

They assured me that couldn't possibly have happened.

After the play, I went next door to the restaurant and called Maria again. It turned out that she had had a fight with Greg. She had gone and bought a kitten without talking to him about it. Then she had it immunized and brought it home.

When he arrived and saw it there, he went into a temper tantrum. It was a big drama and she was calling me for help. No matter where I went,

I always felt like I was on call for everybody... and I was. No matter how much I tried to get away from it, I still felt responsible for everyone.

Strangely, the times I felt most comfortable were when I went to visit Doug in the hospital. We would just be there talking alone together and I would feel better. It was as if he and I were in our own little world and he could talk to me more easily there than at home.

It was funny. At home, we were always talking about a medical problem or a business issue. At the hospital, we talked about personal stuff. He could really just be himself and open up there.

Chapter 67

Now that I'm writing this, I realize a lot of things happened in 2008. That was also the year when Steve called me one day and said, "Mom I'm going to take a job that's really out of the box."

I had never heard that term before. I said, "What do you mean?"

That's when he told me he was going into something completely different from what he had been doing. He was getting out of the computer field to go work on an organic farm in Dundee, New York. He needed to move his belongings out of his place in Princeton and into our house for storage.

Princeton was about an hour from our house, so Steve wanted to borrow Doug's mini-van for his move. It was big and would hold a lot of stuff. So I agreed to help.

On the appointed day, I drove the van down to Princeton and helped him pack everything up and load it. He was planning on putting his mattress on the roof of his own car. I asked somebody if that was okay and they said, "Oh, no, that's illegal. You'll get stopped by a cop, if you do that." So the mattress went into the van too.

We spent all morning loading everything, until we couldn't get any more in there. Steve even sold his sofa that day, because we didn't have room for it. Finally, he told me I could leave, but I refused and said, "No, I came to help and I'll stay till you're finished."

Steve had a modem for his computer, which had to be returned to the Internet company, so I offered to drop it off for him. I did that on my way home.

When I finally got back home at 8:00 or 9:00 that night, I was absolutely exhausted. Steve arrived a little later. We both turned in. There was nothing we could do till the next day, when we would unload everything into the basement of our house.

If you've ever been a parent, you know that's true love – helping your son move all day. Well, in the long run, Steve paid me back, because when Doug died a couple of years later, Steve helped me for many months as I was moving out of our house. It all comes back around.

After Steve started working at the farm in upstate New York, I went up to visit him for a long weekend. A woman owned and ran the place. I was staying with them in the farmhouse.

Meanwhile, Doug was in the hospital. He requested that I ask Steve

275

to come visit him. He even offered to pay Steve's expenses to do so. When I asked Steve, he said the money wouldn't make any difference whether he visited or not...but he did agree to come down.

He had one problem after another doing so though. The farm was over 200 miles away, near Watkins Glen. On his way down, he was about 100 miles from our house, when his car broke down.

He called to tell me he would have to stay overnight in a motel there, because he needed a new radiator and they were going to install it in the morning.

He got that done and hit the road again. Then, lo and behold, his car broke down once more, almost immediately. He was now about 95 miles from us.

Well, for years, I belonged to AAA Plus. It always seemed to come in handy. They would give you a free tow if the distance was less than 100 miles. So I gave Steve the information and told him to get his car towed to a mechanic in our town, whom we had used before. I picked Steve up at the mechanic's and then we finally got to visit his father.

We had a nice visit for two hours. Doug was talking a lot about his childhood and all kinds of fascinating things. He was a great talker. It was really special. Then we went back home.

Steve had left on a Saturday, stayed overnight at the motel while his car was being repaired, and arrived on Sunday. He needed to drive back on Monday, because the woman he worked for went to the farmers' market on Tuesday, and she needed his help.

So Steve picked up his car on Monday and took off. Meanwhile, I went over to the hospital to see Doug again. Just as I was walking in, I got a call from Steve. He had only gotten about 15 miles down the road, when his car broke down again!

I told him to have it towed back to our mechanic and went to get him there. The problem was, he still had to be back to the farm by that night, to work the next day. He asked me to check on bus and train schedules to Ithaca, which was about an hour from the farm.

I couldn't find anything that would get him there on time. Plus, the woman he worked for didn't want to drive those winding, narrow, back roads late at night, to pick him up in Ithaca.

Finally I realized I was going to have to take him up there myself. That was the only way he would make it. It was a six-hour drive. I was a little tired, but I decided to do it anyway.

276

I told Doug I was driving Steve back. Meanwhile, the mechanic said he couldn't fix Steve's car. It was being written off as a total loss. Steve was going to have to buy another one. What a disaster.

Steve actually drove most of the way up to the farm. I only drove for about an hour. We got there about 11:00 pm. I had been there before, so I stayed again. I slept in a bedroom upstairs, while Steve slept in another one across the hall. The owner's bedroom was up there as well.

The next day about 9:00 am, things got even more complicated. I received a call from the hospital that they were discharging Doug that morning. This was unexpected. I was shocked. Somebody had to be at the house to meet Doug, but I was 200 miles away.

Doug always went both to and from the hospital by ambulance. I called Tammy to tell her he was coming home and she should be at the house.

Whenever Doug felt that he had to go to the hospital, one of us would call 911 and they would send the police out. The police would come first and then the ambulance would arrive. The paramedics had to come, take his blood pressure, find out what was wrong with him, and so on. They would check him out and then the ambulance would take him to the hospital, which was about eight miles away.

Whenever Doug was in the hospital, Tammy would stay at her apartment with her husband and son. Technically, she probably shouldn't have, but she did, so I always had to call her to tell her when she needed to be at our house. She had to help Doug get in when the ambulance arrived, open the door, get things situated, and all that.

When Doug was in the hospital, Tammy would go visit him every day. She'd stop by our house first to pick up *The New York Times,* along with anything else he needed.

So they brought Doug home about 1:00 in the afternoon and everything was fine. I had panicked a little, being all the way up there and thinking I had to turn around and rush back when I was so tired. I couldn't possibly have made it.

This is another example of how stressful my life was. How many mothers would even offer to do all that in the first place…drive their son 200 miles late into the night, sleep over, then drive right back home the next day?

Steve ended up doing that organic farming for four years. He really seemed to like it. He worked at three different farms. He stayed for two

277

years in Dundee, where it was beautiful, really serene. The third year, he had a position at a different farm in Saratoga Springs. The fourth year he worked in Western Pennsylvania.

That last year, though, he hurt his back. He called me when he did and I called Greg, who invited him to come to Columbus for chiropractic treatment. Steve went there for a week and felt better. After that, he decided to return to his previous career, working with computers. It's not quite as strenuous as farming.

Chapter 68

Like a true absent-minded professor, Doug was often forgetful of the smallest, most basic things. One time he was flying solo to a meeting overseas. He had a car service taking him to Kennedy Airport. He got all way there, and then suddenly had to have the car turn around and come racing back to the house. He had forgotten his passport. Thank God, he remembered before he got to the airport!

My friends were amazed at how many things I had to keep track of and how organized I was about it. One German female friend is also married to a famous scientist who worked at Bell Labs. He invented the little microphone used in all our cell phones, computers, and so on. He even designed the acoustics at Philharmonic Hall in New York.

Whenever we talked, my German friend would say, "Sylvia, you're the one that keeps your family together." It was true...in many ways. Everyone knew that.

Doug was very slow to do things and loved to procrastinate. For example, when the people at the Rusk Institute originally had him cementing a condom onto his penis to attach his catheter, it took him at least an hour a day to do it. And it had to be done every day.

Doug was just slow with that kind of stuff. I had to just be patient with him. Many of his issues weren't the kinds of things you could do fast anyway. Still, Doug never moved quickly to begin with...ever.

He was a confirmed procrastinator. In fact, that was his philosophy, delay things as much as he could, until he got what he wanted. Believe it or not, he would usually win out in situations because of that. He would just wear people out.

When he was negotiating his position at Rutgers, he didn't immediately accept their offer. He asked for this and he asked for that. It just went on and on. By procrastinating and holding out, he eventually got everything he wanted. It always worked for him. It never backfired.

I don't operate like that. Delaying things makes me nervous. If someone calls me today, unless I'm dead, I'll call them back the same day. It will be the first thing on my mind.

I called a girlfriend of mine, Priscilla, the other day about something. It took her eight days to call me back. I'm not like that. If I don't call someone back right away, they know there's a good reason. I must be out of the country, in a hospital, or dead.

Another characteristic of Doug's was that he was very unrealistic. Sometimes I had to step in and put my foot down, to bring Doug back to the real world. About two or three years before Doug died, he was invited to give a talk in the Netherlands. They were going to give him an honorarium and pay all his expenses, so he wanted to go. I wouldn't let him.

He was on dialysis. That meant he would have had to go to a strange hospital in a foreign country to get it done. It was a big trip and I felt it would jeopardize his life. Either Tammy or I would have to go, to keep him safe. It just wasn't worth it. Even our kids said it wasn't worth it.

Doug thought he could do anything, so I had to lay down the law, and yet compromise at the same time. I said, "If you have an invitation in the States, we'll take you to that."

Lo and behold, he soon got an invitation to be the keynote speaker for a meeting at Temple University. Tammy and I both took him to Philadelphia, where he spoke at the meeting. While he was doing that, I took Tammy out to lunch.

Afterwards, we came back and picked him up again. He got his $1500 honorarium and we went home. That was fine. I was glad we could do it. It was very little risk. But to go to Europe and face God knows what? No, thank you.

Doug was a genius at being theoretical. He just wasn't very practical. If you think about it, that's what put him into a wheelchair in the first place. He thought he could do more than he could.

The conditions were bad on the ski slope that afternoon at Mont-Tremblant. It was very icy. It was so cold, we were both wearing face masks. He had on rental skis, which he wasn't used to. It was too dangerous.

At first, I said, "No, I just want to take the easy slope."

He said, "Oh, but I want to go down one more time."

I said, "What time is it?" I wouldn't ski anything dangerous after 3:00. It was a little after 2:00, so I figured this was a grey area. I gave in, but I wish I had convinced him not to do it.

Doug and I were like equals in our relationship, even though I didn't have a PhD. When he would complain about his life after the accident, I'd have to give him a pep talk. I would say, "Well, Doug, you have a PhD. I don't. That's quite an accomplishment in itself, not to mention all the other things you've done."

At first after his accident, I was really scared. I told him, "You have to help me raise our boys. I can't raise them by myself." Over the years, we became a team and just did whatever needed to be done. And yet we each had our own lives. I would sometimes say, "Do you want to go to New York with me tonight?"

He usually answer, "Oh, no, I just want to work tonight."

That was the way we lived, even before his accident. He never tried to control me and I didn't try to change him. No one could have kept either of us down anyway, even if they tried.

My daughter-in-law once told me that I am a butterfly, but I'm a faithful butterfly. I always come back home, to those I love. I'm faithful to all my friends, but no one can tie me down.

Still, by the last two years of Doug's life, I honestly didn't know how much longer I could hang in there. The winters in New Jersey were so cold and severe and our life was getting so difficult, I was just worn out. The medical problems kept building up: loss of mobility in one arm, decubitus ulcers, dialysis and more. Doug was getting weaker and weaker and needing more care. It was heartbreaking.

As time went on, the decubitus ulcers became really dreadful. They were what killed him. There are three things paraplegics usually die from: decubitus ulcers, kidney failure (which he also had), or urinary tract infection.

For years, we had to take Doug in to see the plastic surgeon at the wound care center every two weeks. The doctor would remove the dead, necrotic flesh with a scalpel.

The sores looked awful. They were huge and embedded in his buttocks. We couldn't do anything about them any more. Doug had no idea how bad they looked. He didn't have any feeling back there, so he couldn't tell.

Tammy would say to Doug, "Oh, they're looking better," but they weren't. Eventually, they became septic. They infected his whole body. That's what killed him.

Just before Doug died, he was in and out of that hospital four times with infected decubitus ulcers. He would receive an antibiotic IV for ten days, go home for five days, and then come back again into the hospital.

As Doug got weaker and weaker at the end, he lost a lot of weight. You could see it in his face. His legs were getting a lot thinner too. Even his friends could see it. Doug used to love to eat, just like my son Steve does. But as he grew weaker, he didn't feel like eating much anymore. He just couldn't.

I don't know how much weight he lost altogether. The only time we could weigh him was when we went to the hospital, where professionals could do it. They would weigh the wheelchair first. That power wheelchair weighed about 300 pounds. Then they'd put Doug in the chair and figure out the difference.

It broke my heart to see him declining. There are different kinds of love, you know. The love we had after Doug's accident was a deeper love in many ways than we had before, but not so much a romantic love.

Since he couldn't have sex and was disabled, I had to do all kinds of things for him that really squelched the romance. I knew what I had to do and I did it. How does that make a woman feel?

What we had was more of an unconditional love.

Chapter 69

Christmas 2010 was really bad in some ways. Greg was turning 40. He, his wife, and his kids had come to our house for Thanksgiving, so they all were going to Costa Rica for Christmas with her family.

Because of all the trouble we had been having with Doug's medical issues, I was having a tough time. Even so, I didn't realize how much Doug was declining. Maybe I was in denial. It turned out he wouldn't be even around for another Christmas.

On top of everything else, my daughter-in-law emailed me that she was going to throw Greg a surprise 40th birthday party in December around the 23rd, a couple of days before Christmas. She was asking me, since Greg was such a wonderful son, husband, and father, did I want to contribute to the cost of it?

We had already paid half their family's airfare to come visit us at Thanksgiving, besides paying for all the food and stuff. I felt we had already done a lot. Still, I didn't want to refuse her completely, so I emailed back I would send her a check for $100.

Then she came back with another email, itemizing all the food and so on she was planning. It totaled about $1500. She was obviously asking for more.

Normally, I take care of all the money in our family, but this time I wasn't sure what to do. So I told Doug about it and he said, "Well, maybe just double the check you were going to send."

As I discussed the situation with various friends, they all said I really shouldn't get too involved. So finally I wrote to Maria, "I wish you had told me about this party sooner. I would have gotten a plane ticket and flown down there for it."

She emailed me back, "Oh, Mom, I thought you were too busy."

Maria didn't realize how much this whole situation was upsetting me. With all I had been through with Doug, I was very sensitive at the time. I went into a full-scale depression. I was thinking things like, *She asks me for money for my son's birthday party, but she doesn't even invite me to come to it.*

I was no stranger to depression. Sometimes on a Saturday night, if we had no plans, I'd go out just because it wasn't good for me to stay home and isolate myself. I might go to a hotel where they had music and enjoy a couple of drinks. In my life, I was dealing with emotional suffering.

Physically, I had everything I needed, but I didn't have a normal marriage. I didn't have the affection or the sexual connection that a normal, healthy couple would have. Of course, a lot of "normal" couples don't have that either. Also, at times Doug would get irritated about something and start yelling, which was understandable, but difficult for me.

In the last few years, as things were getting worse, he would often take his frustration out on Tammy. I had long since learned to just leave the room when he started getting upset.

So anyway, a little after this back and forth with Maria, Greg called me and casually asked how I was. I had to be honest. I said, "Well, I'm depressed. It's really cold here."

I couldn't tell him, "I'm depressed because your wife is going to throw you a surprise birthday party and I'm not invited."

The drama continued. I eventually did send Maria $200. Then she acted like she was mad and was going to send it back, but I said, "Oh, no you don't. You keep it and use it."

Her party was supposed to be on a Sunday. The Friday before that, we were supposed to take Doug to the wound care center for his decubitus ulcers. Tammy was going with me.

That day Greg called me again and once again he asked me how I was. I told him I was still very depressed. I blamed it on the weather, his father not doing well, and so on.

Then Greg said, "Well, Mom, why don't you just come down to Costa Rica for Christmas?"

I almost jumped through the phone to kiss him. I kept my cool though and just said, "Oh, hey, Greg, that's a great idea. After I take Dad over to the hospital, I'll come back home and see if I can get a ticket."

It turned out I had airline points that would cover the trip. They would even fly me down first class. Plus, I would arrive on Sunday, well in time for the party. Greg still didn't know there was going to be one.

I arrived about 1:00 pm, took a taxi to my hotel, checked in, and called my daughter-in-law to say I was there. She suggested I take a taxi over to her parents' house, but I wasn't comfortable with that. I didn't know where they lived and I don't speak fluent Spanish.

So she said she would have her sister and brother-in-law pick me up and bring me over to her parents' house. Later, to keep the secret, when I talked to Greg I said, "I don't know what we're going to be doing tonight, so I'll get a little dressed up, just in case we're going somewhere nice."

I didn't want him to suspect anything when he saw me all dressed up at Maria's parents house that afternoon. Everyone else there would be very casual.

So Maria's sister and brother-in-law picked me up. They thought I was neat. We had fun on the ride over, but, meanwhile, there was more drama to come.

Maria had taken Greg's rental car to pick up lasagna and cake for the party. As she was putting the cake in the back seat, she accidentally dropped the car keys inside the car and locked herself out.

By the time we got there, she was crying. She had called a locksmith and was waiting. I went up, hugged her, and told her everything would be all right.

It turned out I never did see Greg before the party. Maria had to go get drinks and party stuff, so I went with her and waited in the car. Then we went to Maria's half-brother's house for the party.

He was an architect and very suave, with a gorgeous home. It turned out to be a party I wouldn't have missed for the world. It was in San Jose, in an elite area called Escuzu, where Greg had had his practice when he worked there. There were about 50 people attending.

I met a lot of nice people...all of Maria's half-brothers and sisters, whom I'd never seen before, some of her friends, and more. It was just great. When it was all over around 2:00 in the morning, one of her cousins took me back to my hotel.

After that, Greg rented a room in a hotel down in the Jaco Beach area and I did too. On Christmas day, we had breakfast overlooking the water. Then we went up to Maria's parents' house. Her father was totally deaf. He very sweet, but couldn't hear anything.

In the midst of all this fun, we called Doug in New Jersey. Greg and Maria talked to him, but he was really down and complaining. He said it was the worst Christmas of his life. He felt alone. He had asked Tammy to go buy some food, but even that was terrible.

Maria got a little upset. Greg said, "Oh, my father's just trying to make us feel guilty," but he was upset too.

Two days later, I was supposed to go back to New Jersey, but there was a blizzard in New York and I couldn't get a plane. I ended up staying two more nights. That was the last time I was in Costa Rica.

If I had been in New Jersey for Doug's last Christmas, I don't know if it would have been much better for him. I certainly would have been depressed. Doug always worked late. He was a true night owl, so we hardly ever even ate together. He would usually eat late, around 11:00 or 11:30. Tammy would go home, have dinner with her family, and then come back and fix Doug's dinner.

I certainly didn't know that would be Doug's last Christmas. Over the years, he had almost died about a hundred times. We never knew when it might come. Every time Doug went into the hospital, we wondered if he would ever come out again.

Doug passed away on June 7, 2011.

Chapter 70

Starting around 2009, for the next two years, Doug's decubitus ulcers took a major turn for the worse. He had always had them. They're very common with paraplegics.

A normal person shifts their position every now and then when they're sitting down, just to stay comfortable. That relieves the pressure on the area you're sitting on and allows blood to flow though again.

Someone who has no feeling, though, doesn't know to move, unless you tell them or they just remember on their own. That's what causes decubitus ulcers, the lack of blood flow.

At first, the ulcers started as little, minor things, but they just kept getting progressively worse. They were consistent. We were always checking for skin breakdowns. It was a chronic problem. After a while we started having to cancel trips because of them.

When Doug's ulcers got too bad, we would take him to the Wound Care Center at Overlook Hospital for treatment by a plastic surgeon. He was well-known there.

After Doug died, the nurses wrote me a beautiful note about how Doug was always such an inspiration to them. He never gave up. They admired him and missed him.

Sometimes Doug also got urinary infections and eventually had kidney failure. That's why we had to do dialysis, but dialysis just made the ulcers even worse, because it weakens the skin. Doug developed huge wounds in his buttocks. Thank God, he couldn't feel or see them. If he had, he would have been very discouraged.

They were like sores, big openings in the skin. Some of the surrounding skin would become black and dead. After the plastic surgeon removed that dead tissue with a scalpel, we had to put dressings on it, using ointment, bandage and tape. These had to be changed regularly. This is all part of normal care for a paraplegic.

The health aides would change the dressings every day. Once a week a visiting nurse would come check the ulcers. She'd measure the ulcer and write down the information for their records. This went on for a long time.

The last year Doug was alive, 2011, toward the end of March, he wasn't allowed out of bed, because the ulcers were so severe. In fact, his last semester at Rutgers, he couldn't actually teach, because he couldn't sit up in his wheelchair at all.

Still, we had to go in to the university one day, against doctor's orders. We had no choice, because the Dean of the Business School wanted to see Doug. Tammy and I got Doug dressed and took him.

First, we went into the room where his TA, Nancy, was lecturing his class of about 20 students. He explained to them that he wouldn't be able to teach that semester, because he had to stay in a special bed to heal.

Then he introduced me and we listened to the class together for about 15 more minutes, before Doug announced we had to leave. That was the only time he ever saw his class that semester. If Nancy hadn't been able to handle it, the course would have been cancelled.

Nancy got her PhD after Doug passed away. I called and told her when it happened. She was at a meeting out in Arizona. She was very upset and started crying. I still stay in touch with her.

The ulcers put Doug in the hospital a lot. Whenever he went in, I'd always go into his bedroom and spend half a day cleaning up. His $40,000 bed was filled with papers. Plus, he had more papers on the dresser. I don't think he knew where anything was, but he still wouldn't let me move it.

I would try to throw things away, but he always just said, "Well, keep those and put them in a box down in the basement."

We had a lot of papers in the basement, which Doug never looked at. He couldn't get down there and, even if he could, he had no idea what was where.

He was just basically a hoarder. He didn't want to throw anything away. Of course, this was his work and part of who he was, so I understood.

Doug spent half his life in a hospital. It was incredible how he could keep on working, both in and out of there. When he was in, I would have to bring him his work, his mail, whatever.

In fact, he was in a rehab hospital when his mother died. I got the call at 8:15 in the morning that she had passed away. It was okay though. She had had dementia, so it was a blessing.

She had told me for years, "Sylvia, I know you always want to go on a trip, but I just want to go to heaven."

The day she died, I went to see Doug at the hospital about 1:00 in the afternoon. Whenever I visited, I would always ask him, "How are you?" just to gauge his mood.

As usual, this day he just said, "The same."

So, I told him as gently as I could, "Your mother went to heaven this morning." He just became very quiet and closed his eyes.

There was no funeral. She was 91 years old and most of her friends were already dead. She had previously made up her cremation papers and had bought a niche in Fort Myers for her ashes.

Thank God. With Doug in rehab, I couldn't have dealt with going down there and doing all that, like I had for Aunt Betty.

Doug himself never put much attention on religion or spiritual things. Nor did he ever talk to me about it. He did once write something somewhat philosophical, titled "Optimism."

He also wrote a letter to Al Roker, in which he talked about his wish list of things he would love to do before he had to "shuffle off this mortal coil for good." Doug never questioned why he was here or where he was going though. It was all about his work for him.

As I said earlier, in the weeks before he passed, Doug was in Overlook Hospital three times in a row, being treated for sepsis caused by the decubitus ulcers. The infection was all through his body.

The first two times, each time, he was there for a ten-day regimen of IV antibiotics, and then went home for five days. He was still on antibiotics at home. Then he'd get sick again and feel so terrible, he would say, "Call 911 and take me to the hospital."

That happened twice. The third time, he was supposed to only stay in the hospital ten days again, but then they decided to keep him longer. Tammy and I could see how bad his condition was.

The whole time he was there, he was complaining to me that his stomach was upset. I kept asking the staff if they could give him something. If they did, it didn't help.

Doug was getting very weak. He had lost a lot of weight. Tapas Sen and his wife, Sondra, brought dinner over one night and we all ate in Doug's bedroom. Doug hardly ate anything. Even Tapas could see how bad Doug was doing.

Still, Doug wanted to keep working till the day he died. That's what I helped him do. It wasn't easy with all this stuff going on.

Then, as June of 2011 started, I realized my son Greg hadn't seen his father since the previous Thanksgiving. He knew Doug wasn't doing well, but he kept saying, "Keep Dad working. Keep him teaching." He figured that was keeping him alive.

Steve, of course, was just the opposite. He would say, "Mom, why don't you let Dad retire? He's done enough. Let him rest."

I told Greg his Dad really wasn't doing well and if he wanted to see him, he should come soon. He was going to fly in the weekend before Doug passed away, but I said that probably wouldn't be a good time.

I thought Doug was coming home from the hospital that weekend. It always took a half-day to transfer him. We'd have to pack everything up and then call an ambulance. They'd have to put him on his bed and get him situated.

He usually wouldn't be able to have dinner till about 11:00 at night. So Greg didn't come, but then Doug didn't come home after all. They wouldn't discharge him.

We didn't know it, but the clock was ticking down.

Chapter 71

I visited Doug Monday evening, the night before he died. While I was at the hospital, I was talking to the social worker. They were getting ready to discharge him or move him.

She was talking about putting him in a sub-acute unit, which is less intensive than acute rehabilitation. Patients in a sub-acute facility generally only receive one or two hours of therapy per day and stay there longer.

So I asked, "Do they have dialysis there?"

She said, "Oh, no, the patients have to go out for that."

"Well," I responded, "Doug could never do that, because he'd end up lying on a hard table for hours."

I told her we had a better life support system at home, with a live-in health aide and all the equipment he needed. Just then Steve, who was in Saratoga Springs, called me. He said, "Mom, Dad can't even talk." He had just tried to speak to Doug on the phone and Tammy had said Doug couldn't.

He was trying to tell me he felt his father was about to die. I told him I was talking to the social worker and I would get to Doug as quickly as I could.

I finished with her and then I went into Doug's room, which was right around the corner. He hadn't been talking all that day anyway. When I was with him earlier, Hank Gran had called, but Doug shook his head no, he couldn't talk.

So I spoke to Hank for a while and then let Doug say into the phone in a very weak way, "Thank you for calling." He was dying.

I can't tell you how many times Doug had almost died before that. Once I had fallen at home and then went into his room to tell him. I said, "Doug, I almost just died."

He said, "Sylvia, do you know how many times, I almost died?"

I honestly figured it was at least a hundred.

So I was there with Doug again. Since he knew I liked the beach, he said to me, "Are you going to the beach tomorrow?"

I said, "I don't know. " I couldn't really make any plans at that point.

Then I told him I had to go and I would call the next day. I kissed him good-bye and left. I had a quick dinner with a lawyer friend and then went home.

After I got there, I called Greg and said, "Greg, you really better get here to see Dad, if you want to see him. He's not doing well at all."

Greg said, "Well, I can't come this weekend." So we finished talking and I had a couple of drinks. Then I went to bed.

When I woke up the next morning I didn't feel good. I was depressed. On top of the drinks I had had the night before, I was remembering that day was the anniversary of my mother's death – June, 7, 1959.

I called the hospital, as usual, and asked about how Doug was. They said, "Oh, he's not complaining about anything."

I thought, "Well, that's good." Once again, I still didn't realize he was dying.

I was feeling down and sick. I didn't want to go to the hospital depressed, so I went to the beach at Sandy Hook after all. It's about an hour's drive from my home.

There I ran into a friend from Baltimore, who had met Doug once and really admired him. We were talking, when I got a call from a woman doctor at the hospital. She said Doug's heart had just stopped beating.

I froze. I said, "You mean he died?"

She said, "No, we resuscitated him, but he's in the ICU. You'd better come immediately."

It took me an hour and a half to drive up there. I just had my shorts and top on from the beach, so that's how I went into the ICU. Doug was there with a breathing tube down his throat. He was unconscious. It didn't look good.

They said, "The last thing that goes is the hearing. You should go in and talk to him."

So I went in and said, "Hi, Doug. This is your wife, Sylvia. I love you, Greg loves you, Steve loves you, and my mother loved you. But this is not a good day. It's the anniversary of my mother's death."

I guess in a way I was asking him not to die yet. I don't remember what else I said, but then a nurse came up and told me, "I'm sorry, but you have to leave now. We need to run a test on him."

They hadn't said to go to the waiting room, so I drove home, about a 25-minute drive. I had just arrived there, when I got another call. "You have to come back, Mrs. Carroll. He's dying now."

So I rushed back. I missed Doug's passing by about a minute. It didn't matter. I had already said my good-byes.

I waited for the doctor to come and pronounce him dead. I knew all his doctors, but I didn't know this one. I asked if he had known my husband.

He said, "I certainly did. Every time I went in to see him, I gave myself an extra 30 minutes to spend talking. He was the most interesting man I know to speak to."

That made me feel good. But Doug was gone now. He had died, after all, on the same date as my beloved mother.

Chapter 72

After Doug was pronounced dead, I called the funeral home from the ICU. I had already pre-arranged his cremation. I had even bought a niche for Doug's ashes in Basking Ridge. I did this after Greg married Maria. I felt it would be good for the kids to always know where their grandfather's ashes were and have a place to visit.

Before I made that decision, I had been planning on just scattering Doug's ashes on the grounds of Bell Labs. I always said that, when I died, I wanted my body also cremated and my ashes spread at the Esalen Institute. I loved it there and couldn't think of a more peaceful place. I felt Bell Labs would be an appropriate resting place for Doug's ashes.

Anyway, after I made the call to the funeral home, I went back to my own home, to prepare for what was to come. A few months earlier, I had already met with our Unitarian minister, Allison Miller. I knew Doug's health was getting worse and he might go any day. He certainly couldn't live forever.

I was concerned about what my mental state might be when that happened. When someone close to you dies, you're naturally very upset and emotional. Still, you have all these things to do and many decisions to make.

I was living by myself. Steve was working at a farm in Saratoga Springs. Greg was in Columbus, Ohio. I wanted to simplify things as much as possible. When the time came, I wanted to be ready, so I could just grieve.

Allison was a wonderful minister, just the same age as Steve. She suggested we have a Celebration of Life service at the Unitarian Fellowship in Morristown.

She suggested I could have five speakers and each one could speak about ten minutes. So now we planned to do it on a Saturday morning, June 18, about ten days after Doug's passing. I had to allow time for people to make their travel arrangements and so on. We would start the service at 11:00 and end by 12:00, with a reception afterwards.

Next I called the people I wanted as speakers. First was Hank Gran, Doug's best friend, who was living in Tucson. He said he would fly in for the service. Then I asked Tapas Sen and he agreed also.

I also asked Mike Wish, who had been Doug's department head when he had his accident and had helped us tremendously. He accepted.

Another speaker I chose was Stephen France, a graduate student of Doug's from England, who was now teaching at the University of Wisconsin in Milwaukee. He said he would come.

Finally, I asked the Dean of the Business School at Rutgers, because that's where Doug was working when he died. He accepted as well.

Now I had my five speakers. Steve helped me tremendously in the planning. I wanted to hire a pianist to play something by Doug's favorite composer, Beethoven. Steve also suggested we have the pianist play some jazz at the end of the service, to help uplift people as they were going out.

I also asked Steve to find a poem by Doug's favorite poet, Henry Wadsworth Longfellow. Steve looked online and read quite a few of his poems. Then he chose three or four, which he sent me. The one he liked best is the one I selected to be read by the minister at the memorial service.

A lot of my friends, who didn't even know Doug, asked me if I wanted them to come and I said yes. Most of them did. People came from Morristown, Baltimore, Washington, DC, the Netherlands, and more. Most of the attendees were colleagues of Doug's or long-time friends of ours.

Hank arrived first, on Thursday. I had something to do in New York, so unfortunately I couldn't meet him. I didn't really have room for him to stay with us anyway, since my whole family was there at our house.

Doug's room was in no shape for anyone to stay in. It was like a hospital room. Instead, Hank came over to our house on Friday morning and joined us like a family member to reminisce and grieve.

My two boys arrived on Friday, the day before the service. Steve drove down, while Greg and his family flew in. After I picked them up that same morning, we all went to put some of Doug's ashes in the niche I had bought at the cemetery.

We made it like a small family service, including Hank. We had to do it on Friday, because everyone was leaving on Monday and the cemetery wouldn't be able to open the niche on Sunday.

I had made a deal with the memorial grounds. We had to hire someone to open the niche, so we could leave some of Doug's ashes there. We also kept some to scatter later at Bell Labs.

Doug's niche was one tile in a big mosaic of square ceramic tiles on the outer wall of the mausoleum. The overall mosaic depicted a beautiful, peaceful scene. It had lots of grass, a tree, blue sky, golden sunbeams, and a little stream flowing through the whole scene.

Doug's niche had a plaque with his name and the dates of his birth and death on it. His particular tile had green grass and water with sunbeams radiating through it. That's what I like, being outdoors with the sun beating down.

I didn't care for the inside of the mausoleum. It smelled like a funeral home, since there were so many dying flowers in there. That's just depressing to me. I don't like being stuck inside anyway, so I had bought Doug a spot that was outside in an atrium.

After we deposited Doug's ashes in the niche, the family and Hank drove over to Bell Labs, to spread the rest of his ashes on the grass there. Somebody asked me later if I had asked permission first, and I said, "No, I just went there." I felt that was where Doug belonged. It had been his second home for 25 years.

After we scattered the ashes, Steve said, "Let's go into the reception area." The reception area was basically the lobby for Bell Labs. They had a museum of the Bell Labs history and achievements right off the lobby. Hank suggested we check it out. It was full of machines and displays about what they had done. Bell Labs was always known as one of the top places a scientist could work for research and development.

Then Steve typed "J. Douglas Carroll" onto a touch-screen computer they had there. Suddenly all of Doug's work and accomplishments came up on the screen. It was amazing. It was very touching and impressive. Doug would have liked that.

Most people didn't know when Doug was cremated or where his ashes were. We didn't announce any of that at the time. It didn't seem appropriate for the general public. If someone asked, I would tell them, but I felt it was really more just for family.

The next day, Saturday, was our big memorial service, our celebration of Doug's life. Hank went with us on Saturday morning to the memorial and was still with us Saturday evening. I talked to him a lot while he was there. He was a good friend and had always been like an uncle to my sons.

Chapter 73

Doug's Celebration of Life was held in a large, beautiful room at the Morristown Unitarian Fellowship. It was modern, with huge windows on both sides, so you could see the peaceful woods outside.

The building had previously been a mansion, owned by private people. It had been bought by the Fellowship about 30 years before. They had added on this room, where they held services and programs.

Our service began with a musical prelude, *Sonata in E Flat Major*, by Beethoven. Then the minister spoke. She talked about how our family had all supported Doug so much over the years through his difficult times. It was very touching.

Next, she read the poem Steve had found, *Dedication*, by Henry Wadsworth Longfellow. It was very beautiful. Steve always had such good taste for things like that.

Our first invited speaker was Hank Gran. He had been Doug's oldest friend, since they grew up together in Jacksonville. He was the one who was still religious and Doug always asked him why. Hank talked about their childhood. He told a story about Doug I had never heard before.

He described how as boys they both worked together to make sure they didn't develop a Southern accent. Jacksonville was very close to the Georgia border, so most people there do have a strong accent. Doug's mother was from Jacksonville and she certainly did. Doug's father, however, was from Philadelphia, so he didn't. It was a cute story.

The next speaker was Stephen France, a student of Doug's, who was originally from England. He had earned his PhD under Doug. He spoke mainly about what kind of professor Doug was and how he taught.

He said the first day of school, Doug just gave the class about 20 pages of material to go through and then said, "Read these pages and let me know what you think about them."

Doug liked to encourage his students to think for themselves. He was not a very conventional teacher…but then a lot of professors aren't. Next, as a little break, our pianist played another one of Doug's favorite pieces by Beethoven, *Sonata #8 in C Minor, Pathetique*.

The third speaker was another colleague and a very dear friend of Doug's, Tapas Sen. He spoke about what a great person Doug was and got very teary-eyed.

Our fourth speaker was another wonderful colleague from Bell Labs,

Mike Wish. He had been Doug's department head when he was first paralyzed and had helped smooth the path for us in many ways.

We had known Mike for years before he and Doug worked at Bell Labs. We were all friends in New York City, when we lived there. Mike got really choked up. There was a lot of emotion in the room.

The final speaker was the Dean of the Business School at Rutgers. He talked very movingly about Doug's service to the school and what he meant to them there. The flag at Rutgers flew at half-mast for three days, in honor of Doug's death.

After our invited speakers, we opened the floor for community sharing. One of Doug's roommates from grad school, Jim Isbister, talked about how Doug always shuffled his feet when he was sitting and thinking.

He pointed out how it was ironic, because later in life Doug did so much thinking, but he couldn't shuffle his feet any more. That was strange to hear. I had never noticed it myself. It's interesting how people remember different things.

Finally, after the sharing, as per Steve's suggestion, the pianist played a jazz number, something uplifting for people to leave on, *Tuxedo Jazz*.

My grandson was there for the whole service and behaved amazingly well. There was a man in his 90s, who was a member of the Fellowship and did paper cut outs professionally at local libraries. He was doing it for Bradley, who was completely entertained and never made a peep.

I was actually very impressed with Bradley. He was quite young, having just turned five. Doug had spoken to him on his birthday, which was just five days before Doug died.

The whole service was very impressive and touching. I got many compliments about it. Mike Wish's wife, Naomi, said, "Sylvia, you couldn't have done a better job." Of course, I did get a lot of help from Steve. The only thing I regret is that I didn't have it recorded.

After the service, we had a reception line. Greg, Steve, and I stood there as everyone filed past and said something. Then came the fun part, the reception.

Once, years earlier, when Doug was getting dialysis at Overlook Hospital, on the spur of the moment, he yelled out to me, "Sylvia, when I finally die, I want you to serve wine, lots of wine, at the funeral. I want it to be a celebration of my life. I want it to be a party."

The head nurse in charge of the dialysis unit there had said, "I heard that!"

I never forgot it. So the night before the service, my son Steve and I went to the liquor store. We were going to have a catered lunch, but our caterers didn't have a license to sell wine, so we bought a lot of it, both red and white. We took it to the reception and they served it for us. It was a great party...all in Doug's honor, just as he wanted.

On Sunday, Greg went to work out, while Steve took the rest of us to a park about 45 minutes west of where I lived. We just walked around. It was a peaceful family time and very healing.

One of the nicest things that happened that weekend was that Tony Sellitto, a good friend of mine, sent us a whole bunch of cold cuts, macaroni, coleslaw, cheeses, all kinds of things. It was enough to feed everybody for the whole weekend, which was a good thing.

I never would have been able to cook. Tony never knew Doug, but Doug once wrote a letter to help Tony's wife's son get admitted to Rutgers. I guess the food was part of his way of showing his gratitude and appreciation.

On Monday, everybody left. I was all alone, ready to face my next step in life.

To close this chapter, I thought it might be nice to include the poem that was read at Doug's memorial service.

"Dedication"
by Henry Wadsworth Longfellow

As one who, walking in the twilight gloom,
Hears round about him voices as it darkens,
And seeing not the forms from which they come,
Pauses from time to time, and turns and hearkens;

So walking here in twilight, O my friends!
I hear your voices, softened by the distance
And pause, and turn to listen, as each sends
His words of friendship, comfort, and assistance.

If any thought of mine, or sung or told,
Has ever given delight or consolation,
Ye have repaid me back a thousand-fold,

By every friendly sign and salutation.

Thanks for the sympathies that ye have shown!
Thanks for each kindly word, each silent token,
That teaches me, when seeming most alone,
Friends are around us, though no word be spoken.

Kind messages, that pass from land to land:
Kind letters that betray the heart's deep history,
In which we feel the pressure of a hand –
One touch of fire—and all the rest is mystery!

The pleasant books, that silently among
Our household treasures take familiar places
And are to us as if a living tongue
Spice from the printed leaves or pictured faces!

Perhaps on earth I never shall behold,
With eye of sense, your outward form and semblance
Therefore to me ye never will grow old
But live forever young in my remembrance.

Never grow old, nor change, nor pass away!
Your gentle voices will flow on forever,
When life grows bare and tarnished with decay,
As through a leafless landscape flows a river.

Not chance of birth or place has made us friends,
Being oftentimes of different tongues and nations,
But the endeavor for the selfsame ends,
With the same hopes, and fears, and aspirations.

Therefore I hope to join your seaside walk,
Saddened, and mostly silent, with emotion
Not interrupting with intrusive talk
The grand, majestic symphonies of ocean.

Therefore, I hope as no unwelcome guest,

At your warm fireside when the lamps are lighted,
To have my place reserved among the rest,
Nor stand as one unsought and uninvited!

Chapter 74

Even though Doug was in pain and uncomfortable, with his health so poor toward the end, I was depressed about losing him. He had recently talked to a colleague of his, Phipps Arabie. They both knew they were dying, so they just wished each other a painless death. Phipps died two weeks after Doug did.

Now that Doug was gone, I was trying to figure out what to do with the rest of my life. Not only had I lost my husband, I had lost my job as his caretaker...which had actually been about seven different jobs.

No longer would I be monitoring his health, driving him to work, and traveling with him to meetings all over the world. All of a sudden, everything I had done all those years just ended. I really felt the loss.

Doug had known I didn't like living in the suburbs, so he had always said that, when he died, I should sell the house, move to Miami, and buy a condo. That is exactly what I did eventually, but there was a lot to go through before I could.

The Monday after Doug's memorial service, everyone left. I was alone. There was so much work to do, with all this stuff to clean up and dispose of: the Clinitron bed, the dialysis machine, bandages, saline solutions, so much stuff....

I had prepaid Tammy for two weeks just before Doug died. She was always trying to get me to pay her in advance and I usually did. Toward the end, she was probably afraid Doug wouldn't live much longer, so she wanted to get what she could.

When Doug did pass, she had already received at least $1,000 more than she had worked for, but I didn't care. That was her severance pay, as far as I was concerned. She came over and helped me clean up Doug's room and get rid of things.

It was overwhelming. Besides our bedroom, he had an office in Newark, full of all his books, awards, computers, and papers. His TA Nancy was there and she helped me clean that out.

There was a mountain of paperwork I had to go through. I donated all of Doug's books to the Rutgers Newark Library. They were valuable textbooks, which he had written or collected. I took home his computers. Doug's mini-van didn't have that many miles on it, but, when I sold it, I only got $3000.

I also had to recruit two of Doug's colleagues to write his obituaries for the professional journals of two of the organizations he had belonged to. Willem Heiser wrote the obituary for Psychometrika and Tapas Sen did it for the American Psychological Society.

Doug had done so much, it took a long time to research and write them. Willem's was seven pages long. I included it at the back of this book, just to give you an idea of all that Doug did.

At this time, Steve was working in Saratoga Springs, so he came back and forth to help me with the house. Before I could get out of there and move to Florida, I was going to have to get rid of 99% of everything I had ever collected in my life.

After a while, Steve could see that the whole ordeal had drained me terribly. So in October, about four months after Doug's death, he told me, "Mom, I think you should go down to the beach in Florida and relax for about five days." What a great idea.

That was when I found the condo I'm living in now. I flew down and was picked up at the airport by a Cuban fellow I had met there before. He insisted I stay with him on South Beach. I told him I wanted to look for a condo in Sunny Isles Beach, which is on the north end of Miami Beach.

I liked Sunny Isles Beach. I would usually stay there when I came down, because it was close to the clothing-optional beach, Haulover. He said he would help me and he did.

I had an appointment with a real estate agent I knew from my previous visits. He showed us three apartments, right across from the hotel where I usually stayed. One of those condos is the one I'm living in now, so the whole process was quick and easy.

My apartment is a corner unit with two bedrooms, two baths, and a wraparound terrace. It has a northeastern exposure, but it has a view south as well. I can actually see four different bodies of water from my apartment: the Atlantic Ocean, Biscayne Bay, the Intracoastal Waterway, and a canal where yachts moor.

This is a gated community. We have two door people on-duty 24 hours a day, so it's very secure. When we first saw it, my Cuban friend told me, "It's a good buy. Take it."

That same day I put down $100 to hold it. I closed on it a couple of months later, December 5, and paid cash. The market was way down when I bought it. It's worth a lot more now.

Better yet, it was already furnished. I've changed a lot of things, but I kept a lot too. I put in hurricane windows, had it all painted, and bought new appliances for the kitchen. It's a great unit.

My only complaint is that they built this place in the 50s, so they didn't put in central heating with the central air. They were like my father, I guess. He didn't believe you needed heat in Miami. It does get cold sometimes in winter though, so I have four space heaters for when it does.

After that beautiful and productive interlude in Miami, I was definitely feeling better about life. Now I had a place to get away to and start building a future.

Still I had to get back to New Jersey and settle the estate. It took me a year, all told. Our financial advisor came over every week to consult with me. One difficult thing was that I had to figure out our life insurance policies. Doug had policies through the professional organizations he belonged to, which also covered me.

I had to decide whether to continue my coverage, to benefit my family after I passed. I did the math to see what would happen if I lived to this age or that. Finally, I decided to keep the coverage, because it wasn't that expensive.

I did have trouble collecting on one policy, because, before Doug's accident, we had set up a marital trust. Someone at Merck had told me it would be a good idea, but it turned out that it wasn't.

After Doug's accident, I went to the bank where the trust was set up and asked them, "If my husband had died, would I still be able to take a vacation once a year?"

The bank officer's answer was, "Well, I'm not sure about that."

I didn't like that. I was used to taking four vacations a year. So we got rid of the marital trust shortly afterwards. Still, when I went to collect on one of Doug's life insurance policies with Hartford, they said, "Oh, no, this money goes to the marital trust."

It was about $100,000, so that was serious. I said, "I'm sorry. There is no marital trust any more. We canceled that."

They said, "Oh, but that's what it says here. The money gets paid to the trust."

Evidently they had never been notified of the cancellation or didn't make the change if they were. So I had to go through paper after paper, to find the document proving Doug had changed the policy and left it to me personally. Finally, I found this little scrap of paper and sent it to them. I collected.

That's just one example of all the details I had to deal with.

Doug was always into insurance. If anything, we were over-insured, but we both felt better that way. My son Greg is the opposite. He doesn't believe in insurance. Of course, Steve is the opposite of Greg. He does.

After all the financial affairs were put in order, the next big challenge was everything else.

Chapter 75

Once I bought my condo, I was back and forth between Miami and Warren. Steve was helping me a lot. Then, a year after Doug died, Steve hurt his back working on the organic farm. I told him he could stay at our house, since no one else was living there.

I also called Greg and told him Steve had hurt his back. Greg is a chiropractor, so fixing backs is his thing. Greg called Steve and said, "Why don't you drive to Columbus and I'll treat you."

Steve was in western Pennsylvania, which is not that far from Ohio, so he took Greg up on his offer. He stayed with Greg for a week and got better. Then he drove to our house and lived there for a year, while I was back and forth.

Steve helped me clear everything out of the house. For example, we spent nine days, just going through a huge box of photographs from both sides of our family. Steve scanned the photos we wanted to keep and sent copies to Greg, Steve and me. I didn't leave the house for those nine days.

Steve also helped me go through all kinds of other items. You build up so much over 46 years of raising a family in a big house. I even hired a cleaning woman to come help with clearing out the kitchen, linen closet, bathroom, and so on. It was a tremendous amount of work.

To sell the house, I had planned to hire a real estate agent, David, who had been to my home many times. Steve hadn't met him before, but he did meet another agent who came over, trying to get the account. The second agent hadn't seen our house in about two years. Both agents wanted the contract, but Steve liked the second fellow better.

When this guy came over, he inspected the house very thoroughly. He hadn't seen our place in a long time, so he had to. Also, he wanted to ask more money for the place than Dave did. Steve thought he would be the better choice.

I had told Dave before that I would hire him. He had visited many times, when Steve wasn't there. When other people would suggest I should do things like pave the driveway, I would call Dave and ask his opinion. He would generally say, "No, don't bother with that."

Anyway, we hired the second guy and he started showing the house. I spent the winter of 2012 in Miami, while Steve was house-sitting for me and seeking a position in bio-informatics. I had him pay the bills and keep everything running.

When I came back in July, 2013, Steve told me he had good news. There was an offer on the house. The agent had found a young couple with a three-year-old daughter, who wanted to buy it. Steve had just met them.

We went back and forth with them through the agent, to settle on a price. Then it was time for the inspection. When you're selling a house, before you make the final agreement, you have to get it inspected. If you don't, the buyers could come back later and say, "Hey, we found something you need to fix."

These people's inspector had already found about 20 things that needed to be repaired, which I either fixed or offered them money to compensate for. We had an attorney for the sale, so I went over to his office to sign some papers.

The paralegal there told me, "Don't let them into the house again until after the inspection is completed and everyone agrees everything is fine." She was afraid they'd find more to complain about.

The house was scheduled to close on September 11. Since I didn't have to be there, I was planning to leave on the 9th. I had gotten everything done the buyers wanted taken care of, except for the front walkway.

Five years earlier, I had spent $15,000 to have it completely re-done. Still, there was one place that was beginning to fall apart. When their mortgage company inspector came out, he found fault with it. That was the last hurdle. It seemed like it would be okay though, because my real estate agent told me the buyers were probably going to fix it themselves. They just wanted to meet and finalize that.

On Thursday I called my real estate agent about 4:30. He said, "Oh, I'm so happy you called. The buyers want to either repair the front walkway or put in a new one, but they have to get your permission first. They can come over and talk to you about it at 7:30 tonight."

I had a date that night, so, of course, I cancelled it. I needed to get this done before I left. Then I ran into town to grab a bite to eat. I didn't finish my whole dinner, so I put the rest of it in the trunk of my car. Silly me. I accidentally dropped my keys in there and locked myself out of my car.

What was I going to do now? I couldn't reach Steve or anyone else and I needed to be at the house to meet the buyers. Then I saw a guy coming out of the restaurant. I stopped him and asked if he lived in Warren. He said he did, so I told him where I lived and asked if he could, please, please, give me a ride. Believe it or not, he did.

I got there in time and waited. Nobody showed. Finally at 7:50, I called my real estate agent and asked where they were. Can you believe this? He said, "Oh, I'm so sorry. I forgot to tell them to come over."

I was boiling. I couldn't believe it. I held my temper though and just said, "Well, I'm going away for the weekend, but if they can make it Sunday morning, I will be back then. So he said okay and I hung up to simmer.

The next day, Friday, I called him again, to see if they were coming on Sunday. He said he hadn't heard. I called again Saturday. Still no word.

Finally I said, "Screw this. I'm not calling this agent any more."

Steve agreed. I didn't keep that promise though. The following Wednesday, after more attempts, I told Steve, "I've been calling the agent on his cell phone and he's not picking up or calling back. I tried his office and no one picked up there either."

Then I called the paralegal who worked for my lawyer. Someone there said she was on vacation. Finally I called the lawyer and asked him what was happening with the house. He checked his email and then came back with the news. "Oh, the buyers canceled the sale last Friday morning." What?

That was the morning after they were supposed to come talk about the walkway. Our real estate agent really dropped the ball by not getting them there and then didn't even bother to tell me they were canceling the closing.

To me that was beyond unprofessional. It was totally rude, inconsiderate, and irresponsible. To make matters worse, the lawyer said it was legal for the buyers to cancel, since we hadn't closed yet. We even had to return their deposit.

When I finally got that real estate agent on the phone, I found out he was enjoying himself on vacation in Myrtle Beach. He had left without even telling me. He actually said his phone didn't work in certain areas of the hotel down there. Sure.

I told him how upset I was, but I didn't fire him. I decided to just let our contract run out in the beginning of November and forget him. People told me I should report him for incompetence, but I had had so many lawsuits already in my life with Doug, that I didn't want any more stress. I figured I would just go back to the first real estate agent, Dave, and start over again.

I had already arranged to have an estate sale the next weekend, because I thought we were closing. I wanted to sell my furniture, some paintings, clothes, and a lot of stuff that was still in the house. Before the estate sale, I had a moving van take what I wanted to keep down to Florida. Everything else I wanted out.

I hired two women to set up for a one-day sale. It takes a lot of work to figure out something like that. They priced everything, put it all in order, and then arranged displays for it. The sale went off without a hitch. After it was over, I felt I had done everything I could. The house was ready to be sold. Eventually it did, without too much more trouble.

I had also put my car up for sale and found a buyer. Since I had thought I was leaving on the 9th, I had told the buyer he could pick up the car then. When I lost the closing, I decided to leave on the 17th instead. The car buyer needed my car by then and I couldn't live up north without transportation.

Around the beginning of November, I signed a contract with Dave to be my new real estate agent. Winter was coming and I never thought the house would sell soon, but I wanted to give it a shot and see what happened.

So I didn't object when Dave called me in December, as Christmas approached, and said, "I'm taking the house off the market for five days over the holidays. I don't think we'll get any action till Christmas is over."

I said okay, and then, lo and behold, the very day Dave took the house off the market, we got an offer...a good one. These people actually bought the house. We closed on February 27, 2013. My days in New Jersey were over and I could head to Florida for good. What a relief.

I officially became a resident of Florida on January 1, 2013, by putting in a declaration of domicile for Miami. That meant I didn't have to pay New Jersey income tax any more.

I had been a member of the Asia Society in New York City since 1965, so I gave my membership to Steve, who was still living there. All the loose ends were finally tied up.

Now I was ready to start living the dream.

Chapter 76

I was brought up in a very traditional, conventional family. My parents loved me dearly, but they never could have imagined what my life would be like...and what kind of person I would become. The person I am today is definitely not who I was when I graduated from high school.

Today I am honest and caring, but definitely aware of much more than I ever dreamed of then. Just interacting with Doug and his intellectual colleagues in the academic world, plus my experience working in medical research, made me feel like an academic myself. I spent most of my life surrounded by PhDs and so on, but that's the least of it.

I am grateful my parents never knew what happened to Doug and how it affected my life. They would have been devastated. My mother was a lovely lady, but she was the nervous, high-strung type and she had a lot of stress between running their business and raising me.

If anything went wrong, she would get very upset. I knew I never wanted to be like that. I was calmer about things. I learned to handle problems. That ties into the whole philosophy of life I developed over the years. Sure, Doug's back broke and he was paralyzed, but I didn't go crazy. I dealt with it.

Okay, at first I often wished that either Doug had hit that tree and died...or that I had. It was tough being tied to each other like we were. Through the years though, I learned patience. When you live in a situation like ours, you have to have patience...and compassion.

Now, if I see someone who is disabled, I look at that person differently than most people would. I may not necessarily want to get involved, but I understand their situation. And I don't judge.

When I used to go out on a Saturday evening to hear music or get a drink, I never told anyone I was married to a paraplegic. That had nothing to do with why I was there. If I met someone and liked them, then I would tell them the truth about my life, but I didn't introduce myself that way. I wanted people to like me for myself.

When they did hear my story, some people would try to guilt me, saying things like, "You're out tonight, while your husband is a paraplegic and is home alone?" It's so easy to judge, when you haven't lived someone else's life.

I knew there was no shame in taking a break from my daily struggle. In fact, it was the agreement and an understanding Doug and I had. It was what made our marriage work for all those years.

I respected and loved Doug for giving me the freedom to travel, date, go to a nude beach, have sex, and so on. All these things were very private, but they were what got me through the hard times and kept me going.

Maybe I shouldn't even write about this, but as for the people who don't know me, I don't care what they think. The people who do know me, many are already aware of most of this and understand it. I often hear, "Your husband was a special person to allow that." Yes, and we had a special relationship.

Doug felt guilty that his accident had changed my life so drastically. After he got home from rehab and we had moved into our new home, he wrote me a letter about it. He said, "We have to make a new contract. Life will be even more challenging now, because of this accident. How will we survive? We have to build a new life now."

We found the way.

Recently I heard a guy expounding on his view of American women. He said something about how they're not very sophisticated or independent. They just read all these girly magazines.

When he finished, I said, "I don't agree with you. I'm not like that at all."

He said, "Yes, but you're unique. I wasn't describing you. I was describing the typical American woman."

He may have had a point. It's true that I think more like a man does. I'm not into shopping, gossiping, or venting. I never was. If I need to buy a new jacket, I just go to the store and buy one. I don't shop around. I very seldom even go into a mall. If I do, it's usually for happy hour or a movie, not for shopping.

A lot of women go shopping for fun. To me, it's no fun at all. Shopping tires me out. If you need something, you just get it. Even when my kids were little, I'd ask them, "What do you want for Christmas?" They'd make out a list and I'd go to Toys "R" Us and then just check off the list, as I got what they wanted.

I guess I'm pretty practical when it comes to love too. I believe in love at first sight. I fell in love with Doug the first weekend we met. We spent most of that weekend together, then went back and forth for years, before we finally married, and spent our lives together. It just worked.

My most memorable experience from our years together was traveling with Doug around the world for two months in 1968. That was when we had it all and we were doing what I loved best, traveling.

In my life, though, I'm most proud of having had a good career, raising my two sons as a good mother, and helping my husband throughout his life. Doug's greatest recognition was winning the Lifetime Achievement Award in Pyschometrics. I was especially proud that I was recognized with a tribute in Doug's obituary for the help I gave him over his lifetime of achievement.

Other people who know me will probably remember me for being friendly, open, adventurous, fun-loving, independent, and curious. I'd like to be remembered as caring and intelligent, a world traveler, with many friends, as well as a good wife and a loving parent.

My definition of happiness is having peace and serenity in your life. If you're helping others and you're not stressed out, then you're probably as happy as you'll ever be. I'm talking about long-term happiness, not just ten minutes dancing at a great party. That's not really happiness. It's just being happy.

My happiest memory of that type is getting my diamond engagement ring and going to see *Hello, Dolly*, starring Carol Channing, the same night. And, of course, getting married in Miami was another great day.

I've had a happy life. When I think about it, there's really nothing I wish I had done differently, or I would do differently now. It would be nice to be younger, but then I would have to live through all the hassle again. Getting older isn't great, but it's a valuable part of life.

On second thought, the only thing I might have changed would have been to talk Doug into going down the novice slope, instead of that expert slope, where he had his accident.

But then, if he had, who knows if we would have stayed together all those years? I certainly wasn't thinking about getting divorced, but you never know. We don't really know why things happen.

Certainly our life together would have been easier without the accident. So if I could do it again, I probably would have been more insistent. Doug didn't always have good judgment. Men often don't. They take risks.

I was much more practical than Doug. He thought he could do anything, if he put his mind to it. That's how he accomplished so much, but it also got him into big trouble that time.

Doug and I thought very differently about a lot of things. Doug's philosophy was you're not obligated to do anything. You can always do something else. I was more into following one particular path. If it was on my calendar, that's what I was going to do, even if I didn't really want to.

Doug felt you could change anything. Everything was an option. If I had something I had agreed to do and I didn't want to, he'd say, "Well, why don't you just go ahead and change it?"

I felt that, if I had a commitment, I had to do it. That was my attitude. His was, "Hey, you can choose to change." Maybe, it's a good thing I wasn't the one who got injured that day.

As I went through my life, I found myself doing lots of things I never wanted, expected, or thought I could. The big one, of course, was taking care of a paraplegic husband. I was a full-time caretaker.

As a nurse, I had never wanted to work in a hospital with sick people, but I didn't consider Doug as sick. He was disabled. A lot of people don't know the difference.

If someone said something like, "Oh, your husband's not well," I didn't like that and I would disagree with it. Doug did end up in the hospital at times, and was more and more sick as time went on, but it was because of conditions that arose from being disabled. He was overall a very healthy guy.

In the Preface of this book, I mentioned the idea that a true test of one's love is if you could stay with your partner after they were paralyzed. Evidently my love was true.

It wasn't easy, but I made the choice to stay and raise our children with Doug. If we had split up, I would have had to take the boys. Doug always told me that if I divorced him, I would have to take them. Most couples fight over custody, but we wouldn't have. There was no way he could take care of them.

Even though at times I did think about possibly leaving, a number of years before Doug died, I realized I had definitely been right to stay with him though it all. It was a good feeling to know I had done the right thing.

So the moral of my story is....

The major qualities I've come to value and practice in my life are patience and love. I had love all along, but I learned patience, and that taught me how to love even more, especially my family and friends.

I've also learned the importance of peace and serenity. I never really had them before, with so much weight on my shoulders. The last few years, though, I have finally found peace and serenity in my life and I love it.

Whatever your challenges and hurdles may be, I can only wish the same for you.

About the Author

Sylvia Booma Carroll grew up as an independent, only child in a loving, traditional family. Her dreams were always to work in medical research, travel the world, and have a loving family. She accomplished all three in a very untraditional manner.

She was never a homebody. She has traveled to 91 countries in her life and still plans to add more to the list. Today she lives happily in Sunny Isles Beach, Florida, in view of the Atlantic Ocean. She teaches water aerobics every morning and goes out for some kind of fun activity every night.